2001

Airspaces

TOPOGRAPHICS

Airspaces

David Pascoe

REAKTION BOOKS

Published by Reaktion Books Ltd
79 Farringdon Road, London EC1M 3JU, UK

www.reaktionbooks.co.uk

First published 2001

The author and publisher gratefully acknowledge permission to reprint
copyright material as follows: W. H. Auden, 'In Transit'. Copyright 1950.
Reprinted with permission of Harcourt Brace Jovanovich Inc., and Faber
& Faber Ltd.

Printed and bound in Great Britain by
Biddles Ltd, Guildford and King's Lynn

British Library Cataloguing in Publication Data

Pascoe, David
    Airspaces. – (Topographics)
    1. Airports
    I. Title
    629.1'36

    ISBN 1 86189 090 7

Contents

Midnight mass, Christmas Eve, Orly airport, 1966.

Preface

Though airports are familiar zones of modernity, their larger significance tends to be overlooked, either by accident or design. This book attempts to provide a fresh topography of the airport by considering its place in history; the creative destruction it wreaks on the landscape in which it is located; its views on abstract space; its assumption of political roles; its awkward sense of the aesthetic; and the perceptions of finality it inevitably generates. Throughout, my arguments seek to present the airport not as some inert architectural project existing under clouds of exhaust gas and an air of the terminal but as a space which, more effectively than any other framed by the last century, reflects and shapes the narratives of those who process through it.

Over the last 3 years, I have been fortunate to hear countless travellers' tales. Those recounted by Spilios Argyropoulos, Richard Boyd, Susan Castillo, John Coyle, Alice Jenkins, Stephen Johnson, Thanassis and Nana Loupas, Paddy Lyons, Willy Maley, Adam and Diane Piette, Stephen Prickett, Mark Rawlinson, Irina von Wiese and Alec Yearling have been particularly compelling. I would also like to express my thanks to all the airports, picture archives, libraries and other organizations without whose assistance and generosity *Airspaces* could not have been written.

At Reaktion Books, Harry Gilonis responded to my choice of artwork with a nice balance of enthusiasm and alarm, while Andrea Belloli asked exactly the right questions about the entire text. Any shortcomings that remain are mine alone.

Vassiliki Kolocotroni has been my companion on many journeys home; the book is dedicated to her.

Introduction

Airspace was once so simple to comprehend. English common law guaranteed the bearer of a fee title – a manor in Hounslow, West Middlesex, say – that his fiefdom stretched as far as the Heavens above and deep into the Earth. Despite the fact that the terms of this ownership could be imposed only at or close to the ground – the level at which one might cultivate or construct – that perception of privilege gave landlords an extraordinary sense of infinite power. In epic fashion, the law exploited a third dimension, connecting man, the gods and the Devil himself; but it was too easy a bargain: Faustian ones always are. In due course, with the advent of powered flight, the price would have to be paid. As the basis of air-traffic systems, the newly established operational and legal abstractions – namely, airways and flight paths – ensured that airspace would become a complex, crafted network invisible to the spectator on the ground. Now enshrined in international legislation as that zone of strict enforcement above a country, where rules of sovereignty apply, and where ignorance or infringement can be lethal, airspace is divided into several discrete areas of control.[1] The most secure, 'Positive Controlled Airspace' (PCA), ranges from 18,000 to 60,000 feet above sea level; between these altitudes, at various levels, transverse the commercial airways, the 10-mile-wide superhighways of the air. All movements here are subject to regional and national air traffic control clearances and orders, and must proceed on the basis of instrument readings alone; pilots must not rely on what is visible through cockpit windows. The next discrete area, 'Terminal Controlled Airspace'

An aerial view of Los Angeles International Airport, 1996.

(TCA), reaches up from ground level to a fixed safety height of between 3,000 and 6,000 feet, under the aegis of, and within sight of airport authorities (weather permitting). It is this exclusive zone that is the subject of this book, the site of complexes large enough to be regarded as fully self-contained cities with lives and names of their own, and also the location of the most hazardous of aircraft manoeuvres – take-off and climb-out, final approach and landing.

A basic premise here is that it is not simply through the basic physical manifestations of airspace that we can discern the shapes of our modernities; we must also be aware of its *representations*. Versions of airspace are so common that twentieth-century culture resounds with whirling propellers, the whistling roar of jet engines and the shockwaves of accidents smashing into the vacuity of the terminal. Airports, lying as they do at the threshold of airspace, should be treated not as the sterile transitory zones with which we are all familiar, but as 'vessels of conception' for the societies passing through them. More than any other building type of the last century, their

The runway at Milan Malapensa International Airport under construction, 1958.

being seems to depend on cultural identification no less than architectural use, on their aesthetic properties no less than technological function. Yet such manifestations in photographs, poetry, novels, theatre and cinema seem to be almost unduly overlooked when set against the overall mechanism of the airport itself, whose morphology is best viewed not as a discrete structure, but as an array of functionally diverse spaces designed on various scales, a network of ticketing checks, security searches, customs inquiries and transit zones through which food, fuel, mail, cargo, baggage and air traffic are circulated. Airspace provides a familiar sequence of services for travellers, the most fundamental of which may be lavatories, telephones, *bureaux de change*, restaurants, duty-free shops, news stands, as passengers 'in transit' are forced to proceed in ways that prevent them from seeing that the expanse through which they are flowing is a state within a state, a fragmentary territory nipped off from the ordinary laws of the urban fabric. In 'Narita', the poet Allen Curnow described 'the door for arrivals' and 'the door for departures' at Tokyo International Airport, and claims that 'Between the two the meantime is all there is. / It passes of itself.'[2] There is a larger aspect to the 'meantime', for, as the novelist Brigid Brophy claimed in *In Transit*, a work set entirely in a departure lounge, to be in airspace means to 'perpetually or for a simulacrum of perpetuity remain in the present moment, in at least *semi*-sempiternal transit between departure from the past and arrival at the future.'[3] As is so often the case, Brophy's representation attributes to the airport a certain philosophical dignity that derives from its being considered a symbolic instrument, endowed with mysterious properties and seductive charms, surrounded by taboos and an air of danger – a repository of illicit pleasure, a conduit to the transcendental and a spur to repression.

Consider the work of the French critic and philosopher Michel Serres, who, in 1993, published *La Légende des anges*, a strangely haunting *mélange* of speculations about the modern fascination with the transmission and deciphering of messages, and with

An underground passageway leading from the main terminal of Roissy-Charles De Gaulle International Airport to a satellite terminal, 1975.

the emerging global information networks that are transforming the globe. Much of Serres' text is set within Roissy-Charles De Gaulle International Airport. Pantope is a 'travelling inspector' for Air France, permanently on the move. His friend, Pia, is a doctor at the medical centre; 'she stays in one place while everything else moves around her.' Hence, they both exist as part of a much larger system of relations; 'between the two of them, a whole universe flows.'[4] This universe is later identified as Newtown, a modern 'city of light' which has its 'centre everywhere and its circumference nowhere' and is organized around 'a single ribbon, the outside of which goes from a pedestrian footpath to a wide boulevard, or, if you prefer … an airport runway'.[5] Ultimately, Newtown is synonymous with airspace, a network without localizable boundaries (other than the perimeter fence of the airfield) and extending towards the Heavens, where at any given moment, hundreds of thousands of beings live. In the upper reaches of this vertical city, they remain 'absolutely stable, albeit moving at subsonic speeds'; Pantope's address here is 'A340; OSA-CDG; 14F': that is, seat F, row 14, of an Air France Airbus A340, *en route* from Osaka-Kansai International Airport to CDG. To live in airspace is to be defined in such encoded forms, as a virtual object, a bearer of messages:

> By means of this single highway, the intersections of which are constructed out of multiple choices, Newtown creates linkages between all spaces, whether concrete and abstract, of this world and of any other; it creates links between towns, houses and offices, women and men, science and information, idea and motions ... But also, and more particularly, between cities and men, women and emotions, offices and ideas.[6]

The literary critic Christopher Ricks has written on the complex workings of the preposition 'between', which, he observes, displays 'an intersection' of 'three prepositional functions: Space, Time and Relation', as well as manifesting simultaneously 'a joining and a separation, disconcertingly accommodating itself both to acts of mediation or meeting and to acts of obstruction or

An Air France Airbus A340 in flight over Nagoya, Japan, en route for Paris-CDG, 1998.

disjuncture'.[7] Applying such perceptions to Serres' Newtown, one might say that subjects within it are nothing other than go-betweens. Pia admits:

> All we really are is intermediaries, eternally passing among others who are also intermediaries. But the question is where is it all leading? Because I spend my life here, in this never-ending flow of passengers, communications, conveyors, messengers, announcers and agents, because my work is at this intersecting point of a multitude of networks all connected to the universe … I hear the sound of angels … How else are we to understand these sounds in this hurly burly world where nobody actually lives and everyone's just speeding though.[8]

Clearly, by way of this fundamental and immediate tension between movement and immobility, in terms of space, time and relation, Serres was drawn to the exciting aesthetic possibilities of the airport. Architecture, obviously, is an art of immobility, of frozen time, of suspended movement, and in a society where transit looks like flight, and where perpetual motion abolishes places, its practitioners seek to affirm the values of stability, identity, presence, by resisting movement, by preventing everything becoming an indistinct flow. Such an affirmation is not a negative reaction; rather, it is a mediation between flight and confinement. Existing within the aegis of such an antithetical concept, airports should never be taken for simple thoughts; they are neither monuments to immobility, nor instruments of the mobile society, but instead, the improbable conjunction of both.

As an architectural array, this nexus usually manifests itself in the thresholds of airspace itself: the airfield – the arrangement of aprons, taxiways, runways – or the terminal, the intricate system which accomodates the flow of the travelling public. Yet airports should not be regarded as mere complexes, or even as machines meant to expedite people and cargo. Instead they should be seen as organic entities whose success depends on the ability to fit into the pre-existing infrastructure, and simultaneously adapt to the new technologies, economic trends, or social dynamics emerging in their environments. Airports also derive their character from an ever larger set of conditions ; they stage, so to speak, an engrossing image of the aspiration to break out of the element into which we are born and to move into that in which we breathe. It is not, therefore, surprising that they are often experienced as such edgy zones, places in which to experience oneiric moods, loss of agency and imprisonment within the confines of a technological system. As Andy Warhol put it:

> Today my favorite kind of atmosphere is the airport atmosphere. If I didn't have to think about the idea that airplanes go up in the air and fly it would be my perfect atmosphere. Airplanes and airports have my favorite kind of food service, my favorite kind of bathrooms, my favorite peppermint Life Savers, my favorite kinds of entertainment, my favorite loudspeaker address systems, my favorite conveyor belts, my favorite graphics and colors, the best security checks, the best views, the best perfume shops, the best employees, and the best optimism. I love the way you don't have to think about where you're going, someone else is doing that, but I just can't get over the crazy feeling I get when I look out and see the clouds and know I'm really up-there. The atmosphere is great, it's the idea of flying that I question. I guess I'm not an air person, but I'm on an air schedule, so I have to live an air life. I'm embarrassed that I don't like to fly because I love to be modern, but I compensate by loving airports and airplanes so much.[9]

One should always be suspicious when nouns are pushed so wilfully into the realm of adjectives just so that they can be seen to work as terms of hyperbolic approval; here, Warhol suggests tautologically, airports are so 'airport'. It is not to deceive by exaggeration that Warhol overshoots the mark in this way, but to allow the basic value, the underlying truth of what is insufficiently valued, to appear. The very artless monotony is an effective endorsement of the uniformities of airspace, which offers commodity while at the same time narrowing one's choices. The question might be posed: Who, in their right mind, would willingly suffer the deprivation that follows from the 'airport' version of mind, a version screened off from reality and the external world, receiving only vicarious projections of things as they are? But that is the point; one must accept the insulation, or start screaming. Brigid Brophy was attempting to do just this when she claimed: 'Airport alone vindicates our century ... The true pure feel of the twentieth century is a rarity to catch on the wing. Catch it at airport. Sense yourself, at airport, at home; be, for once, in your own period.'[10] The dumping of the definite article before 'airport', turning a place into a state of mind, exposes Brophy's hyperbolic approach to her own century. The truth that exaggerations such as these may convey relies on a principle well recognized by those approaching an airport, finally; occasionally, aiming to overshoot the runway is the condition of not missing it.

In the opening words of her novel *Between*, the British experimental writer Christine Brooke-Rose also responded to airspace by creating a world which, compounded simultaneously out of stasis and movement, reflected its own dislocation: 'Between doing and not doing the body floats.' In her conception, such space creates strange demands, especially on language; her text, written without any recourse to the verb 'to be', shows that, for the subject moving in airspace, to be can only ever to 'be-tween'.[11] The novel begins: 'Between the enormous wings the body of the plane stretches its one hundred and twenty seats or so in three on either side,' a familiar enough description of the interior of a big jet, but it ends: 'Between the enormous wings the body floats', which seems to refer to the great piers of the terminal at Orly Airport, where much of the novel is set. In between, Brooke-Rose flies a holding pattern around two locational figures, progress and containment, as the narrator is first presented travelling between cities in aircraft, and is then seen stranded in airports between flights. Such reversibility mirrors the condition of being suspended between ideologies, languages and countries; but such suspension assumes many other forms too. It may take place in the womb-like interior of an aircraft, on the surface of the body, at the border between countries or even at the boundary between beliefs. Ultimately, however, within airspace, 'air and other such conditioning ... prevent any true exchange of thoughts.'

16

The tendency towards enclosure and fixed meanings within this topos is political and personal, as well as spatial – hence, Brooke-Rose's description of an arrival at Orly:

> … the concrete corridor encased in glass slopes up straight from the tarmac where the yellow bus has stopped, and on into the airport hall of clean glass galleries coffee-bars teak stairways with wide frightening space between the steps and queues of plastic luggage moving unowned, unmastered up the conveyor belt over the edge and straight along toward the small metal swing gates where men half-hidden in booths consult secret lists with a quick lift of the eye on to this or that face.[12]

This is a place of enclosure, of clean lines and straight edges, of conveyor belts and constant surveillance; in this world of arbitrary negativity ('unowned', 'unmastered'), any possibility of escape is forestalled. Even a stairway, with 'wide frightening space between the steps', is too contained ever to be regarded simply as a 'flight' of stairs. When the contrary tendency towards flight does emerge, the erosion of borders is manifested most explicitly in terms of language:

> … one day even airports will have no frontiers and no passports per assistere anche una persona priva de conoscenza. Aber natürlich. He stands by his pigskin hold-all his thick black briefcase in his left hand, shaking the right with the president of the congress the secretary the most important delegates male elderly female and doesn't introduce his team of three interpreters English – German French – German English – French besides himself French into English and they simultaneously stand about and smile in English German French.[13]

Translation becomes the central metaphor for escape; the narrator, an interpreter by profession, crosses the borders with such ease that origin and destination, the here and there of air travel, cease to be antithetical states. For airports to exist without frontiers would mean, of course, that the zones the authorities once so strictly contained had become multiple, and ubiquitous; having emerged from airspace, such places would be co-terminous with the modern world.[14]

'The airport hall of clean glass galleries': Orly *c.* 1966.

Under the influence of such diverse representations of air-space, it is tempting to think of airports, in particular, as metaphors of modern existence. However, to describe them in such terms is to realize that since reality so easily skids off into the service of representation, the line separating the former from the latter is as easily crossed as a runway threshold. Nevertheless, that division has the virtue of making it possible to specify and emphasize, so it will be seen that the overall emphasis of *Airspaces* falls more on real than on represented airspaces – more, that is, on the space itself than on the state of being that recreates it; more on fixity of purpose than on flight of fancy. On arriving at the airports from which their represented counterparts have previously departed, what is communicated, I would suggest, is not so much single-mindedness but a resonant duplicity: the double feeling of hating control and yet cherishing it; of reaching for the sky and yet being fixed in place; of wanting to take off and yet not wanting to. And over and above this doubleness, streaking like exhaust trails through all airspace, is the sensation of imminent disaster. Technology may have extended the powers of the human to manipulate, domesticate and transform the elements which surround us; once deployed, however, this power then demands that its scope be extended ever more fully, with the consequence that these powers escape our abilities to manage them. Hence, an overwhelming cloud of catastrophe pollutes airspace, which in turn only creates the desire to escape still further, to accelerate away from established holding patterns.

HOPELESS DEPARTURES

Flight is, broadly speaking, a sublime combination of attitude and motion. When an aircraft is in the right attitude – that is, once it has struck the precise 'angle of attack', the point at which the wings are set in regard to the lengthwise axis of the plane, and once it has reached sufficent velocity so that the nose is lifting – it cannot but leave the ground. At the moment at which it begins its 'rotation' and its nose lifts, a flying machine such as Concorde is pushing into the air at over 250 mph. The wing, so rigid and awkward on the ground, is now an aluminium blade sufficiently sharp and delicate to slice through interfolding tissues of air and lean into the void. Its four giant Olympus turbojets – engines originally developed to power the Vulcan nuclear strike bomber – are burning fuel at a rate of 8 gallons a second, and, as the plane begins to climb, the temperature of its exhaust gas will reach 1000°. The effect of this interplay of thrust and lift is both to frighten with threats of constraint and to beckon with hopes of flight. The ambient air, so thickly present over Heathrow, will be filled with the crackling, rocketing boom that J. H. Prynne described in his 'Airport Poem: Ethics of Survival' as 'the century roar', a sound which, at well over 100 decibels, measures out the terminal point of the epoch of flight: 'The century roar is a desert carrying / too

An Air France Concorde, 1977.

much away; the plane skids off / with an easy hopeless departure,' undertaken seemingly without friction, but also, perhaps,
without control; to be so much a part of such a 'hopeless' movement is to be confirmed as a passive subject, a mere spectator.[15]

On a spring afternoon in 1997, the photographer Wolfgang
Tillmans, standing on the threshold of a runway at Heathrow,
pointed his camera in the direction of this 'century roar'. The
result, one of a series of photographs exhibited the following
year under the title *Concorde*, carries that familiar sense of a dispossessed spectator watching aircraft take off, but places it
within a vanishing perspective set against a background of sky
that seems variously to be framed by, or infinitely far removed
from, the architectural manifestations of airspace; the distant
terminals glistening in the fading light. Built to exclude unau-
thorized intrusions, the tall perimeter fence seems highly secure,
to military standard; prefabricated concrete panels are sur-
mounted by wire mesh, and topped off with barbed wire. In the
still, chill air, several pieces of shredded translucent plastic, the
remains of wind-blown carrier bags, dangle limply from the
wire, while in front of the fence gorse and brambles grow vigor-
ously from a ditch, despite the fact that the water it contains is
polluted by anti-freeze and jettisoned fuel. The pervasive stench
of kerosene must have made the dusk seem even more vividly
substantial to Tillmans; his photograph shows the air stretched
over the perimeter fence like painted silk. In the centre of this
theatre of movement, a white, delta-shaped machine has reared
up on its haunches, its flexible nose dropping down, its great jets
invisible in their speed, save for the tremor they make against
the solid blue, and the turbulent cloud of brown soot rising from
the spent runway. Concorde seems to be floating free into the
airspace above West Middlesex.[16]

What is most remarkable about Tillmans's photograph, however, is the way that it captures the demands powered flight
makes on the spaces which accommodate it. The field itself is
entirely in thrall to the impeccable machine making use of its
splendid expanses; the runway, effectively a jetty projecting out

towards the light and air, effaces the landscape to provide, at once, an ending and a beginning; the airport buildings, low and aloof, stand their ground against the thin ruled line of the horizon; and, above and beyond, the threshold of the runway is the blue void, now pierced by a dirty cloud of pollution. Of course, what this image fails to capture, what very few photographs of airspace can ever contain, are what might be termed the accidents of history.

On 25 July 2000, at CDG, Paris' main airport, there was the usual high-season chaos. Summer thunderstorms had delayed many flights and, having missed their scheduled connections, disgruntled passengers besieged transfer desks; the less exercised dozed in packed departure halls. At Gate 2A of Terminal 2, 96 Germans, two Danes, an Austrian and an American waited to board an Air France Concorde, chartered to carry them to New York, on the first leg of the trip of a lifetime. At 4.30 pm, after an hour's delay, the passengers filed out of the terminal, and processing down a tube, entered the aircraft's narrow fuselage. Fifteen minutes later, the Concorde began to accelerate down runway 26. Having covered just over two miles of runway, and attained a speed of almost 200 mph, its needle nose began to twitch upwards, as expected; just as it became impossible to abort the take-off, flames appeared under the left wing. As the rear wheels left the ground, passengers delayed in the gate lounges watched aghast as the burst of orange lengthened into a massive stream of fire and thick black smoke. The transcript of the Cockpit Voice Recording picked up air-traffic controllers scrambling to call the airport's fire brigade, clearing runway 26 and coolly telling the crew: '... you have fierce flames behind you. At your convenience, you have priority to return to the runway.' But the stricken jet could not; with fire klaxons sounding in the cockpit, the pilot, Christian Marty, was heard to say: 'Too late. No time, no.' The last recorded words were from the co-pilot, Jean Marcot: 'Negative. We're trying Le Bourget ... No.'

Within a few days of the accident, an explanation was beginning to emerge. A small strip of rivetted metal which had fallen from a Continental Airways DC10 a few minutes before the Concorde began its take-off run, cut deep into one of the four high-pressure tyres. Already hot from friction with the concrete, the tyre exploded, sending pieces of the wheel's brittle magnesium rims and heavy chunks of rubber flying upwards into the huge delta wing, shearing hydraulic lines and puncturing fuel tanks. Almost as soon as the thinly insulated tanks were pierced, leaking kerosene, now ignited by a spark or shard of hot metal, was flung back by the airflow, and the Olympus turbojets became, in effect, huge blow torches. For some time, noises, described in the accident report as 'sounds like exertions', were heard before communication with the aircraft was lost. The control tower announced, 'For all planes listening, I'll get back to you in a minute. We're going to pull ourselves together and restart take-offs.'[17]

Incessantly, the main runways at CDG dispatch aircraft directly west over the town of Gonesse. Once famed for its exquisite white bread rolls and its lacework, since 1974, when the new airport opened nearby, ringing it with dual carriageways and industrial estates, it has become known as the home of the National Mine Testing Centre, and as a dormitory town for airport employees. One in eight of its 25,000 inhabitants work at CDG, driving the buses, pouring coffee, cleaning terminals. In fact, the residents of Gonesse entered the world of aviation early. On 17 August 1783, frightened by a monster, they skewered it with forks and pumped buckshot into it, then had it sprayed with holy water and exorcised by a priest; it deflated with a sinister hiss, giving off a foul smell. The creature was M. Charles and Robert's hydrogen balloon, a sphere made from taffeta coated with elastic gum, 36 feet in circumference, which, earlier that day, had risen from the Champ de Mars into the clouds before disappearing from view, carried north east on the prevailing wind.[18] As a result, the locals claimed that the twice-daily flypasts by the world's most famous passenger jet were nothing to get excited about.

However, for those beneath the flight path, Concorde's climb-out this time sounded different. Flames spurting from its underside, the plane started to bank to the left and lose height. Describing a huge arc, it was soon almost facing back the way it had come, but it had bled too much speed, and, as it began to stall, its nose came up until it was almost vertical: '... it was as if it just fell gently from the sky like a leaf in autumn, with its tail and one wing pointing downwards.'[19] To the last fraction of time in which the jet was no longer hovering, witnesses could not believe their eyes; then it banked stiffly onto one wing at a 100 feet, stalling into its own shadow, and fell onto an airport hotel. By design or accident, the pilot had managed to avoid the main part of Gonesse, the stricken jet dropping and exploding 'like an atomic bomb'. The hotel, modern and functional, typical of the architecture round any airport, seemed to 'vaporize'; only a single charred wall remained upright. Arriving at the scene, local people and the emergency services found metal fragments, scattered like grain; fluids unidentifiably human or hydraulic; and bodies heaped and burned, like so much timber from the copse only a few hundred yards away.

All 109 passengers on board the jet died instantly; on the ground, five people were consumed by the explosion. In the hours that followed, helmeted firemen carried stretchers amid the debris and marked out the charred corpses and body parts with small plastic cones. Unlike many crash sites, it was a curiously compressed scene, the wreckage not pulverized and strewn around a large area but blackened beyond recognition, and contained in an area about the size of a couple of tennis courts. Such was the brief intensity of the fireball, that within a couple of days the smell of fuel and smoke had evaporated from the crash site; within a month, it seemed as though it could never have happened.

Yet what was most extraordinary about this accident was that it was so comprehensively captured. Even a quarter of a century after the Concorde came into service, each flight, for many of those on the ground, was regarded as extraordinary, an event in

The Concorde crash outside Paris, 25 July 2000: 'A dull smudge in the sky'.

itself. As a result, in the 77 seconds between the time the controller spotted the fire, and the last sound was recorded, amateur
photographers found themselves recording the end of a dream.
A Japanese tourist, *en route* to Florence, strapped in the window
seat of another jet as it waited to be cleared for take-off, fired off
a sequence of photographs with his motor-driven Nikon; his
graphic pictures would provide the answer to the accident investigation. An anonymous businessman about to board a private
aircraft snapped at a dark smudge across the sky, framed by arc
lights and service vehicles; at the edge of the cloud's darkness, a
blur of light marks the point of no return. Andras Kisergeley, a
Hungarian student lacking the means to travel by air, had spent
several weeks parking on the perimeter roads of European airports, sleeping in his car under final approach paths, indulging
his hobby of photographing airliners. His famously grainy picture, syndicated globally in the hours following the accident, is
even more affecting, not simply because it captures the burning
jet streaking low across the sky, leaving a white-hot line of flame
in its wake but also because it incorporates the 'fraying edge' of
airspace: lamp posts, 'squat buildings / With their strange air
behind trees', and a long-stay car park.[20]

25

Three days after the crash, the town of Gonesse held a march to commemorate the dead. Some 2,000 people – locals, relatives of the crash victims and Air France staff – processed down the high street, past the light-industrial estates and warehouses, through the fields and out to the crash site. They were led by the mayor, Jean-Pierre Blazy, incandescent in his grief, railing against the seemingly heedless jets passing low overhead, and by Michele Fricheteau, owner of the destroyed hotel, who wept inconsolably. Five hundred yards from the charred wreckage they halted, and fell silent. Above them, the engines of expensive delicate jets pushed on through the sky; these aircraft had 'somewhere to get to and sailed calmly on', further into airspace.[21]

1 Thresholds of Modernity

In the earliest days of aviation, the airfield (or more grandly 'aerodrome') was simply a platform, a grass jetty which permitted the take-off, landing and parking of flying machines. It only occupied itself with the needs of the aircraft, not with those of the passengers, and its gaze was directed uniquely upwards, towards the possibilities of the sky, the unknotting of new latitudes. An airport, however, is a larger proposition whose function is announced verbally by its compound form: it is an aerial port, and that implies many corresponding functions. In its earliest days, aviation was a spare activity, aerodromes peopled only by magnificent fliers, specialist engineers and, as an afterthought, the occasional paying passengers. Since the Second World War, building on the platform offered by airports, aviation has become a gigantic enterprise undertaken, above all, in the name of economy and commerce. Rigas Doganis defines modern airports as 'complex industrial enterprises', factories devoted to the processing of people and cargo, that act 'as a forum in which disparate elements and activities are brought together to facilitate, for both passengers and freight, the interchange between air and surface transport'.[1] The issue is now no longer one of making machines fly, but of managing their movements and choreographing them with those of the passengers they carry; hence the airport does not simply look at the sky but also, equally, at the ground, concentrating not simply on winged containers – the planes themselves – but also on the terrestrial installations which fill and evacuate these vessels.

A 1997 exhibition at the Photographers' Gallery, London, claimed that 'the history of airports is the history of our century. A history of modernity and urbanism, of flight and light and speed. A history of the future.'[2] In their celebration of such history, the curators, Steven Bode and Jeremy Millar, clearly found it difficult to strike a suitably convincing tone, and relied perhaps too much on theoretical works which sought to present the airport as a 'heterotopia', or a 'non-place'.[3] Nevertheless, the catalogue accompanying the exhibition was distinguished by the inclusion of a specially commissioned essay by J. G. Ballard, whose novels have so obsessively inhabited the airspace in the vicinity of his home town in Shepperton, West London, to create a topography even stranger than fiction. In his most famous work, *Crash*, the deranged advertising executive *cum* 'TV scientist', Vaughan, regularly drives out to London Airport via the old Western Avenue, to photograph arriving celebrities, his zoom lens watching their every move 'from the observation platform of the Oceanic Terminal'. At other times, prior to picking up airport prostitutes, he and his voyeuristic friend, James, the narrator of the story, gaze through the perimeter fence at 'the deserted standby runways', across which, despite the movements of gigantic airliners overhead, 'immense peace seemed to preside.' In Ballard's utopian vision, even the curtain-walling of the terminal buildings and the multi-storey car-parks behind them belonged to an enchanted domain; such houses 'of glass, of flight and possibility' are, according to the narrator (whose surname happens to be Ballard), 'the departure point for our own lives and deaths'.[4] Almost a quarter of a century later, this stark view of airspace seems unchanged: 'Airports and airfields have always held a special magic, gateways to the infinite possibilities that only the sky can offer.'[5]

In the circumstances, writers and artists have perhaps found that when representing airports, hyperbole, the rhetorical figure that thrusts its objects up, excessively, way above their just deserts, is required in order to create 'infinite possibilities'. Consider the work of Chris Goode who, in a recent pamphlet, asks: 'Has the idea of airports lived inside us for as long as we've dreamed of sex and home, and of flight?' It sounds like an impertinent question, but the answer he provides is apposite:

In the evolution of the airport we perceive, as with rapid eye movement, merely a small and cumulating betrayal in the material world of the activity of the human imagination. There was no first airport, no statement of intent. We could bookmark the first paved runway, developed during the Great War; or the rudimentary Newark airport of 1928. Or we could look backwards, to the Rose Window at Notre Dame, to Tallis's forty part motet, to the Sermon on the Mount. Or forward to the major edifices of the virtual sublime, or the nodal termini of remote viewing expressways.[6]

Goode wrote this out of the knowledge that one cannot celebrate airports at present without seeming to be perverse; one can only overpraise them, hoping that the reader, hearing the excessiveness of the hyperbole, will not dismiss the extravagance but instead restore what has been immoderately debased to a level more closely approaching its actual worth. (Proceeding in this way, Goode was in good company; in 1940, F. Scott Fitzgerald wrote in his unfinished final novel: 'airports lead you way back in history like oases, like the stops on the great trade routes.'[7]) Consequently, Goode claims that in order to trace the airport aesthetic, rather than alighting at the 'rudimentary' Newark

The exterior of Eero Saarinen's TWA building (1956–62) at John F. Kennedy International Airport, New York.

The interior of the TWA building at JFK, 1981.

airport, whose terminal building was once adorned with murals by Arshile Gorky, we might as well begin in 'Altamira, in northern Spain, 25,000 years ago'.[8] Here on the walls of caves,

> ... stone-age man used fat and dyes derived from the bodies of destroyed birds, and the colours of the scorched earth, to capture for the first time his vision for the TransWorld terminal at John F. Kennedy airport in New York: a vision which would take nearly eight hundred generations to be realised.

The world's most famous terminal building, Eero Saarinen's great concrete bird at John F. Kennedy International Airport, is indeed cavernous, consisting of four intersecting barrel vaults, each separated from the other by narrow strip skylights; it is also almost primitive in its decor. The entire interior was originally finished in whitewash, but its carpets, signage and detailing were carmine – TWA's corporate colour – a crimson pigment

30

made from cochineal, the dried bodies of female insects raised on Mexican cactus. As one moves through the 'organic' interior, the form of the building seems to grow, presenting a series of subtly changing shapes and patterns; in an extraordinary architectural trick, the air-bridges leading to the satellite terminals curve, meaning that all sense of perpective disappears.[9] Paul Andreu, the designer of CDG, observes: 'When you go in, you cannot see the end of the tunnel. Instead of this horrible impression of a fixed perspective, you genuinely get the feeling that you are going somewhere.'[10] For Goode, travelling through Saarinen's Terminal 1 is only ever going back in time, and he concludes:

> Clearly, then, the idea of the airport predates not only the reality of air travel but, in some respects, the idea of the aeroplane itself. And this delicate conception, of the airport as a tenet of prelapsarian harmony and universal intercourse, obtains even while we perceive the airport as it is lived: as crisis and crucible, as an ulcer in the undifferentiated sheen of decadent globalism.

The effort of imagination Goode required in order to establish airports way beyond their accepted history allows him to plumb the depths to which their value has fallen. To say that airports are both 'harmony' and 'crisis' instals an opposition that allows one to conclude that they are not simply abysmal.

J. G. Ballard arrived at his sense of airports by means of a more circuitous flight-path. In 1991, he visited Shanghai for the first time in almost half a century:

> An hour before midnight, after flying through the darkness from Hong Kong, we approached the western rim of a vast metropolis of lights, and touched down at Shanghai International Airport, on the site of the old Hungjao aerodrome where as a boy I had played in the cockpits of rusting Japanese aircraft. A sea of superheated air covered the tarmac, carrying the forgotten scents of the Yangtse countryside.[11]

The superheated and scented air also suppresses what lies below, a secret history which had already emerged in *Empire of the Sun*, Ballard's autobiographical account of growing up in Shanghai under Japanese occupation. At the end of the first part of the novel, in a chapter entitled 'The Runway', Jim witnesses construction work proceeding at the airport:

> Watched by the Japanese sentries, hundreds of captured Chinese soldiers in ragged tunics were carrying the tiles and cobblestones from the tip and laying the bed of a concrete runway … Many were emaciated to the point of death. They sat naked in the trampled nettles, a single roof tile held in their hands like the fragment of a begging bowl. Others climbed the shallow slope to the edge of the airfield, wicker baskets laden with stones clasped to their chests … He knew that the Chinese soldiers were being worked to death, that these starving men were laying their own bones in a carpet for the Japanese bombers who would land upon them.[12]

'Carpet' is a deft but ruthless touch, as it prefigures the US Air Force's carpet bombing of the facility, at the end of the war. The passage derives its most shocking effect from the clear-eyed revelation that the very fabric of Shanghai's runway is built out of the pulverized bodies of slave labourers.

Ballard enjoys airport environments precisely because they have succeeded in evacuating history, and replacing it with worthier alternatives. In his contribution to the Photographers' Gallery *Airport* exhibition, he eulogized Heathrow, celebrating it for its 'transience, alienation and discontinuities, and its unashamed response to the pressures of speed, disposability and the instant impulse'; for the fact that 'under the flight paths of Heathrow, everything is designed for the next five minutes.'[13] Ballard was comfortable in his fundamental premise that mobility and communication, both technically imparted and supported, are the central values of post-industrial thinking, and can be experienced as the spectator stands 'under the flight paths' of an international airport and observes jets descending over the city, in some kind of sustained offensive. The rest of his essay proceeds with the verve of a writer of science fiction, as he argues that the airport is an area on which future structures, conditions and patterns of behaviour are tested out; a contingent place, the physical limits of its expansion yet to be decided. Ballard looks forward to seeing at Heathrow, 'the new terminal 5, and beyond that … terminals 6 and 7, and the transformation of Britain into the ultimate departure lounge', and describes '747 tailplanes … cruis[ing] the tarmac like the fins of amiable sharks'. For other writers, these machines are not so benign; Martin Amis, for instance, senses only disaster: 'As I stood in some stalled passage and listened to the canned instructions, I looked down on the lots and runways through the layered insult of dawn rain: all the sharks with their fins erect, thrashers, baskers, great whites – killers. Killers every one.'[14]

As soon as one drives into an airport car park, one finds oneself integrated into an unparalleled conglomeration of communication and control systems which refuses any dissent. Once one is inside the terminal, the computer at the check-in desk has first to be consulted. Hundreds of annunciator boards constantly provide updated flight information, and television

Tailplanes at Frankfurt/Main International Airport, *c*. 1995.

monitors purvey global news, 24/7. The voice over the loud-speaker, calling out in several languages, reaches into every conceivable space, even the toilet cubicle; uniformed personnel are encountered at every step, wired with walkie-talkies, some carrying machine pistols across their padded chests like dark medals. Everything seems a little more modern and ordered than in the world beyond the airport perimeter; indeed, one might claim that throughout the century, airspace, an island of advanced development where familiar standards and defini-tions begin to seem uncertain, has provided a glimpse of how the world outside the terminal might look in 10 years or so. *In Transit*, Brigid Brophy's extraordinary paean to the airport, set out its unique properties:

> It is not the limitless anarchic space of everyday life, where you must scrabble a living. It is circumscribed. It is newer, cleaner and smarter than everyday life; and services wait to spring to the salute when you press the button. You are free to supply your own wants, but all the sources of supply are within stroll.[15]

In such a space, time zones and time lags begin to assume con-crete reality; the idea of 'border' loses its physicality and reveals itself to be a theoretical construction which can materialize any-where. The airport functions as a national frontier on the out-skirts of a major city in the middle of a country; that in itself should suggest the beginning of a different spatial dimension. Within airspace, indeed, there seems to be a split in the very constraints on time and place, and for Ballard that, ultimately, may represent the most exciting possibility: 'The terminal con-courses are the ramblas and agoras of the future city, time-free zones where all the clocks of the world are displayed, an atlas of arrivals and destinations forever updating itself, where briefly we become true world citizens.' The 'time-free' zone is nothing other than an infinite loop; such places efface both the past and the future, and leave only the relativity of the present. In particular, the proliferation of clocks provides a means of

An annunciator board at Zürich-Kloten International Airport, 1997.

short-circuiting the past, of freeing us from Time; historical and also predictive time, that is. For Ballard, the loss of history that results from the airport's modernity provides social glue to hold the departure lounge together as a political prototype: 'Air travel may well be the most important civic duty that we discharge today, erasing class and national distinctions and subsuming them within the unitary global culture of the departure lounge.' Oddly enough, however, for Ballard, the central point of Britain's main airport does not lie within the hundreds of departure lounges themselves, nor its runways, nor its control tower; instead it is manifested in the Heathrow Hilton, designed by Michael Manser in 1986, which Ballard terms 'the most inspiring building in England today … its vast atrium resembl[ing] a planetarium in the way that it salutes the skies above its roof'. In typically skewed fashion, Ballard celebrates an amenity from whose glazed areas the gazer can observe the machines orbiting within airspace, or, like Vaughan in *Crash*, watch the stars passing through.

Marcel Plantevignes, one of a series of young men whom
Marcel Proust had befriended during summers spent on the
Normandy coast, later recalled an evening spent in the writer's
rooms at the Grand Hotel in Cabourg. As they dozed after
dinner, a plane passed very low overhead, and Proust, suddenly awoken from his reverie, pointed at the noise coming
from the sky, and said: *'Ecoutez Marcel, écoutez, les temps futurs
qui sont en marche!'*[16] What this meant for the past emerged periodically in Proust's life's work especially when he considered
familiar places of transition, such as ports and harbours.
Consider his account of the vista from the windows of the
dining room at the Grand Hotel in Balbec, the fictionalized version of Cabourg:

> Alas for that sea-wind … it seemed cruel for my grandmother not
> to be able to feel its life-giving breath on her cheek, because of the
> glass partition, transparent but closed, which, like the front of a
> glass case in a museum, separated us from the beach while per-
> mitting us to look out upon its entirety, and into which the sky
> fitted completely so that its azure had the effect of being the
> colour of the windows and its white clouds the many flaws in the
> glass. Imagining that I was 'sitting on the jetty' or resting in the
> 'boudoir' of which Baudelaire speaks, I wondered if his 'sun's
> rays upon the sea' were not something rather different from the
> evening ray, simple and superficial as a shifting golden shaft –
> just what at that moment was burning the sea topaz-yellow, fer-
> menting it, turning it light and cloudy like beer, frothy like milk.[17]

As he wrote this passage, Proust was attempting not simply to
remember wasted time, *'temps perdus'*, but also the lost textures
of Baudelaire, whose work undertakes, according to the French
critic Marc Augé,

> The spelling out of a position, a 'posture', an attitude in the most
> physical and commonplace sense of the term, [which] comes at
> the end of a movement that empties the landscape, and the gaze

of which it is the object, of all content and all meaning, precisely because the gaze dissolves into the landscape and becomes the object of a secondary, unattributable gaze.[18]

Hence, in a Baudelairean landscape, such as that which Proust was here invoking, 'everything is combined, everything holds together … What is seen by the spectator of modernity is the interweaving of old and new.'[19] Proust accurately recalls 'boudoir' and the 'sun's rays upon the sea' ['*soleil rayonnant sur la mer*'] from Baudelaire's 'Chant d'Automne', poem LVI of *Les Fleurs du mal*: '… not even your love nor the boudoir nor the hearth, means so much to me as the sunlight glittering on the sea' ['*Et rien, ni votre amour, ni le boudoir, ni l'âtre, / Ne me vaut le soleil rayonnant sur le mer*'].[20] However, the earlier allusion to the prose poem 'Le Port' is a more meaningful gesture to the past. Baudelaire's speaker, a man 'sick of the struggles of life', has allowed himself to be carried away into the blissful anonymity only a port can offer, and as he 'reclines on the terrace or leans on the jetty', there is something ghostly about his identity; he seems adrift between what he once was, and what he no longer can be.[21] Proust, 'sitting on the jetty', also seems to identify with the progressive loss of selfhood which lies at the heart of Baudelairean modernity; indeed, his rendering of Baudelaire's own act of 'leaning' ['*accoudé sur le môle*'] as 'sitting' ['*assis*'] is even less strenuous and more passive. But where Baudelaire saw open skies, Proust glimpses a looking glass coterminous with the view of the sea, which, so precisely framed by the dimensions of the window, now exists only as a virtual spectacle. His grandmother may miss the touch of the elements but Proust, ever more circumspect, plays it safe, pressing his face against the chill of the 'glass partition, transparent but closed' ['*du châssis transparent mais clos*'] which functions as a *vitrine*; simultaneously, a plate-glass window, and a show case in a museum.

A similar partition will encountered, when Proust describes the camaraderie of aviation enthusiasts:

Others, keen on aviation, seek to keep in with the old boy in the glazed bar perched above the aerodrome ['*du bar vitré perché au haut de l'aérodrome*']; protected from the wind, as in the glass turret of a lighthouse, they can follow the manoeuvres of a pilot looping the loop in the company of a flier who at that moment is not airborne.[22]

Faced with such terrifying exhibitions in the new aerodromes, it is little wonder that the aviation enthusiasts now remained, like Proust at Balbec, caged behind the glass, insulated from the touch of the elements. He saw such thrilling aeronautical manoeuvres echoed in the unlikeliest of spaces; even, for instance, in the flying angels of Giotto's frescoes for the Arena Chapel in Padua,

> ... real creatures, effectively flying, can be seen soaring upwards, following curves, 'looping the loop', diving towards the earth head first, assisted by wings which enable them to support themselves in positions contrary to the laws of gravity, and make one think of an extinct species of bird, or of young pupils of Fonck practising gliding, than of the angels of the Renaissance and later periods.[23]

As he recalls the designs, Proust finds himself remembering aerodromes, often run by such air aces as René Fonck, to which young men and fallen angels naturally gravitated.[24]

On the afternoon of Saturday, 30 May 1914, at the aerodrome at La Grimaudière near Antibes, a young airman by the name of 'Marcel Swann' climbed into a flimsy aircraft and took off from the grass runway. He had only enrolled for flying lessons two months earlier and yet here he was, already making his second solo flight; as before, as he was carrying in the pocket of his khaki overalls a wad of 7,000 franc notes given by his benefactor. Joseph Garbero, the chief flying instructor, had warned this eager novice – whose real name was Alfred Agostinelli – to stay close to the aerodrome after take-off; but the young man, carried away by the feeling of take-off, ventured north-eastward out over the Mediterranean. As he set himself up to fly back towards the runway, he failed to gain height and speed for the turn; and, as the right wing dipped, his monoplane stalled and crashed into the sea several hundred yards from the shore. The spectators watching from the shore saw the young pilot standing on his seat waving and shouting for help as the wreckage began to sink. He was a non-swimmer, and even as a boat made for him, the plane and the airman disappeared under the waves. The following evening the wrecked aircraft was hauled to the surface, empty; a week later, on Sunday 7 June, a fishing-boat working near Cagnes, 6 miles north-east from the crash scene, found the corpse and brought it back to the jetty. The wad of money was never located.[25]

The dead man's benefactor, of course, was Marcel Proust, who thought his chauffeur had the potential to be a great writer, even if Agostinelli, on their frequent motor jaunts through Normandy lanes, succeeded only in driving his employer to distraction. In late 1913, Proust, furious that his driver had eloped with the intention of learning to fly, had written to him: 'you can tell your wife that if (which heaven forbid) you should have an aeroplane accident, she will find in me neither a protector nor a friend, and will get never a halfpenny from me'.[26] In the years that followed, Proust relented and gave the 'wife', Anna, some financial support, just as he placed her lover at the centre of his sequence of novels. Ineluctably, Alfred Agostinelli became Albertine Simone; and consequently, the type of aviation facility Proust frequently visited with his young employee, in order to watch the planes, and from which Agostinelli took off to his death, assumes a pivotal function in his sequence of novels.

In *La Prisonnière*, for instance, the narrator recalls days spent with Albertine at the aerodrome at Buc:

As there had recently been established round Paris a number of aerodromes, ['*des hangars d'aviation*'] which are for aeroplanes what harbours ['*les ports*'] are for ships … I often chose to end our

day's excursion – with the ready approval of Albertine, an enthusiast of every form of sport – at one of these aerodromes ['ces aérodromes']. We went there, she and I, drawn by that incessant stir of
departure and arrival which gives so much charm to strolls along
jetties ['les jetées'], or merely along the shore, to those who love the
sea, and to hanging around an 'aviation centre' ['un centre d'aviation'] to those who love the sky. From time to time, amid the
repose of the machines that lay inert and as if at anchor, we would
see one being laboriously hauled by several mechanics, as a boat
is dragged across the sand at the request of a tourist who wishes
to go for an excursion on the sea. Then the motor was started, the
machine ran along the ground, gathered speed, until finally, all of
a sudden, at right angles, it rose slowly, in the stiff and almost
static ecstasy of horizontal speed suddenly transformed into
majestic, vertical ascent. Albertine could not contain her joy, and
demanded explanations from the mechanics who, now that the
machine was in the air, came back.[27]

In this beautifully precise passage of flight, Proust fixes upon
the sudden shift from the horizontal plane, that zone which
contains mundane, banal and habitual, to the vertical, representing the new dimension of freedom, vision and will. In what
may have been one of the last textual revisions he made before
he died, Proust added the words *'verticale'* before *'ascension'*;
hence, that phrase 'in stiff and almost static ecstasy' [*'l'extase
raidie, comme immobilisée'*] freezes the moment at which the pilot
crosses the threshold between earth, the element on which we
stand, and sky, the element in which we breathe, before Proust
goes on to describe the circumstances of the flight itself:[28]

The passenger, meanwhile, was covering mile after mile; the
small craft, upon which our eyes remained fixed, was now no
more than an almost indistinct dot in the sky ['l'azur'], a speck
which, however, would gradually recover its solidity, its size, its
volume, when, as the time allowed for the excursion drew to an
end, the moment came to return to the field ['rentrer au port'].[29]

After it has taken to the air, the narrator watches the plane diminish to the size of 'an almost indistinct speck' ['*un point presque indistinct*'] and then, in due course, grow again; so that at the point of landing it has reacquired the volume, the shape, the dimension that it began to lose as it made the shift from one space to the next. Something, inevitably, is lost in this process of elevation; and not just contact with the earth.

Like an aircraft on the point of stalling, Proust's account of the flight wavers and becomes unstable just when it abandons any attempt to come to terms with the facilities from which these activities commence. As a means of identifying the aviation facilities, Proust provides three new terms: '*hangars d'aviation*'; '*aérodromes*'; '*centre d'aviation*'; finally, however, the plane, which late in the passage is nothing more than 'the small craft' ['*l'esquiff*'] lands at the 'port', a topography familiar from Baudelaire's prose poem. Yet by the time the sentence comes to rest, Proust's earlier '*azur*' has itself become indistinct, since it could either denote either element, sea or sky; and since the account of the process of departure and arrival is couched entirely in conditional voice ['*reprendrait ... serait venu*'], it becomes clear that finally, Proust is using the image of the boat returning to jetty (so familiar from Baudelaire's prose poem) as a metaphor for an aircraft returning to an aerodrome; the past is being used to *transport* the present.

For Proust, after the death of Agostinelli, the aerodrome became a place where the difference between past and present, truth and fiction became blurred, a place of illicit *rendez-vous* and of downright lying. In *Albertine disparu*, the narrator recalls:

One day she [Albertine] had told me that she had been to an aerodrome ['*camp d'aviation*'] where one of the airmen was a friend of hers (this doubtless in order to divert my suspicions from women, thinking that I was less jealous of men), and that it had been amusing to see how dazzled Andrée was in the presence of this airman, by all the compliments he paid Albertine, until finally Andrée had wanted to go up in his aeroplane with him. However, this was a complete fiction; Andrée had never even visited the aerodrome in question.[30]

This is a type of 'transference' which strongly suggests – because we can be quite sure the pilot was male – that Proust was chiefly jealous of Agostinelli's relations with the many women who flocked to the aerodromes. It seems that, because such a place abolished the ordinariness of landscape, undermined the authority of the status quo, and flattened aesthetics, the aerodrome was somehow complicit in this destabilization of the identity of self and other. Indeed, by naming it *'camp d'aviation'*, Proust here queried its very status, suggesting it was impermanent; and yet on so many occasions in his fiction, the place offered itself as nothing less than the platform from which his own aesthetic could take off.

In the second novel of his sequence, *A l'ombre des jeunes filles en fleurs*, Proust discusses Bergotte, a successful writer of humble origin, and observes that:

> To move in the winds it is not necessary to have the most powerful of motors, but a motor which, instead of continuing to run along the earth's surface, along the horizontal which it began by following, intersects with a vertical line, and so is capable of converting its speed into lifting power. [31]

In order to ascend, to take to the skies, Proust argued that it was not required to possess the most powerful vehicle, but simply the one which, as it moved across some notional runway, could most efficiently convert velocity into altitude ['*convertir en force ascensionnelle sa vitesse horizontale*']; Bergotte, the 'pilot' of a vehicle which, although unprepossessing in appearance, and no match for others in terms of style, is able to gather speed, transform itself into an aircraft, and overfly those critics, who, 'in their fine Rolls Royces might return home expressing due contempt for the vulgarity of the Bergottes; but he, in his modest machine which had at last "taken off", soared above their heads' ['*de son modeste appareil qui venait enfin de "décoller", il les survolait*'].[32] Proust places the verb '*décoller*' in inverted commas since at the time he was writing, the noun from which it was formed, '*décollage*', was yet to acquire the modern French sense of 'take-off' and meant literally 'to become unstuck'; the opposite of collage. What is most crucial in this usage is that, for Proust, the airport was proving itself as a platform on which horizontal velocity could be converted into aspirational energy, and then back again.[33] On the other hand, there were other artists who, like experimental aircraft, never left the runway: 'These sterile and whimsical amateurs are as touching to contemplate as those first machines which tried to leave the ground and could not, but which yet carried within them, if not the secret, the still to be discovered method, at least the desire of flight.'[34] And, in Proust's imagining, flight was inevitably asssociated with desire; the yearning for that which has been lost.

On a final excursion with Albertine to Versailles, the narrator looks at the bright blue airspace overhead and thinks of his grandmother, who used to enjoy gazing at the steeple of Saint-Hilaire at Combrai 'soaring into that same blue':

> Suddenly I experienced once again a nostalgia for my lost freedom on hearing a noise which I did not at first recognise and which my grandmother would also have loved. It was like the buzz of a wasp. 'Look' said Albertine, 'there's an aeroplane, it's very high, very high.'[35]

It takes a few moments for him to locate the aircraft flying at an altitude of several thousand feet in the 'unalloyed blue'; when he does, it is clear that even this most modern of machines carries with it a cargo of the lost past, a history rather than a future. During the epiphanic section towards the close of *Le Temps retrouvé*, the same machine is equated with the steeple as an embodiment of spatial splendour: 'grandeur, for example, in the distant sound of an aeroplane or the outline of the steeple of Saint-Hilaire' ['*la grandeur dans le bruit lointain d'un aeroplane, dans la ligne du clocher de Saint-Hilaire*']. The key term here is '*ligne*', suggesting an order of architecture as well as a trajectory of descent. Since the impetus of Proust's fiction amounts to a seeking out of wasted time, of a lost life, then the church at Combrai matches this quest, as it is 'an edifice occupying, so to speak, a four-dimensional space – the name of the fourth being Time' ['*un édifice occupant … un espace à quatre dimensions – la quatrieme étant celle du Temps*']; and aircraft, taking to the skies from aerodromes, occupied a similar space. As both objects demonstrate, the recovery of lost time is possible, but only through a precise elevation beginning from some solid foundation.

After Albertine's accidental death – she falls from a horse, rather than out of the sky – the narrator, suffering from writer's block, and a range of physical ailments, retires to a sanatorium outside Paris, where he lives, chronically unwell. Regarding himself as an artistic failure, he returns to Paris and is driven though the city to attend a *matinée chez* La Princesse de Guermantes. As his car traverses the badly paved streets near the Champs-Elysées, so familiar to him as a boy, the narrator suddenly experiences the feeling of flight:

> The solid earth knew in itself where it had to go; its resistance was vanquished. And like an aviator who hitherto has progressed laboriously along the ground, before abruptly 'taking off' ['*décollant brusquement*'] I soared slowly towards the silent heights of memory ['*je m'élevais vers les hauteurs silencieuses du souvenir*'].[36]

Up until this point in his career, the narrator has perceived himself as just another one of those who could never rise to the occasion, artistically at least, because the artistic vehicle he piloted could never gain sufficient velocity to leave the runway. Now, however, as he moves down the great runway of the Champs-Elysées, he realizes that he is experiencing a 'take off' whose disconnecting force might furnish a way across that unprecedented distance between himself and his past, and enable him to come to terms with the ultimate loss and gain. Merely the sense of an aerodrome provides him with a platform from which to fly '*vers les hauteurs silencieuses du souvenir*', in order to arrive at his '*temps perdus*', his lost opportunities and wasted time.

Hence that extraordinary moment in *Sodome & Gomorrah*, when the narrator, riding through the woods near Balbec, sees an aeroplane for the first time, and bursts into tears:

44

... the airman seemed to hesitate over his course; I felt that there lay open before him – before me, had not habit made me a prisoner – all the routes in space, in life itself; he pushed on, let himself glide for a few moments over the sea, then quickly making up his mind, seeming to yield to some attraction that was the opposite of gravity, as though returning to his native element, with a slight movement of his golden wings he headed straight up to the sky.[37]

Of course, as far as Proust is concerned, the golden-winged pilot here can only be Agostinelli, uncertain of his course (just as he was on the day of his death) and abandoning himself. The difference here, however, is that this pilot succeeds in pulling the plane into trim, and climbing away from the ground. Little wonder the Narrator is in tears, for this is the ultimate fiction, one strong enough to countenance the reversal of gravity, a death defied. Even though there is not an aerodrome in the vicinity, what is clearly present in this passage is an early version of that act of empathy with (and desire for) flight so often experienced this century by those left behind, standing on jetties or sitting behind glass.

PORTS-AVIATION

Scattered in villages around Paris, the aerodromes Proust visited were uniformly unprepossessing in terms of clientele and appearance. In October 1913, Maurice Paléologue wrote of Jean Cocteau's friend the Grand-Duchess Anastasia: '... she is fifty-three, she lives openly with an Argentinian blackguard, dances at Magic City with all comers till two in the morning, and associates with all the scum of the aerodromes.'[38]

In January 1911, Jacques Lartigue, one of France's most distinguished photographers, had been recording images of aircraft in flight at Issy-les-Moulineaux, a famous airfield formerly used by the army for training. To his trained eye, it looked like nothing other than a ploughed-up plain, 'immense and deserted ... On one side, a few small houses; on the other, the fortifications with trees and the railway track of the little commuter train by which I arrive'. Skirting the aerodrome were several tall chimneys belching smoke; Issy, situated south west of Paris, had recovered quickly after the rising of the commune in 1871 (which destroyed three-quarters of the town) and was now a centre of heavy industry. The place had also acquired a reputation as a cultural attraction: the upper part of the town and hillside were often visited by two great artists, Auguste Rodin and Henri Matisse, the latter living there from 1909 to 1917; the airfield itself was visited frequently by Picasso, Braque and the Delaunays.[39]

However, Issy was only ever an ad-hoc airfield; the first aerodrome, constructed in late 1908 at Juvisy, 15 miles south of Paris, was modelled on the hippodrome at Longchamp. Known as Port-Aviation, it was nothing more than a large flat field, covered in grass, about 800 yards in diameter; around its edges, the owners erected hangars, workshops and, uniquely, grandstands withh rudimentary catering facilities to accommodate several thousand visitors. The attraction for the visitor to Port-Aviation was simple: the aerodrome – the flat space on which planes arrived and departed – had became the new, modern threshold between one element and another, whose very design was, as it were, unlimited; it could define itself only spatially, only in terms of aircraft entering and leaving the frontier of airspace. Louis Blériot having crossed the channel, there were no more state boundaries. Such was the familiar cry, anyway, uttered across Europe. Stefan Zweig remembered the reaction to Blériot's achievement in the cafés of Vienna:

> We shouted with joy when Blériot flew over the channel as if he had been our own hero; because of our pride in the successive triumphs of our technics, our science, a European community spirit, a European national consciousness was coming into being. How useless we said to ourselves, are frontiers when any plane can fly over them with ease, how provincial and artificial are customs-duties, guards and border patrols, how incongruous in the spirit of the times which visibly seeks unity and world brotherhood.[40]

A photograph by Jacques Lartigue of Issy-les-Moulineaux, December 1911.

Roland Garros photographed by Lartigue as he flew over the aerodrome at Issy-les-Moulineaux in 1911, from *La Vie au grand air*.

The young architect Charles-Edouard Jeanneret, then working in Paris at the offices of the Perret brothers, witnessed the typical response as his employer, Auguste Perret, burst into the *atelier*, a newspaper in his fist, and shouted: 'Blériot has crossed the channel! Wars are finished: no more wars are possible! There are no longer any frontiers!'[41] It was not so much that frontiers no longer existed; it was that they were changing, and with them, perceptions and behaviour altered too. In *Aircraft* (1935), Jeanneret, better known as Le Corbusier, remembered the impact a series of historic flights made on Parisians during 1909:

> ... from my student's garret on the Quai St. Michel I heard a noise which for the first time filled the entire sky of Paris. Until then men had been aware of one voice only from above – bellowing or thundering – the voice of the storm. I craned my neck out of the small window to catch sight of this unknown messenger. The Comte de Lambert, having succeeded in 'taking off' at Juvisy, had descended toward Paris and circled the Eiffel Tower at a height of 300 metres. It was miraculous, it was mad! Our dreams then could become reality, however daring they might be.[42]

In previous years, 'scattered madmen in the flat fields of lucerne', famous fliers such as Santos Dumont, the Wright brothers and Voisin had 'captured the chimera and driven it above the city'. The fanciful conception in question was the possibility of powered flight; the aviators were based at such places as Issy and Juvisy, and using them as launching pads for a new perception of the world. The sculptor Léon Delagrange, one of the finest pilots of the early days, provided a curious insight to the way in which crowds at aerodromes behaved, in his account of the opening of Juvisy in May 1909. Huge numbers had gathered for the first day's flying, and nine machines were announced to appear, but only three were wheeled out onto the field. Delagrange made what was considered a cautious little flight, and another pilot, one De Bischoff, attempted to take off, but could not get his machine off the ground. Thereupon the crowd of 30,000 people lost their tempers, broke down the barriers surrounding the flying course, and remonstrated with the officials, who were quite unable to maintain order.

In *Aircraft*, Le Corbusier also offers an account of the break-down in public order at Port-Aviation in 1909. He recalls being one of 'three hundred thousand people' who woke early one morning in Paris ('The sky was blue. It was spring') resolved to journey out to Juvisy, where Hubert Latham and other aviators had announced that they would fly at 2.00 pm. By his own admission, Le Corbusier is generally unreliable as a narrator: the 'meeting' took place in October, and even generous esti-mates put the size of the crowd at no greater than 100,000. Even so, the railway authorities were completely taken aback by the demand; although extra coaches were procured, and trains ran in duplicate, neither arrangement could begin to deal with the huge mass of spectators determined to make their way to the aerodrome. Le Corbusier left central Paris at midday, but when his train pulled in at Juvisy it was 7.00 pm and already dark. During their interminable journey, his frustrated fellow passen-gers had vandalized their own carriage. On arrival at the sta-tion they headed in search of food, only to discover that the gates had been closed and were guarded by soldiers with fixed bayonets. On the platform, having missed the fliers in action, a mob was waiting impatiently for coaches that would transport them to Paris:

> There was then a beautiful manifestation of the human intelligence, human solidarity and the collective spirit. The mob, one knows, generally becomes inspired when it is necessary to take action …
> As our train did not leave and other trains arrived in the night, filled with would be spectators for the 'aviation meeting,' we set to work to demolish the station. The station at Juvisy was a big one. The waiting-rooms went first, then the staff offices, then the station-master's office. I still see the room with its overturned furniture, its innumerable electric wires in wild strands: a gentleman armed with a cane, indomitable, carried on javelin-play at the centre of each mirror, methodically … At eleven we returned to Paris.[43]

This account carries a potent symbolism. Juvisy's railway station, the sign of a nineteenth-century means of transport, is smashed up, and the glass of its numerous mirrors, offering nothing but the opportunity for aimless self-regard, is shattered. Instead, attention is directed to a new space, a new platform, about to announce itself: the first airport.

Notwithstanding the unleashed energies described in Le Corbusier's account, other early airports tended to accommodate more passive visitors. The largest plane-spotting event ever was the meeting which took place in the last week of August 1909 – a month after Blériot's channel crossing – at Rheims in northern France. 'La Grande Semaine de l'aviation de la Champagne' was organized by a syndicate of French businessmen, incorporated under the name of the 'Compagnie Générale de l'Aérolocomotion' and presided over by the Marquis de Polignac, a champagne magnate. The site selected for the event was the plain of Betheny, just north of the city on the road to Neuchâtel; over this flat expanse, a 7-mile-long rectangular flying course was pegged out, using wooden towers. Railway tracks were laid to transport spectators from Rheims to the airfield, and a terminal named Fresnay-Aviation – in imitation of Port-Aviation – was constructed to greet them. A few hundred yards from this building, four elegantly appointed grandstands were erected, large enough to hold 3,500 wealthy spectators, as well as a large terrace restaurant, which would prove equally popular; 3,500 bottles of champagne were consumed during the meeting. In front of the grandstands, strewn over the open field, stood the less affluent spectators; on average, about 50,000 each day. Over the next week, 500,000 people visited, among them the President of France, Roosevelt and the First Lady, David Lloyd George, the future King of the Belgians and numerous high-ranking military figures. On the last day, over 250,000 visitors paid up, and saw Latham break the altitude record, circling higher and higher until he attained the dizzy height of 508 feet, before descending slowly to the runway. It was the ultimate spectacle; as the correspondent of *Le Petit Parisien* wrote: 'Yes, to be honest everything that has happened astonishes you, surprises your imagination, leaves you deeply moved and disconcerted, your head a bit dizzy as if you'd had too much to drink.'[44]

The early passion for watching planes propel themselves over the lucerne runways had little to do with prospects of public transportation or thoughts of commercial utility, present or future. What drew spectators was the risk involved. Just over a week after the Rheims meeting, Eugen Lefevre, one of France's most charismatic pilots, famous for his daring manoeuvres, was killed at Juvisy: having lost control of his machine while making a low turn, he crashed in front of the airport restaurant where he had just enjoyed a meal with some friends. Spectators were drawn into the danger, too. In May 1911, a flying machine piloted by Train made a steep turn, stalled and careered into a crowd of dignitaries assembled on the runway at Issy to watch the start of the Paris–Madrid air race; among the dead was the French Minister of War.

Some writers were troubled by the spectacle the airport itself presented. Franz Kafka was one of 50,000 people who had paid to watch an airshow in Brescia in September 1909. Having arrived at the aerodrome, Kafka and his friends, Max and Otto Brod, were confronted by a large expanse of grass around which were arrayed a number of sheds bearing unexpected designations: garage, snack bar and so on.[45] Over each of the hangars, which, with their curtains closed, recalled 'the packed-up stages of a touring dramatic company', flew the flag of the aviator's country; across each was written the aviator's name. They sought out Blériot but instead found Glenn Curtiss, sitting alone and patiently reading an old copy of the *New York Herald*, waiting for the moment when the wind would fall sufficiently so that he could take off. On their return to his hangar half an hour later, Curtiss was still staring at the same page. Gazing at this oddly lifeless scene, Kafka observed: '… order and accidents ['*Ordnung und Unglücksfall*'] seem equally unlikely.'

At first glance, Kafka's piece contains distant echoes of Baudelaire and Proust, but unlike the vistas of Normandy, this

51

An air meeting near Rheims in 1909, showing grandstands with hangars and the airfield in the background; from *Livre d'or de la conquête de l'air*.

great expanse is perplexing. Rather than the simple pleasures of watching boats, there is the tedium of waiting for aircraft to leave the ground; rather than natural exuberance, there is fragility; rather than a sense of space, there is a strange sense of contraction. Indeed, the longer Kafka spent at the airport, the more uncomfortable he became. Gazing across its wide expanse, he saw nothing but an 'artificial wasteland' ['*eine künstliche Einöde*'] in an 'almost tropical land' ['*in einem fast tropischen Lande*']; the Italian nobility, fine Parisian women and all those other people in the grandstands were gathered here 'in order to spend several hours, staring with narrowed eyes across this sunny desert' ['*diese sonnige Einöde*']. Given the fact that this was a sporting meeting, the few scattered objects to be seen on the field seemed scant compensation for what they replaced; Kafka missed 'the lovely hurdles of racecourses, the white lines of tennis courts, the fresh turf of soccer matches, the stony furrows of automobile and cycle tracks'. But there were even larger issues to confront here. Milling around in the mass of spectators, Kafka suddenly realized that, viewed from the perspective of the expensive, tall grandstands which loomed behind him, the crowd of which he was now a part must appear to melt imperceptibly into the 'empty plain' ['*leeren Ebene*']. Even in 1909, he was beginning to sense that a world enthralled by the plane was somehow diminished, and would soon be under threat. As they watch Blériot fly 70 feet above the ground, imprisoned in a wooden frame, and defending himself against an invisible danger, the spectators standing below are 'pushed away, without existence' ['*wesenlos*']. This is an amazingly pre-scient account of the modern airspace, with Kafka perceiving (and being perplexed by) a profoundly inhuman space which shatters and effaces the individual. The great aerodrome, a seemingly benign threshold between earth and sky, swallowed up the present; devotedly, everyone looks into airspace, with the consequence that 'there is no room in anybody's heart for anything else' ['*in keinem Herzen ist für anderen Platz*'].[46]

ON THE JETTY

In 1989, the French writer François Maspero, accompanied by the photographer Anail Frantz, undertook a journey on the Paris RER B line from CDG down to Saint Remy les Chevreuse, 38 stations away. As they began their journey in the vast machin-ery of Terminal 1 at CDG, they asked themselves ruefully whether an attractive airport had ever existed. Frantz suggested, simply, that one might consist of 'a hangar at the end of a runway: Ziguinchor [in Senegal], say, with the delighted chil-dren surrounding an old DC-3 at the end of the tarmac'; Maspero travelled farther afield, suggesting 'Murmansk or a hut in the Far North in the midnight sun' before returning to Paris and settling on Orly:

> Orly in its first year – was it 1963? – with is gleaming high steel-
> blue outline, pure and clean, standing alone at the end of the
> motorway rushing towards it, into it, under it; he used to finish
> work at midnight and drive from the centre of Paris to Orly; the

inside of the airport was huge and brilliantly lit, the echoes crystal-clear; as the last flights took off, there was time for one last cup of coffee.[47]

When in late February 1961, De Gaulle opened the new terminal at Orly, seven miles south of the French capital and within earshot of the ancient aerodromes at Juvisy and Issy, he described it grandly as the 'meeting place of sky and earth' ['*la rencontre du ciel et de la terre*'].[48] Within a year the airport had, much to the surprise of the authorities, become one of the biggest attractions in Paris; by 1964 it was receiving three million visitors a year, making it more popular than the Palais de Versailles. For the first time ever, a place existing to facilitate one of the great myths and rituals of modernity, air travel, had been designed with a desire to communicate emotion and comfort passengers.

Orly's architect, Henri Vicariot, created a terminal consisting of a massive rectangular box frame fabricated out of stainless steel over which, in order to absorb ambient sound, curtain walls were elastically suspended. Resistant to weathering, the steel offered the advantage of always looking like new, even on the window mullions. In total, the terminal building presented a surface area of 12 square miles, of which over half was glass. This daring use of materials, intended to create totally new façades, patterns and spaces, marked a key moment in the architectural awareness of an entire continent. For the first time since the war, Europe seemed, perhaps, to be capable of creating its own image of modernity, drawing on its native canons and interacting with the present on a more objective basis than, say, Saarinen's TWA terminal at JFK. For Orly was, in effect, a massive *vitrine*: a window on the world, and a display case.

Straddling the A7 'Autoroute du Sud', this extraordinary terminal contained a new world consisting of a 300-seat cinema; several hotels; an exhibition space; a Michelin-starred restaurant; a chapel fitted out with marble detailing; a crèche strangely decorated with brightly coloured birds; and, of course, shops stocking luxury products from all over France and its colonies. Men and women would hang around its vast air-conditioned concourse, enjoy an espresso, take in a film. Above it all, aloof from the commodification going on down below, were observation terraces open to the public, the piers along which the great jets docked, along which, every Sunday, families would range themselves with picnics to spend the afternoon contemplating the movements of aircraft.

Indeed, Orly's attraction did not manifest itself as much on the level of architectural singularity as on that of symbolically rich experience. Its airspace provoked an emotional disequilibrium, placing into question the individual's sense of selfhood. Take Gilbert Bécaud's 1964 hit record 'Dimanche à Orly', whose

Orly at night, 1962.

The tower and terminal at Orly, *c.* 1966.

Apron and terminal at Orly, *c.* 1966.

lyrics by Pierre Delanoë tell of a young man's sense of entrapment in the consumer culture of the Fourth Republic. Living in a nice apartment that his father, if all goes according to payment plan, will own outright in 20 years, the young man is surrounded and stultified by all the mod cons. On Sundays, his mother does the housework, his father watches the sport on television; he, however, travels out to Orly to watch the jets taking off for new worlds, and spends his time there dreaming of leaving on board one of them. In the evening, back in his parents' apartment, *'J'entends les Boeings chanter là-haut / Je les aime, mes oiseaux de nuit / Et j'irai les retrouver bientôt'* ['I hear the Boeings singing above, I love them, my night birds / And I will go back to visit them again']. Being the vessel of his aspiration, even its momentary vehicle, the airport produces a number of internal effects on him: a capacity to dream, a resilient certainty, a faith and a moral vision according to which everything that lies outside the airport's ambit is unworthy. Orly is entitled to its privileged position in this song, its radiance beyond its verses, not by virtue of any intrinsic merit or luminiferous capacity that it may be thought to possess, but because a chance representative of humanity has chosen to declare his enrapturement for the *'oiseaux de nuit'* which move through its airspace. Increasingly evident in Delanoë's lyrics is the degree to which the young man is reliant upon the airport; it has become an all or nothing affair, as aircraft flying to 'tous *les pays'* are linked with the continuity of 'toute *une vie'*, and then, with the speaker imagining himself on board a jet, its altitude reduces his apartment block to little more than 'tout *petit point'*. While affirmative throughout, the young man, like Proust's narrator, only discovers his full capacity for affirmation as he identifies with the feeling of take-off. But at the same time, his motivation is much more reckless, since the speaker seeks to be transported by a defiantly optimistic aspiration, the dangers of which were only too clear to the regular spectators on the Orly terrace.

On 3 June 1962, the usual crowd of sightseers and planespotters thronged the airport. On this particular Sunday, the weather was fine, if a little chilly, as a breeze was blowing across the airport from the north, scattering the clouds. Just after 1.30 pm those on the terrace saw a 2-year-old Air France Boeing 707 push back from the gate and heard the whine of its turbines. The jet, named *Sully* after the château near Tours, was carrying 10 crew and 122 passengers, and had been chartered by the Atlanta Art Association to fly to Atlanta and Houston, via JFK. The group, 121 strong, consisted of amateurs, academics, art historians, architects and artists on a three-week field trip to Europe; some of the party had done the Grand Tour of the continent's capital cities, but most had opted to remain in and around Paris. They were now on their way home in the gleaming white machine which would carry them and, their memories of a Europe newly rebuilt, back across six time zones.

The aircraft taxied across the airport, turned onto runway 08 and aligned itself for take-off. After final checks to the flap settings, full thrust was applied, and, with a sudden roar, the great jet began to accelerate along the centre line of the runway. Forty-eight seconds after the beginning of the run, and approximately 1800 yards down the runway, in full view of the spectators, the aircraft reached the take-off speed, 158 knots, and the pilot pulled backwards on the control column. According to accounts of witnesses, the aircraft then lifted its nose, and held this position for several seconds; by which point, the 707 was 2,600 yards from its starting point and had reached its maximum speed of 179 knots. Then, rather than finally lifting away from the concrete strip, the nose wheel kissed the ground again with a puff of burnt rubber; the brakes were instantly applied, and clouds of smoke began to issue from the red-hot undercarriage. Now out of control, the aircraft veered slightly to the left and then listed heavily in the opposite direction, barrelling off the runway and onto the grass threshold. At this point, owing to the high speed of the jet and the roughness of the turf, the left-hand landing gear snapped off, causing the underwing engines to dig into the ground and break away. Still moving quickly, the aircraft now crossed the airport perimeter road,

58

A young plane-spotter at Orly, 1960.

struck the approach lights, and started to disintegrate; the nose broke off and struck a house and garage, while the rest of the fuselage came to a stop 100 yards further on in gardens on the edge of the village of Villeneuve-le-Roi, narrowly avoiding a terrace of houses. The kinetic energy of this collision caused all 18,000 gallons of kerosene to spurt out of the massive wing tanks, and explode. The fireball was huge, immediately engulfing the main fuselage; such was the intensity of the blaze that firefighters were unable to approach the wreckage to free the bodies for an hour and a half. Amazingly, two air hostesses sitting on jump seats at the rear of the aircraft escaped with shock and minor injuries after being hurled into vegetation; one of them told reporters: 'We didn't have time to realize what was happening … it was all so quick, so sudden.' After the fire was extinguished, a steward was found alive in the wreckage, but shortly after his rescue, he succumbed to his burns. In all, 130 people died, a small death toll by today's standards, but, at the time, it was the worst air accident Europe had seen, and the world's worst disaster involving a single aircraft. Furthermore, it had taken place not over a desert, or in the middle of an ocean, but at the world's most modern airport in front of the crowded jetty.[49]

In New York the following day, Andy Warhol was lunching at 'Serendipity 3', a coffee shop *cum* general store on East 60th Street, accompanied by his associate, Henry Geldzahler. Warhol was in a good mood – his 'soup cans' were about to be exhibited at the Ferus Gallery in Los Angeles – and he was looking forward to one of the extravagant desserts for which Serendipity was renowned. His friend, however, was impatient. In Warhol's recent works, there had been, for him, sufficient 'affirmation of soups and Coke bottles', 'too much emphasis upon the consumerist aspect', and so he sought to bring the artist back down to earth, telling him: 'It is enough life. It is time for a little death.' To illustrate his pronouncement, he picked up a copy of that day's *New York Mirror*, whose front page carried a report on the Paris crash. Waving the tabloid at Warhol, Geldzahler said: 'This is what's really happening.'[50]

In response, Warhol painted *129 Die in Jet (Plane Crash)*, now in the Museum Ludwig, Cologne. This canvas, completed in the summer of 1962, reproduces the very image of the disaster which the media sent out from the airport immediately after the crash; Warhol even records the photo credit: '*UPI RADIOTELE photo*'. But here the image has been deprived even of the human interest the news photograph contained. The crash investigators picking through tangled wreckage in the photograph have disappeared into the monochrome haze of Warhol's canvas; the policemen watching the grim labours of rescuers, have become shady and secretive, more like Gestapo than *gendarmerie*. Furthermore, the landscape at the edge of Orly has been

The aftermath of the crash at Orly on 3 June 1962.

bleached of its features, scarred and entrenched like some World War I battleground; bushes and trees have died back into abstract space or broken lines, and a birch sapling, snapped in half by the explosion, becomes, in Warhol's representation, a stark cross, or gallows. While the large stanchions of the approach lights on the left have gone, the striped poles on the right are represented by mysterious blocks of paint which seem to hover in mid air. This is echoed in Warhol's rendering of the tailplane, the charred *empannage*, whose expensive delicate ribbing, clearly visible in the UPI image has been painted out, to create a monolith. Where the photograph showed the tail attached to the rear of the fuselage, which rested on the ground, in Warhol's reproduction it seems to float, a questionable shape – a black void – flagging the finality which is officially announced on the newspaper's masthead.[51] In Warhol's painting, all that remains of substance is the endless present of the headline '129 DIE', the record of an interminable tense. Yet, in terms of his career, the painting itself was oddly final. Perhaps intended as a memorial to a group of connoisseurs of fine art, *129 Die* was the last of Warhol's works to be executed using brushes; from here on his reproduction would be undertaken mechanically. The speed of the jet age demanded it.

At the time, the jet was exciting many other cultural commentators. Roland Barthes, celebrating the culture of thrust in relation to La Tour Eiffel, suggested that the new aviation technology could even lead to time travel:

> Indeed, iron provides human communication with a new image, that of the thrust ['*jet*']. The work of metal, as if cast at a single stroke (even though, in fact, it is minutely assembled), seems to be hurled ['*jeté*'] above obstacles, thus suggesting that time itself is conquered, curtailed by a sharp turn and prefiguring once more the thrust ['*jet*'] of the plane above continents and oceans.[52]

At the time, the great metal wings of Orly, stretching either side of the main terminal, had become as strong an image of modernity as Eiffel's structure. Chris Marker chose to begin *La Jetée*, the remarkable short film he made in 1962, at the airport on a Sunday afternoon, shortly after the completion of the new terminal. The '*jetée*' of his title refers to the famous roof terrace where, as a child, the main character used to come with his parents to watch the jets: 'On this particular Sunday, the child, whose story we are telling, was bound to remember the frozen sun, the setting at the end of the jetty.'[53] The reason why he will never forget is the nub of the film, even though, at the airport, time seems to be 'frozen', to have acquired a near-solid presence, in the form of the jetty itself. J. G. Ballard describes Marker's opening image in the following terms: 'The long pier reaches out across the concrete no-man's-land, the departure point for other worlds. Giant jets rest on the apron beside the pier, metallic ciphers whose streamlining is a code for their passage through time.'[54] Though he is not discussing Marker's film, Jacques Derrida is nevertheless interested in the means by

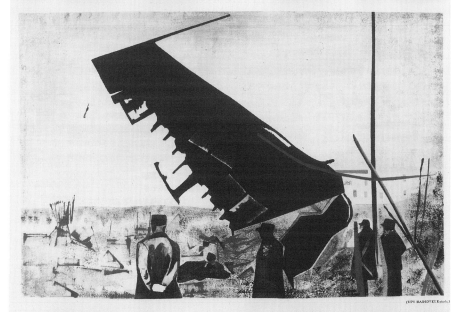

Andy Warhol, *129 Die in Jet (Plane Crash)*, 1962, synthetic polymer paint on canvas.
Museum Ludwig, Cologne.

which a concrete *image* of a jetty, along with other images resting on it, might serve as a point of departure:

> I'll use again the word 'jetty,' in which I distinguish, on the one hand, the force of the movement which throws something or throws itself (*jette* or *se jette*) forward and backwards at the same time, prior to any subject, object, or project, prior to any rejection or abjection, from, on the other hand its institutional and protective consolidation, which can be compared to the jetty, the pier in a harbor meant to break the waves and maintain low tide for boats at anchor or for swimmers. Of course, these two functions of the jetty are ideally distinct, but in fact they are difficult to dissociate, if not indissociable.[55]

Having established a similar disjunction between 'the force of movement' and the 'institutional consolidation', Marker's film leads into a meditation upon human aspiration, time and memory, repeatedly questioning the stability and reliability of the jetty as a departure point for memory and imagination. What follows is a series of grainy stills, accompanied by a monotonous voice-over, recounting experiments carried out on a prisoner in the subterranean camps to which everyone has been forced after the holocaust of World War III, a conflict Marker ironically represents by archival images of the damage done to French cities during World War II. These experiments, which involve the despatch of messengers into both the past and the future to bring back help, will purportedly save humanity; for as the hero is informed, '… space was off-limits. The only hope for survival lay in Time.'

The prisoner has been selected, it emerges, on the strength of his obsessive attachment to a single image of the past; a childhood memory of the jetty at Orly, at the end of which stands a beautiful young woman. Through a combination of psychopharmocology and Electro Convulsive Therapy, he is eventually able to 'arrive' in the past he so vividly recalls, and like a ghost, appear to the woman at various times and places in her life. Satisfied with this achievement, the experimenters send him on his real mission: to travel into the future to catch 'some waves of the world to come', and bring back 'a power unit strong enough to put all human industry back into motion'.

Once back in the devastated present, the prisoner is transferred to 'another part of the camp' to await liquidation along with 'somewhere inside him, the memory of a twice-lived fragment of time'. However, before the scientists can dispose of him, the people of the 'world to come' travel back through Time, ready to accept him as one of their own in the 'pacifed Future'. He declines their offer, but requests that they now help him return to the world before the carnage,' to the world of his childhood ... to the woman who was perhaps waiting for him'. They agree, and so the film closes with a return to the airport: 'Once again on the main jetty at Orly, in the middle of this warm pre-war Sunday where he could now stay, he thought in a confused way, that the child he had been was due to be there too, watching the planes.' But as the time traveller runs down the jetty to join the woman he recognizes from a former life, he is confronted by a man from the prison camp staff (who have had time, of course, to perfect their own technologies) who 'shoots' him. As he falls to the ground, 'the time traveller understood that one doesn't escape Time, and that this moment that he had been shown in his childhood, which had continued to haunt him ever since, was the moment of his own death.'

La Jetée chronicles a death foretold. A man foresees his own future death on the roof terrace at Orly; but this is not so much an intimation of mortality as a reminder of the future. Early in the film, the first photographic image of the woman – 'the only peacetime image to survive the war' – is a close-up of her face, bearing a pensive expression; behind her stretch the flat and depthless spaces of the airfield. The sequence of frozen images that follows, and that accompanies the narrator's description of 'the madness to come', is central to the remainder of the film. First we see a Comet jet – an airliner notorious for its mid-air break-ups – flying low in the air, followed by two still images of the woman, seemingly reacting to external stimuli. The first is

'A woman's face …':
a still from Chris Marker's
1962 film *La Jetée*.

'The sudden roar …':
a still from *La Jetée*.

'A body in motion': a still from *La Jetée*.

'Blurred by fear': a still from *La Jetée*.

an agitated face looking out, along the jetty, hands moving to the face; the second makes it possible to identify the object of her gaze as a body in motion, seemingly spinning out of control and about to fall to the ground. Next come the reactions of bystanders, and then the image of another plane on the apron, this time 'blurred by fear'. This last shot, implies some kind of shock, a tremor strong enough to rock the terminal; it could only be an explosion, in or around Orly. In this justly famous sequence, Marker is playing with expectations of what might befall spectators on a Sunday afternoon at the airport. After all, his title, *La Jetée*, implies a projectile, something thrown out or expelled, like exhaust gas from a jet turbine. Clearly, as the time traveller sprints down the pier, we are meant to think of the fate of an aircraft moving down the runway, perhaps even that doomed Air France 707 which crashed the year the film was made.

Of the last moments of Marker's film, Ballard writes: 'Rather than leave the young woman, he throws himself from the pier. The falling body is the one he glimpsed as a child.'[56] This is a serious misreading, since to leap is precisely what the traveller cannot do; that would be to actively escape from Time. Instead he is someone who is thrown; who finds, in time travel, no real freedom, just a space for his own passivity. In the end, he simply fades, leaving no trace other than that sequence of frozen images which, in the course of the experiment, we have seen 'well up, like confessions': 'A peacetime morning. A peacetime bedroom, a real bedroom. Real children. Real birds. Real cats. Real graves. On the sixteenth day, he is on the jetty at Orly. Empty. Sometimes he recaptures a day of happiness, though different.' This sequence is particularly affecting, because, with the benefit of hindsight, it is clear that it is a visual transcription of a man's dreams and aspirations; he is projecting still images on the screen of his desires. One moment, he is nostalgic for those good times spent 'on the jetty at Orly' (illustrated by a still of the airport's great terrace); the next, he recaptures another 'day of happiness, though different' (represented by an image of a boat approaching a small pier in calm seas). These happy

'On the jetty at Orly. Empty': a still from *La Jetée*.

'A day of happiness, though different': a still from *La Jetée*.

memories are not really 'different', however; they are variants of the same contemplation of departure and arrival so familiar from Baudelaire and Proust, and experienced by all those other spectators of modernity who have ever stood at its threshold, on a jetty.

11 Landscapes of Pre-Emption

CREATIVE DESTRUCTION

The last phase of Goethe's *Faust* shows a hero striving to construct a new world over the landscape of the old. It begins in open country, with a wayfarer making a pilgrimage back to the place of his shipwreck, to meet again the much-loved elderly couple who rescued him from the 'whelming' tide. He soon learns that their world has changed utterly; where once 'the cruel surge was booming' from the North Sea, relentlessly assailing their cottage, now they have 'a garden blooming'. Philemon, the old man, explains:

> Hardy knaves, with masters clever
> Delved the dykes, the ground to gain,
> Foreshore from the sea to sever
> Making it their own domain.[1]

He walks the traveller to the foreshore; where once there was a wild expanse of sea, famous for its shipwrecks, now vessels navigate across permanently calm waters:

> Sails afar will glide from light,
> Seeking port with star-lit prow,
> Like the birds in homing flight,
> Harbour will they find there now.[2]

This great work of infrastructure was, it transpires, undertaken swiftly and at great cost by construction teams under the command of the Emperor, Faust. At the time, he made an offer for the old couple's homestead, since it stood in the way of his expansion plans, his *'Wohngewinn'*. However, they turned his

71

Terminal, aircraft and canal at Amsterdam-Schiphol International Airport, 1961.

proposal down, preferring to stay where they had always lived; and since that time, reports the old man, he has 'lusted / to possess our home and glade'.

The scene shifts to Faust's Palace and, more precisely, the great airy spaces of his gardens, through which runs a great canal, wide and straight-cut ['*gradgeführter*']. It is by means of this strip of water, constructed out of the reclaimed land, that the ships arrive at the harbour. They are overseen by Lynceus, the Keeper of the Watch Tower, who now picks up his amplifer and provides a commentary on the final arrivals of the day:

> Sundown, and a sound of cheering
> As the last ships make the port;
> Closer, a big vessel steering,
> In the canal to moorings brought ...
> Glad sight with freshened evening breeze,
> The gallant vessel inward sails,
> Comes towering proudly through the leas
> Deck laden high with chests and bales.[3]

As the ships dock, the chorus of mariners sing: 'And so we land, / See us arrive' ['*Da landen wir, / Da sind wir schon*']. The vessels, as usual, are freighted with sumptuous and exotic cargoes, commodities to be turned into Faust's capital. A few minutes later, Mephistopheles indicates the shape of his progress to the Emperor, reminding him of the origins of his 'world-control' :

> Form this same spot your power was spread
> Here stood the first rude wooden shed
> Here first a ditch was cut on shore
> Where now they ply the splashing oar.[4]

Faust is not satisfied; he seeks to expand still further to create a spacious view of the sky. However, his plans are still thwarted by the old couple, on whose land grow several tall lime-trees which 'Mock and destroy my wide domain'. He instructs Mephistopheles to evict the couple and rehouse them but the Devil simply sets light to their cottage without first evacuating its occupants. Faust watches the flames from his balcony; from the 'charred horror' will emerge 'boundless space'.[5]

Though Goethe was writing over 200 years ago, and more than a century before powered flight, there are extraordinary prefigurations here of the patterns of development seen in twentieth century airspaces. As Marshall Berman has observed: 'It appears, that the very process of development, even as it transforms the wasteland into a thriving physical and social space, recreates the wasteland inside of the developer himself. This is how the tragedy of development works.'[6] Reading back from the perspective of our age, it is not beyond the realms of possibility to regard the boundless empire created by Faust's clearances as an anticipation of airspace; in this case, his palace, once no more than a wooden shed, would correspond to an airport terminal, and the watch tower would double as a control tower. The wide canal may be regarded as a runway along which ships – a term still used to denote aircraft under construction – move in order to land their cargoes. In such a scheme, Faust himself, the port's operator, would represent the creatively destructive energies of aviation itself, prepared to push the consequences of technical and social innovation to extremes.[7]

The theory of creative destruction is central to understanding the airport space precisely because it derives from the practical dilemmas that faced the pioneers of civil aviation. Sufficient airports exist to make this more than a Faustian trope, but it seems that in more recent engagements between landscape and airspace, creative destruction is emerging in unexpected ways. Consider the case of Amsterdam-Schiphol International Airport. Four miles south-west of Amsterdam, the facility is 13 feet below sea level and built on land reclaimed from the Haarlemmermeer which lay between Amsterdam and Haarlem and covered about 30,000 acres in the sixteenth century. The extreme north-eastern part of the lake was funnel-shaped and in south-westerly gales it became so dangerous to shipping that it became known as *Schipshol*, the ship's hole. During the eighteenth and early nineteenth centuries, the lake grew until it was decided that to protect nearby cities, a system of dykes would need to be constructed. In 1848, the engineering was completed, and the removal of water began by means of three steam-powered pumping stations, a task that took over 4 years to complete and which left the lake bed between 10 and 15 feet below sea level.

After the reclamation, a garrison named Fort Schiphol was built on a piece of land jutting into the *ringvaart* (ring canal); in 1917, just west of the fort, a military aerodrome was prepared. An almost square grassy field of 200 acres, it had six wooden hangars in a row. Three years later, on 17 May 1920, KLM's first commercial flight, a cross-Channel service to London (Hounslow), operated jointly with Aircraft Transport & Travel, took place. In the quagmire that was then the airport at 'Schip Hol', passengers often had to be carried to and from the planes through the ankle-deep mud and water on the backs of strong porters recruited from the nearby farms. Understandably, older smallholders who had quietly worked the fertile lands of this *polder* for three-quarters of a century were not pleased with the intrusion of newfangled flying machines, and so pelted them with turnips, potatoes

An aerial view of Schiphol in 1967, with piers C, D and E and the polder in the background.

and other root crops. The airport grew steadily, nonetheless, until by the early 1960s it boasted two runways, with a full complement of the usual passenger facilities.[8]

In 1967, in a development calculated to sustain its internationally competitive position and to accommodate the imminent 'Jumbo' jet aircraft, Schiphol underwent a huge expansion. For over four decades, the airport had been an isolated settlement on the rim of the Haarlemmemeer; even this new scheme, consisting of the construction of an advanced terminal, Schiphol Central, and four new runways, left three quarters of the *meer* intact, so that the polder could still be regarded as an independent farming area, cheek by jowl with the airport. Now, 30 years later, however, the situation is markedly different. The justification for the *polder*'s existence – farming as a stabilizing force on the landscape – has, to some extent, faded, thus providing new opportunities to reclaim the ground for transport. The airport's future development plans – substantial extension of the termi-

75

nals, the construction of numerous ancillary buildings, and the creation of a fifth runway – mean that Schiphol's terrain will almost entirely be swallowed by airport infrastructure; the limits of the present space have been reached, and what remains of the farms will be destroyed for the creation of a 'Mainport', a transport city employing 60,000 people.

Yet so long as Schiphol remains the national airport of Holland, its environs will be haunted not just by the spectre of a *polder* whose destruction was the result of entrepreneurial voracity, but also by the human conseqences of the construction of the Buitenveldert runway in 1967, and Zwanenburg runway a year later, whose configurations resulted in huge jets taking off and landing low over the suburbs of Amsterdam. Just after Mephistopheles tells him of what has befallen the elderly couple, Faust is dumbfounded; he realizes that the light of his scheme is fading and dying, and that the debts he has built up must soon be paid. Looking out from the balcony across his great flat spaces, he sees something approaching in the sky and asks: 'What means this shape of hovering shade?' ['*Was schwebet schattenhaft heran?*']. On the evening of 4 October 1992, alert inhabitants of the *Bijlemeer*, an estate a couple of miles east of Schiphol, witnessed just such a dark shape overhead. Known to the locals simply as *Bijlmer*, this densely packed area of huge seventies tower blocks, joined by leafy avenues and ornamental lakes, and sandwiched between two motorways on the southeast of Amsterdam, was home to at least 100,000 people, most of whom originated from Holland's former colonies, and Surinam, in particular, where the twice-weekly KLM flight to Schiphol became known as the 'Bijlmer Express'.[9]

Earlier that day, an El Al Boeing 747 cargo plane, en route from New York to Tel Aviv landed for refuelling at Schiphol. It left an hour or so later, carrying 114 tons of cargo, including Dutch flowers and perfume loaded at the airport, and 80 to 90 tons of fuel for the 5-hour flight to Tel Aviv. The weather was poor, a stiff north-easterly wind was whipping across the runway, as the jet lifted off. Just before 6.30 pm with the aircraft by now 17 miles east of the airport, climbing slowly but on track, the captain sent out a May Day call, reporting a fire in a starboard engine and requesting clearance for an emergency landing; by now the 747 was at 5,000 feet circling to lose height, and dumping fuel over the water at IJsselmeer. Air Traffic Control advised the pilot, Yitzhak Fuchs, to land the freighter back on the Kaagbaan runway from which it had taken off 6 minutes before, a recommendation based on the wind direction, and on the knowledge that this approach would also take the aircraft over less populated areas. But as it was an emergency, Fuchs had the right to overrule the ground controller; realizing that his 350-ton plane, so heavily laden with fuel, would not stay airborne much longer, he sought the shortest approach to the Buitenveldert runway, which runs east to west, with the wind behind the jet. Five minutes after his May Day call, catastrophe struck: both starboard engines broke from the wing, and fell in the Naardermeer lake. Soon afterwards, Fuchs reported that the flaps were not responding and he was losing control of the jet; at 6.33 pm local time, he radioed his last words – 'Going down'.

The final approach to the Buitenveldert runway would have taken the stricken freighter across the *Bijlmer*. Living directly under the Schiphol flight-path, residents of the estate were accustomed to the sound of aircraft lumbering overhead, but on that evening witnesses on the ground knew that a plane as large as this was flying far too low; indeed, it almost appeared to be hovering. At 6.36 pm, with one wing dipping, because the plane was hopelessly out of balance, the pilot steered the stricken jet vertically through a 45-foot gap between two nine-storey blocks of family apartments; he could not avoid a third, packed with residents settling down to eat their dinner in front of the Ajax match. The night sky was lit up by a lurid glow, as a colossal red fireball mushroomed into the night sky, followed by a huge cloud of billowing black smoke. As the smoke cleared, it could be seen that the side of one of the apartment blocks was completely destroyed, the 747 having sliced into about 100 of the flats; in some households, occupants in one room survived while others in adjacent rooms were instantly vaporized. After months of careful investigation, it was established that along with the four crew members, at least 39 residents of the *Bijlmer* died in the crash. However, the heat of the blaze and the high proportion of illegal immigrants on the estate meant that the exact death toll would never be established.

In the aftermath of the disaster, residents of the *Bijlmer* began to ask questions. Why, a year after the accident, had the huge gap where the jet had ploughed through the flats not been repaired? An unconvincing official explanation was that demolition work had been hampered by the delicate state of the remaining adjacent buildings, and by extensive tests to check for soil and water pollution after the fire. At the same time, doctors on the estate began to be concerned about persistent complaints of malaise, lethargy, hair loss and respiratory difficulties from many of the surviving inhabitants. It was commonly known that Boeing 747 freighters incorporated several tons of

The aftermath of the *Bijlmer* crash, October 1992.

depleted uranium in the wings and *empannage* as ballast, and so scientists speculated that a few residents and rescue workers may have suffered poisoning following inhalation of uranium oxide. Finally, in 1998, a parliamentary inquiry was commissioned by the Dutch Government, and the authorities finally admitted what they had known all the time: as well as the explosives and ammunition for the Israeli army, the 747 was carrying a range of flammable and toxic substances, including 50 gallons of dimethyl methylphosphonate (DMMP), a chemical used in the manufacture of Sarin nerve gas. The consignment is believed to have been destined for Israel's biological weapons institute in Nes Ziona, although the authorities claimed it was to be used in testing filters. In any event, the official line – that the cargo was harmless – was exposed as a lie. A former head of air traffic control at Schiphol played a tape recording of a conversation, within minutes of the crash, between the airport and an El Al official, who initially warned the authorities about the jet's cargo, and then, in a further call half an hour later, urged the airport to withhold the exact nature of the freight. For the residents of the estate, it was already too late for camouflage by the airport. What had been feared since the Buitenveldert runway opened 25 years earlier, had now come to pass in the midst of the *Bijlmer*; Faust's 'shape of hovering shade' had fallen from the sky.

SURVEYING THE SITE

Just off the A4, between Heathrow police station and the airport's perimeter road, lies a half-buried cannon marking the site of what was once King's Arbour, a hamlet on the edge of Hounslow Heath. Exactly 27,406.19 feet, or 5 miles, to the southeast, in the centre of a housing estate in Hampton, on land originally occupied by the village's poorhouse, an identical memorial is situated. Together, these incongruous objects mark the terminal points of an invisible line measured out in the late eighteenth century, across an area which was then heathland and which proved to be a major innovation in the history of cartography. In the late spring of 1784, soldiers from a regiment stationed at Windsor cleared the ground in a straight line between the two points, and on 16 June that year rough measurement of the distance, using a 100-foot steel chain, started, followed a month later by more precise measurements using wooden rods. Undertaken under the supervision of the Scottish cartographer Major General William Roy, F.R.S., the intention was to establish, as a prelude to a precise survey of Great Britain, a 'baseline' of accurately measured length.

Major General Roy selected the site, now largely occupied by the airport, 'because of its vicinity to the capital and the Royal Observatory at Greenwich, its great extent and the extraordinary levelness of the surface without any local obstructions whatever to render the measurement difficult'.[10] It is for the same reasons of proximity to the centre of power and flatness of terrain that the world's busiest international airport was built on the edges of Hounslow Heath, 14 miles from central London; ironically, over 200 years later, the experiments carried out by Roy, the first stage in the Ordnance Survey of Britain, provide a means of marking the relentless encroachment of air facilities across the wide open spaces of London's western approaches.

In Don DeLillo's novel *Players*, Tammy Wynant drives to La Guardia airport outside New York City to catch a flight: 'When the land began to flatten and empty out, she knew they were in the vicinity of the airport. It was a landscape that acceded readily to a sense of pre-emption.'[11] 'Pre-emption' describes that action or process of setting aside or over-riding something; more precisely, it is a legal term denoting the purchase, or right of purchase, in preference and at a nominal price, of public land. At the outbreak of World War I, the British Army pre-empted the common land of Hounslow Heath and began to make use of it as a training aerodrome for the newly established Royal Flying Corps. H. G. Wells's *War in the Air* had caused many to fear that rogue German airships would flatten London, just as they had attacked New York in the novel:

> As the airships sailed along they smashed up the city as a child will shatter its cities of brick and card. Below, they left ruins and blazing conflagrations and heaped and scattered dead: men, women and children mixed together as though they had been no more than Moors, or Zulus, or Chinese.[12]

In an echo of the 'Flying Stages of London' encountered by Graham in *The Sleeper Awakes* (another of Wells's Edwardian visions of aviation), a crescent of defensive aerodromes was established around the city, and Hounslow Heath was made its H.Q.[13]

At the cessation of hostilities in 1919, the world's first sustained international scheduled service began from Hounslow, operated by Aircraft Transport & Travel. As a means of navigation, pilots followed landmarks, called air stations, which often had their names whitewashed on their roofs. However, the service was not a success, and within a year Hounslow closed down, making way for the more modern aerodrome at Croydon, south of the capital, which was better placed for continental destinations. The grass grew long again on the heath, and the tin shacks that had served as passenger shelters burnt down in 1929. Shortly after, Richard Fairey, an aircraft enthusiast who had formed his own aeroplane company in Hayes, began to look for a new site that would incorporate both assembly plant and testing ground; he found the ideal site, purchasing 150 acres at Heathrow from the vicar of Harmondsworth. He chose the land because of its *flatness*, the lack of suburban sprawl and the fact that unlike at Hayes, there were no railway lines to constrain its development. Even then, local farmers were concerned by the impact of the facility on the environment. They were placated with the knowledge that there would only be a few flights a week, as it was only a 'test aerodrome'. It was called by several names: Harmondsworth, The Great West Aerodrome, The Fairey Aerodrome and, simply, Heath Row.

A decade later, while Britain reacted haphazardly to German rearmament, the Air Ministry began to concern itself not only with the development of the RAF but with civil aviation as well.[14] By this time, Croydon Airport was too small; it was also built rather unpractically on the side of a hill in the middle of a residential area. The Port of London Authority campaigned for a combined sea and air facility on the southern side of the Thames, but Harold Balfour, then Secretary of State for Air, realized the need for a new super airport close to the centre of London. Applying a celluloid grid over a large-scale Ordnance Survey map, he found only one undeveloped place with the 7 square miles necessary for such a project: Heath Row.

In early May 1944, tenant farmers, several generations of whom had made a good living from the land they had cultivated around Hounslow Heath, received the following letter, headed 'Property at Heath Row', from C. Jarrett, an Under Secretary of State, at the Air Ministry:

> I am directed to inform you that the airfield at Heath Row is to be enlarged in the near future and it will be necessary for this purpose to take over your property possession of which, it is anticipated, will be required not later than 24/7/1944. Formal Notice of Requisition, in duplicate, is enclosed, one copy of which should be signed and returned in the accompanying franked envelope ...
>
> Before any work is done on the property a Lands Officer will visit the site and discuss with you detailed arrangements for taking possession. Subject to essential Air Ministry requirements, every facility will be given to enable you to remove your movable property and effects and any growing crops.
>
> The property is being taken over under the Defence Regulations but this will not preclude sale and purchase by agreement if the Air Ministry decides that it is required for permanent retention.[15]

This terse comunication was no doubt intended as a restatement of the blindingly obvious: there was still a war on. However, the declaration that the compulsory purchase was taking place under the jurisdiction of 'Defence Regulations' was duplicitous, for there was never any doubt that the arrangements would be permanent. In fact, a couple of ministers and several civil servants had deceived the War Cabinet into believing that a massive new aerodrome was needed for RAF Transport Command to supply the war in the Far East. Although Churchill believed this, he also felt that to start it in 1944 was a waste of scant resources. But he had more important things to think about – namely, the Normandy landings – and eventually consented.

Despite the fact that the fruits of their labours were still vital for the war effort, the farmers were evicted from their homes in late 1944, and poorly compensated for their loss of livelihood, so that three massive stressed-concrete runways could be laid over rural West Middlesex. In fact, the war was ending before the base could be completed; on 10 May 1945, barely a week after VE Day, but some months before victory in Japan was secured, it was decided by the Atlee government that Heathrow, still under construction, was to become London's principal airport. Had the Air Ministry told the truth in 1944, and not camouflaged the project as a military necessity, it would not have been able to proceed with the scheme; it could not have compulsorily turned householders out of their homes, and built on their land.

In any event, on New Year's Day 1946, control of Heathrow passed from the military to the Ministry of Civil Aviation. While Lord Winster, the man in charge, saw this as a triumph for British aviation, he felt that 'Heathrow' was overly difficult to pronounce for foreigners, and so it was signposted as 'London Airport, Heath Row'. The airport was officially opened on 31 May 1946, and the first transatlantic services arrived, Lockheed Constellations of American Overseas Airlines and Pan American Airways. At the time the control tower was a temporary construction, airline staff worked from old caravans, a few huts, and a departure tent whose passenger facilities consisted of Utility furniture, a post office and a W. H. Smith kiosk. At least while they waited for their flights to leave, passengers could read the local papers, such as the *Middlesex Advertiser Gazette*, which in December 1947 proclaimed: 'An atomic bomb dropped at Heathrow could not spread devastation more widely than the disruption caused by the construction of an airport on this spot'; indeed, it was as if nothing had existed here, other than devastated landscape, before the airport was built.

In fact, because the well-drained loam of West Middlesex was so suited to intensive agriculture, by the time that it had been covered by the new airport, the village of Heath Row lay at the centre of West London's market garden. The inherent fertility of the soil had been greatly improved over the nineteenth century by the addition of huge quantities of organic matter produced by the horses of London. Disposal of such large amounts of stable muck would have been impossible within the capital; the authorities there were grateful that the wagons driving into London each day with fresh produce were able to make the return journey laden with manure. Even when the horse population declined in the early years of the twentieth century, alternative fertilizers were found for the market gardens; the most popular source was the Perry Oaks sludge works which opened in 1935 at Heathrow, and provided some farmers with as much as 50 tons of powdered sewage per acre. Over many decades, the smallholders systematically invested in the fertility of their land, and such was the enrichment of the earth that, valued in terms of capital improvements, the soil was often of greater value than the property on which it rested.

In order to exist, airports do not simply pre-empt and efface such territory; they also evacuate the historical significances of areas. The northern perimeter of Heathrow is marked by the A4, a trunk road prone to some of the worst traffic congestion in Europe, whose air quality is consistently below guidelines set out by the World Health Organization. Known locally as the Bath Road, during the eighteenth century the stretch of highway around the Heath was similarly notorious both for its polluting fogs and for robbers, including Dick Turpin, who would take advantage of these conditions to prey on the gentry heading west in packed stagecoaches. Along the south side of the airport, a section of the elaborate sewage system for Cardinal Wolsey's great palace at Hampton Court runs through old brickwork canals; the last wolf in England was killed nearby. Under Terminal 2 lies one of the most important pre-Christian temples ever to have been found in Britain. The site was alluded to in William Camden's *Britanniae* (1586): 'On the north edge of (Hounslow) Heath towards King's Arbour is a Roman camp; a simple work and not large.' Although ploughed over in the centuries that followed, much of it was still evident when examined by a team of archaeologists who visited Heath Row in 1944 before the landscaping of the airport was completed. The leader of the dig, W.F.A. Grimes, later reported that the rampart and ditch of the encampment were much spread and reduced; the enclosing earth bank stood nowhere more than 2 feet high, its clearest indication being provided by the creep of the plough soil away from its crest, which exposed the light soil of the rampart beneath.[16] The entrance, to the south, was barely discernible. At first, the team's findings were unremarkable: excavations showed that in the northern half of the enclosure had been a series of eleven huts, a relatively small household area with a large vacant space probably used as a farmyard and enclosure for livestock. However, it soon became clear that this was no ordinary encampment. Trenches dug along the west side, near the base of the bank, were of much greater significance since they revealed the existence of a remarkable rectangular building, which, Grimes concluded, could only have been a temple and of a type earlier than anything previously recorded in this country. The structure consisted of a central shrine, which must have had solid wooden walls, enclosed by an outer rectangle of thick wooden posts. It was probably covered by a thatched roof that extended downwards from a central ridge-pole to the outer posts. The edifice has been likened to a Classical Greek temple, with the stone columns replaced by wooden posts and the stone-walled sanctuary by a structure not dissimilar to a log cabin. This important, indeed unique, site was buried under the concrete of the main runway lay-out in 1944; it is unlikely that it will be ever seen again. Ironically, the hamlet of Heath Row, first mentioned in 1453, and vacated by its residents almost five centuries later in 1944, now lies buried under a 'short-stay' car park.

Surveyed from above, Heathrow looks distinctive, like a set of drawing compasses laid out on a cluttered and mottled green baize table; one of the instrument's legs seems shorter than the other, and both are clamped round the terminals. This arrange-

Plan of the airport in Heathrow's Air Traffic Control tower, 1973.

ment, first patented by the Austin Company of Cleveland, Ohio, in 1944, is named a 'Star of David', and its use at Heathrow was based not so much on aesthetic considerations but on the RAF's requirement to provide simultaneous landings and take-off in any of six different directions, according to the wind. (Bizarrely, the airport was, in fact, built out of line of the prevailing south-westerly breeze.) The original design, as laid down in 1947 by Frederick Gibberd, consisted of a terminal and control tower in the middle of the existing military runway lay-out. Then, as the demand for air travel exploded, accommodation for other services had to be built in the limited space within this 'star', and all these buildings were to be supplied via two service tunnels which burrowed underneath the runways. The first permanent buildings in the central area were the control tower block, the Queen's Building (an administration block) and the short-haul terminal, now known as Terminal 2; the long-haul 'Oceanic' terminal, now Terminal 3, came into operation in 1962, and the third terminal (Terminal 1), intended mainly for domestic use by British European Airways (BEA) was opened on 17 April 1969.

As passenger-handling facilities were constantly augmented, three of the original runways were decommissioned, the lay-out dwindling to a parallel east–west pair and a shorter diagonal strip, all of which were enlarged to cope with wide-bodied jets. In the late 1960s, huge cargo-handling and maintenance areas were established on the southern and eastern boundaries, and in December 1977, Heathrow Underground station was opened, finally linking the airport with the whole London Underground network. The following year, the government had decided that proposals by the British Airports Authority (BAA), the national-ized airport authority, for a fourth main terminal, on the south-eastern edge of the airport, should be the subject of a public inquiry. This was held over a period of 96 days, ending in December 1978; BAA was permitted to build a fourth terminal which opened in 1986 (and would increase the airport's capacity to 50 million passengers per year) but was warned that this expansion would be the last to be permitted. By the early 1990s, however, Heathrow was still growing inexorably, and had devoured so much land that its four terminals, two runways, roads, car parking, freight and service areas covered close to 3,000 acres; according to environmental pressure group, Friends of the Earth, the tarmacked area alone was now equivalent to 200 miles of road. Under pressure from the airlines, and its shareholders, the newly privatized BAA plc announced its intention to build Terminal 5; under pressure from local residents and councils, the government held another public inquiry, the longest and most detailed in British planning history; it lasted almost 4 years. At the end of the Inquiry in March 1999, the Inspector intimated that it might take him up to 2 years to prepare his report and make his recommendations to the government; in any case, the final decision would rest, as it did in 1944, with the relevant Secretary of State.

If constructed, Terminal 5 (T5) will be within the airport perimeter road and lie between the two existing runways, on Perry Oaks, the old sewage works, a site which Sir Colin Marshall, chairman of British Airways has described, without irony, as 'a blight on the environment', even though these works, and an adjacent farm which would also be demolished, both *predate* the airport. Heathrow sits in the middle of the Thames floodplain, with the Colne Valley on its western flank, an area that provides diverse habitats and a green corridor for wildlife, as well as a 'lung' amid the roads and the airport. Furthermore, because most of the once-marshy and shallow-water regions in the Thames Valley have been drained, Perry Oaks is one of the most important sites in the London area for wildfowl and waders. During the public inquiry, BAA's expert witnesses presented little evidence on the ecology of the areas threatened by its proposal, and failed to find what local naturalists have always found in abundance: some of the rarest plants in south-east England thrive around the sewage works.

Richard Rogers's design for T5 (awarded in 1991 in a limited competition which included Renzo Piano and Michael Manser as assessors) proposes to build over this environment. His plan

Richard Rogers's proposed design for Heathrow Terminal 5, 1995.

calls for the construction of a core terminal building, three mini 'satellites', aprons, taxiways, a maintenance hangar, a fuel farm, roads, car parks, offices and a 600-room hotel. Dimensionally, the development is very large; T5 would be the largest structure ever built in the supposedly protected 'Green Belt' and should be regarded more as a transportation interchange capable of handling around 30 million passengers a year than as just another terminal building. In effect, it will amount to another airport, as busy as CDG, built within the confines of Heathrow. However, Rogers's development of T5 is particularly striking not just in terms of its size, but also in its attitude to the land-scape which surrounds it. Throughout his proposal, materials and architectural forms have been chosen, it seems, so as to diminish the new building's visual impact on the environment. To reduce the apparent scale of the terminal, a stepped profile has been embraced; the roof undulates in order 'to reduce light spillage at night from the large rooflights, thereby minimizing night-time sky pollution and potential hazard to pilots'. The east and west elevations, which consist of inclined glazing, and the massive overhanging canopies on the north and south eleva-tions, are intended to reduce the glare of the building, espe-cially when the sun is at low angles. One might also suggest, however, that the roof's wavy profile and soft metallic finish are designed to imitate the neutral tones of a Middlesex sky. Similarly, the predominantly glazed walls, set in frames and

89

An aerial view of Lydda airfield before and after RAF camouflage treatment, 1940.

panels of neutral greys and pale greens, will blend the building into the apron areas and adjoining grassland. This is deliberate, since vegetation – trees, hedges, shrubs and earthen banks – will play a key role in reducing the environmental impact of the whole development; the parapets of each level of the car park, for instance, as well as the hotel and office roofs, will be planted with creepers, which, in time, will cascade down the walls and mask the concrete framework. From the landside, at least, the appearance Rogers envisages will be one of greenery concealing the peripheral buildings and ancillary facilities; of course, this also means that the terminal design is resorting to a form of camouflage, that visual subterfuge undertaken around airports in times of crisis.[17]

EARTHWORKS

The clarity of Rogers's visualizations of T5 contrasts with the chaotic jumble of the existing airport. At ground level,

Heathrow is a shabby maze of brick and concrete, whose ground plan, along with any sense of perspective of the landscape itself, was mislaid in some forgotten planning application. Yet when the airport is seen from the air, its original Star-of-David conception is still faintly recognizable; it resembles, suggests the novelist David Lodge, 'a piece of earth-art'.[18]

In describing Heathrow in such a way, Lodge perhaps was mindful of the work of the Conceptual artist Robert Smithson, one of the originators of the 'Land Art' movement in the United States. Smithson died in 1970 when the plane in which he was making a routine aerial inspection of a work entitled *The Amarillo Ramp*, an ascending jetty forming an open circle 150 feet in diameter on the shore of an irrigation lake on a ranch in West Texas, crashed, killing him, the pilot and a photographer. Smithson had spent the previous few years engaged upon several projects which depended upon aerial topography for their effect; their very titles incorporated features familiar from airspaces: ramps, jetties and so forth. Ideologically, he felt that it was inappropriate to attempt to recreate a perfect 'natural' world and endeavoured, instead, to evolve an avowedly artificial landscape that nevertheless acknowledged that technological use could be artistically enriched.

In this respect, the airport-as-site was perfect for Smithson. One of his late essays lays out a series of concepts for aerial art; that is, art made on the ground and viewed from above:

> How art should be installed in and around an airport makes one conscious of this new landscape. Just as our satellites explore and chart the moon and the planets, so might the artist explore the unknown sites that surround our airports. The future air terminal exists both in terms of mind and thing. It suggests the infinite in a finite way. The straight lines of landing fields and runways bring into existence a perception of 'perspective' that evades all our conceptions of nature. The naturalism of seventeenth-, eighteenth- and nineteenth-century art is replaced by non-objective sense of site.[19]

As a means of making the site of this 'future air terminal' intelligible, Smithson proposed the following:

> On the boundaries of the taxiways, runways or approach 'clear zones' we might construct 'earthworks' or grid type frameworks close to the ground level. These aerial sites would not only be visible from arriving and departing aircraft but they would also define the terminal's man-made perimeters in terms of landscaping.

Smithson had first come to see the aesthetic and intellectual possibilities when in July 1966, he had been approached by the architectural firm Tippetts-Abbett-McCarthy Stratton to provide a kind of artistic 'survey' as part of their submission for the new Dallas-Fort Worth International Airport, to be built on 17,500 acres of low-yield farmland midway between the great cities of northern Texas. Defending his collaboration later, in a narrative report *cum* critical essay *cum* poetic fiction entitled 'Towards the Development of an Air Terminal Site', Smithson claimed that his 'discussions do not operate on any presupposed notion of art, engineering or architecture', but, rather, were explorations of, as it were, the common ground between differing discourses. His essay laid considerable emphasis on the importance of 'survey', the process by which a surveyor, by means of some form of objective 'measure', and the examination of various sites within a network of lines and angles, can identify 'the points of identical elevation' and locate 'the boundaries of land tracts'. By such means, Smithson set out the basis of 'DFW', the proposed Texan airport: 'The entire project shall rest on an elevation of about 550 feet to 620 feet. The area is well drained and practically free of trees and natural obstructions. The subsurface site of the project contains sediments from the Cretaceous Age.'[20] That last piece of geological information was irrelevant in the era of the airport, which effaced 'subsurface', both topographically and historically; indeed, within the vicinity of the airport terminal, 'all air and land is locked into a vast lattice,' a pattern created and held through a 'new meaning based on instantaneous time', synchronic rather than diachronic,

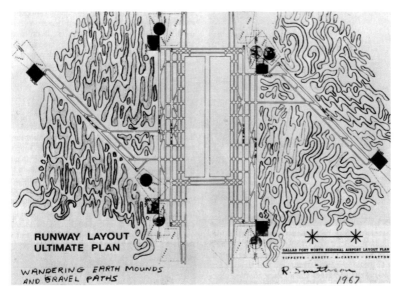

Robert Smithson, *Dallas Fort Worth Regional Airport Layout Plan: Wandering Earth Mounds and Gravel Paths*, 1967, blueprint with collage and pencil. Estate of Robert Smithson.

crystalline rather than fluvial, and consequent on the 'immobilization of space', which becomes more apparent if we consider the high altitude satellite: 'The farther out an object goes in space, the less it represents the old rational idea of visible speed. The streamlines of space are replaced by the crystalline structure of time.' The farther away one gets from, and above, the airport site, the closer it seems to approach an ideal state, the abstract impression of a modernity bereft of historical context; and it was, Smithson felt, this frame that aerial art should attempt to match. As he wrote in 1969:

> Aerial art can therefore not only give limits to 'space', but also the hidden dimensions of 'time' apart from natural duration – an *artificial time* that can suggest galactic distance here on earth. Its focus on 'non-visual' space and time begins to shape an aesthetic based on the *airport as an idea*, and not simply as a mode of transportation. This airport is but a dot in the vast infinity of universes, an imperceptible point in a cosmic immensity, a speck in an impenetrable nowhere: aerial art reflects to a degree this vastness.[21]

An aerial view of Dallas-Fort Worth International Airport, 1975.

Robert Smithson, *Spiral Jetty*, 1970, earthwork. Great Salt Lake, Utah.

For the DFW project, Smithson had commissioned a number of pieces from his friends and collaborators. The artist Robert Morris proposed an 'earth mound' circular in shape and trapezoidal in cross section. Its surface would be turfed, and its radius might be extended as much as 1,000 feet so that it could be easily viewed by passengers on arriving and departing aircraft. Carl Andre offered either 'a crater formed by a one-ton bomb dropped from 10,000 feet', or, alternatively, 'an acre of blue-bonnets, the state flowers of Texas'. Sol LeWitt's submission was 'non-visual' and operated at the level of the 'sub-stratum of the site': it would emphasize the 'concept' of art rather than the 'object' that results from its practice, and would consist of a small cube of unknown contents cast inside a larger cube of concrete, which would then be buried on the airfield, its precise location never revealed. Smithson himself planned a whorling progression of triangular concrete pavements that 'could be built as large as the site would allow, and could be seen from approaching and departing aircraft'. This concept would result in his most famous work, *Spiral Jetty*, whose shape, in any event, echoes that of the terminal zones of DFW.

The most immediate effect of the airport proposals was that they caused Smithson to re-evaluate his conception of the large scale. Before his involvement in DFW, he was formerly attuned to thinking in terms of the gallery space; when he came to deal with such gargantuan areas as the proposed landing strips for the airport, which were to be between 11,000 and 14,000 feet ('or,' he remarked, 'about the length of Central Park') his whole notion of space was amended. Consequently, Smithson's conception of the air terminal depended on the expectation that the human scale of the art gallery must submit to the scale of 'the actual land as medium', a medium constantly in flux, and to be filled, soon enough, with aggregate and concrete:

> The process behind the air terminal endlessly plans and replans its concessions, agencies, and facilities from masses of information. Here unit terminals are not conceived as trip terminus points. Here no gate position has a unique location. The distribution of car traffic is maintained by a central axis of roadways that develops according to statistical probability. Extra terminal space may crystallise off this central linear axis. Framing this central complex of terminal units are the runways and taxiways.[22]

The airport, therefore, represents the purity of process promoting a radical contingency which means that, as an entity, it is never satisfied with its limits, and expands voraciously:

> The air terminal – also known as the Universe – rests on a firmament of statistics. Here statistics are the abysmal archetypes that engender the entire complex of buildings. This terminal area of approximately 600 acres is enclosed by a two-way taxi system approximately 9,000 feet in length by 3,000 feet in width. This inscrutable terminal exceeds and rejects all termination.[23]

Dominated space (i): Madrid Barajas Airport, 1992.

Smithson opens the terms of the discussion ever outwards, in the direction of the stars, and of medieval astronomy and numerology; the 'firmament'. The new airport, larger than Manhattan Island on its completion, will be distinguished by its inscrutable accountancy, its intricate mathematical formulae and inexorable statistical processes. Taken together, such elements form the dark 'abysmal' archetype of the modern terminal: its interminability, the fact that it is endlessly present. This might seem 'abysmal' only if we refuse to cast off our nostalgia for a past that may never have existed and our desire for an ultimate future that turns out, sadly, to be a self-cancelling reflection of the past. For Smithson, his apocalyptic rhetoric notwithstanding, it is, finally, the present that most urgently matters, and the most important features of the runways and taxiways rolling across the prairie can be reduced to a list of measurements:

96

Width of Land strip	500ft
Width of Runway (RAN)	150ft
Width of Taxiway (TAN)	75ft
Distance between RAN Centreline and TAN Centreline	500ft
Distance between Parallel TAN's	300ft
Distance between Centreline TAN and Aircraft Parking	300ft
Distance between Centreline and Obstacle	250ft
Distance between Centreline and Building Line	750ft
Maximum Runway Effective Gradient	0.25%
Maximum RAN and TAN Longitudinal Grade	1.00%
Maximum RAN and TAN Transverse Grade	1.50%

This only accounts for the runway. And since everything lies within its dimensions, it is a monument to the absolute incongruity of the air terminal site.

In his humane account of the reconcilitation between real space (those physical and social spheres in which we all circulate) and mental space (the space represented in culture) Henri Lefebvre observes that, at the time he was writing, space was also 'being recast in response to the growth of air transport, particularly in its geopolitical dimensions'. There was a political explanation for this modification: Lefebvre repeatedly points to the central role of planned space in the perpetuation of capitalism. Its industrial phase, he notes, is followed by an urban one, in which the production of things gives way to the production of space. In this way, capital reproduces itself in even greater measure – a process that increasingly meets with local resistance (not least of all due to its ecological consequences). While the Fordist method of production had aimed at the mass consumption of houses, cars and leisure activities and thus revealed its own spatial dimension, the flexible, post-Fordist method of production reacted to these ecological problems and the increasing resistance with selective and flexible appropriation. The result is an accelerated process of centralization and decentralization, concentration and the multiplication of concentration, in which external constraints increasingly lead to the internal condensation of spatial functions:

Capitalism and neocapitalism have produced abstract space, which includes the 'world of commodities', its logic and its worldwide strategies, as well as the power of money and that of the political state. This space is founded on the vast network of banks, business centres, and major productive entities, as also on motorways, airports and information lattices. Within this space the town – once the forcinghouse of accumulation, fountainhead of wealth and centre of historical space – has disintegrated.[24]

Abstract space effaces the physical, then. And when it introduces the concept of dominated space, Lefebvre's book is even more precise: 'a space transformed – and mediated – by technology, by practice'. He claims that, in the modern world, such a species of space is ubiquitous and immediately intelligible: '... one only has to think of a slab of concrete or a motorway.' What is decisive is the appearance of a clean, pure, isolated sphere while at the same time, an attempt is made to merge with the landscape, in order to abolish the traditional distinction between natural and built environment, real space and image. A prime example of such condensed spatiality is the airport: a small city with hotels, shopping malls, bars, restaurants, discotheques and gyms, all grouped around the centre of the complex, a climate-controlled vacuum. The special quality of a landscape, bound to a particular place, becomes a reproducible atmosphere; the unique experience becomes a staged one. Such virtual space can be created anywhere there is a demand for it. Of course, the obvious artificiality of this fictive landscape is opposed to the idea of originality and authenticity; no one should be fooled by it. Yet Lefebvre goes further, and explains how such spatial domination is so easily effected:

In order to dominate space, technology introduces a new form into a pre-existing space – generally a rectilinear or rectangular form such as a meshwork or chequerwork. A motorway brutalizes the countryside and the land, slicing through space like a great knife. Dominated space is usually closed, sterilized, emptied out.[25]

Lefevbre does not mention airspace; but his account of the placing of new 'meshwork or chequerwork' forms over pre-existing spaces, unintentionally perhaps, must include the airport, which, 'rectilinear' in its form, 'brutalizes' the countryside, and its runways, like motorways 'slicing though space like a great knife'.

A version of this spatial domination emerges in the film version of Arthur Hailey's novel *Airport* (1968). Mel Bakersfield, the general manager of Lincoln Airport, a mid-Western hub, dreams of new runways and extra terminals. In his office, he keeps a scale model of the airport's planned expansion, and when things get too much, he fingers these new facilities, touching them with a developer's hand. His model terminal has a paradoxical effect: its imitation landscape derives its abstract identity from its relation to an international world of images and signs, but also from its homogeneity. Unlike the mundaneness of Lincoln's everyday spaces, it is marked by density and enclosure. The future terminal presents itself as a tidy whole, isolated from its surroundings and exerting a stabi-

Dominated space (ii): an aerial view of the environs of Los Angeles Airport, 1976.

99

The airport developer's hands, in a still from George Seaton's 1970 film *Airport*.

lizing effect. Its design provides Bakersfield with relief from the current demands of his job – averting disasters – producing in him a feeling of resolve:

> After new runways, other projects, so far only talked about or hoped for, must be pressed on; among them – an entirely new terminal and runway complex; more imaginative ground flow of people and freight; smaller, satellite fields for the vertical and short takeoff aircraft which were coming soon.
>
> Either Lincoln international was in the jet age, or it wasn't; if it was, it must keep pace far better than it had.[26]

However, local opposition to the airport's expansion is strong; the residents' association is demonstrating outside the main terminal, and a TV interviewer, 'a handsome man with a Ronald Reagan haircut', is asking the questions:

> 'Mr Freemantle why are you here?'
> 'Because this airport is a den of thieves.'
> 'Will you explain that?'
> 'Certainly. The homeowners of Meadowood community are having thievery practised on them. Thievery of their peace, their right to privacy of their work earned rest, and of their sleep. Thievery of enjoyment of their leisure; thievery of their mental and physical health, and of their children's health and welfare. All these things, basic rights under our Constitution are being shame-

lessly stolen, without recompense or recognition, by the operators of Lincoln Airport.'[27]

Mr Freemantle may bear the mantle of free speech, but above the noise of the airport he struggles to make himself heard. For him, Lincoln is criminal; but in his accusations of theft, one sees merely another effect of the kind of spatial domination identified by Lefevbre, whereby a disputed zone is progressively 'closed, sterilized, emptied out', and finally built over.

The first chapter of William Faulkner's *Pylon* (1935), a novel about barnstorming aviators, is entitled 'Dedication of an Airport' and incorporates the following newspaper report:

FEINMAN AIRPORT

NEW VALOIS, FRANCIANA

DEDICATED TO

THE AVIATORS OF AMERICA

AND

COLONEL H. L. FEINMAN. CHAIRMAN

SEWAGE BOARD

Through Whose Undeviating Vision and Unflagging
Effort This Airport was Raised Up and Created out
of the Waste Land at the Bottom of Lake Rambaud
at a Cost of One Million Dollars[28]

As a setting for his novel, Faulkner had in mind the newly inaugurated Shushan Airport, New Orleans, completed early in 1933 and opened the following February. Named after Colonel A. L. Shushan, the airport, consisting of a Spanish Renaissance-style terminal, and four runways of between 3,600 and 4,000 feet each protected from tidal incursions by a retaining wall, was constructed on 300 acres of 'Waste Land' reclaimed from Lake Pontchartrain through the dumping into its shallow waters of thousands of tons of oyster shells and other 'organic' matter. Faulkner's first description of the airport records the approach from the road:

Now the bus, the road, ran out of the swamp though without mounting, with no hill to elevate it; it ran now upon a flat plain of sawgrass and of cypress and oak stumps ... a pocked desolation of some terrific and apparently purposeless reclamation across which the shell road ran ribbon-blanched toward something low and dead ahead of it, something low, unnatural: a chimera quality which for the moment prevented one from comprehending that it had been built by man and for a purpose.

The process of reclamation is 'apparently puposeless', occurring only in order to foster something 'low', 'dead' and 'unnatural'. The suggestion is that this is a journey into an underworld, entirely appropriate given the airport lies below sea level. Then, as Faulkner accelerates towards a 'chimera quality' – a distant echo of Le Corbusier's description of the 'chimerical pursuit of flight', published concurrently – the description takes off on a flight of fancy:[29]

> The thick heavy air was full now of a smell thicker, heavier, though there was yet no water in sight; there was only the soft pale sharp chimera-shape above which pennons floated against a further drowsy immensity which the mind knew must be water, apparently separated from the flat earth by a mirage line so that, taking shape now as a double-winged building, it seemed to float lightly like the apocryphal turreted and battlemented cities in the coloured Sunday sections, where beneath sill-less and floorless arches people with yellow and blue flesh pass and repass: myriad, purposeless, and free from gravity.[30]

The previously abstract 'chimera quality' now materializes into the 'chimera-shape' of the terminal, decorated with streamers, set against the sea. Seen from a distance, the building is, appropriately enough, 'double-winged', a design feature which no doubt helps it to 'float lightly ... free from gravity'. However, this terminal does not simply serve flight; it *conveys* flight too:

> Now the bus, swinging, presented in broadside the low broad main building with its two hangar wings, modernistic, crenel-

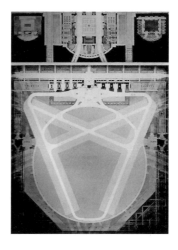

An F-shaped airport: M. E. Boyer's design for the 1929 architectural competition sponsored by Lehigh Portland Cement Company of Allentown, Pennsylvania.

lated, with its facade faintly Moorish or Californian beneath the gold-and-purple pennons whipping in a breeze definitely from water and giving to it an air both aerial and aquatic like a mammoth terminal for some species of machine of a yet unvisioned tomorrow, to which air earth and water will be as one.

The perspective continues to change as the narrator nears the airport. Note that the 'air' of the building is simultaneously poised between elements, 'aerial and aquatic'; 'mammoth' invokes the Neolithic fossils crushed in the ground which supports it; while the runway layout finally announces the facility's underlying origins:

> ... the flat triangle of reclaimed and tortured earth dragged with slow mechanical violence into air and alternations of light the ceaseless surface of the outraged lake notched by the oyster – and shrimp – fossil bed, upon which the immaculate concrete runways lay in the attitude of two stiffly embracing capital F's.

The runway lay-out is not untypical of the time; but here it is made to stand for something larger. Richard Gray has suggested that the description of the capital F's 'reverberates with implications of power and control – locating the airport, in effect, as a product and producer of hard cash rather than the site of dreams'.[31] But this ignores many obvious possbilities. The letters could stand for Faulkner, the author; Feinman, the visionary; the Flights which will take off and land here; the Future which is embraced; the Faeces on which the complex is constructed. Most likely, however, the letter introduces the figure whose energies lie so clearly behind this structure, and behind so many other airports: Faust.

AIRPORTS AND ISLANDS

At the time of the 1992 Schiphol crash, David Learmount, an air-safety expert at *Flight International* magazine, was widely quoted as saying: 'At the end of the day, if you want to avoid aviation accidents you will have to stop aviation.'[32] A reasonable alternative might be to halt the development of airports. By the early 1960s, Tokyo International Airport, built on reclaimed land at Haneda on the edge of Tokyo Bay, was running at full capacity. Consequently, plans were drawn up for a new airport solely for international trafffic, which would consist of three runways, two parallel and one crosswind, covering a total land area of 2,600 acres. In 1966, eager to begin the project, the New Tokyo International Airport Authority, the governmental body set up to run the new facility, announced that it would build on the plain at Sanrizuka, an area 40 miles east of Tokyo which, in the late nineteenth century, had been owned by the Emperor and comprised large estates and stud farms which supplied prized horses to the Tokugawa Shogunate. Indeed, Narita was beautiful enough to have been regarded by European travellers as the Barbizon of Japan; visitors would journey from throughout the country to witness the blossoming of the 10,000 cherry trees the Emperor owned there.[33]

In the twentieth century, the area gradually fell into neglect, and at the time the Airport Authority was making its plans, little was to be seen there except sleepy villages, ramshackle farmsteads and a crossroads skirting a water meadow and horse ranch. Legally, the Authority had every right to pre-empt the land by compulsory purchase, but it also assumed, naively perhaps, that for the good of a new international airport, local farmers would give up, without a fight, the soil which they had worked for generations. Hence, the Japanese government unveiled its airport master plan in 1966 without consulting any of the 360 families who owned the land in question. For the locals, however, the transformation of imperial property in Sanrizuka into runways and terminals lent the area an unavoidable political and metaphorical significance; to site an airport in this paradise was to destroy fertility, and mutilate the empire of the sun.

As the site surveys were carried out, supporters of the farmers purchased tiny symbolic patches of land and moved onto the fields around Narita so as to make it even more awkward for the authorities. Violent confrontations began when officials tried, finally, to sequestrate the land: petrol bombs were thrown, and several people were grievously injured by riot police. The government set up checkpoints to monitor the farming 'families', so hardening the opposition even more. When construction finally began in the early 1970s, only 1,360 acres had been secured, just enough for one runway and a terminal building. The main theatre of war was the road that skirted the airport complex; a secondary front was opened up around the scraps of no man's land for which the second stage of the scheme was planned. This first phase of airport facilities was virtually complete by 1974, but, having discovered that the Authority had not sought to obtain rights to the land at the thresholds of the 13,000-foot runway, the farmers erected telescopic steel towers at both ends to prevent planes from landing. These were destroyed by the police, only to be replaced by a pair of three-storey reinforced concrete fortresses, the first situated directly over the site of the demolished towers, and the second on farmland due to be used for the next stage of the airport. It was when these fortress towers were sacked in a dawn police raid in May 1977 that a martyr was created: Higashiyama Koaru, a student militant, was killed after being struck by a tear gas grenade. The following February, the protestors erected another 65-foot-high tower over the remains of the second fortress; its total height of 100 feet was enough to endanger air traffic. The day after it was erected, it was besieged by riot police who attacked it with water cannons, tear gas and a mobile crane. The 45 farmers and militants inside showered Molotov cocktails and stones on the police. Four protesters climbed to the top of the tower and held out for two days in sub-zero temperatures; when police water cannons were aimed at them, the hoses froze.

Between 1974 and 1978, the farmers caused the opening of Narita airport to be postponed eleven times, periodically breaching the perimeter fence and vandalizing many of the installations, including, on one occasion, the newly commissioned control tower. They obtained detailed plans of the airport site, showing the main electrical cables, and the vast underground network of drainage channels and sewers, and having studied them carefully, emerged into the compound through a manhole near the tower. Ten of them managed to gain entry to it, despite being fired upon by police. Six made it in the lift to the sixteenth floor, and once inside the secure control room, they pulverised the electronics with sledgehammers, dumped equipment and documents out of the windows, and displayed a huge red flag.

In the days leading up to its inauguration in May 1978 the protests against the airport, now defended with electric fences, razor wire, moats and 14,000 armed police, became even more elaborate. Just before Narita was formally opened with a Shinto rite, saboteurs severed an underground coaxial cable, the mainstay of Tokyo's air-traffic control centre at Saitama. Radar screens turned blank, and communication with aircraft was silenced; later that day electricity to 19,000 residences was cut off when saboteurs toppled a steel pylon. After the mains cable had been reconnected, the farmers then used a radio transmitter to jam communications between Narita control tower and incoming aircraft including the first passenger flight, a Japan Air Lines DC8 arriving from Frankfurt. As it approached the airport, hundreds of balloons were released into its flight path and, as it touched down, a huge pall of acrid smoke rose from the perimeter of the airport as the farmers, along with over 3,000 demonstrators, set light to pyres of car tyres.

Even now, over two decades later, Narita still resembles a military installation, with a large contingent of troops and armoured cars permanently stationed around its perimeter, and numerous watch towers, fences, moats and gates. On lonely, arid patches of land, weathered billboards proclaim, in huge vibrant characters, the interminable struggle against the airport, whose vicinity is defined by razor wire. It is now clear that part of the farmers' original tactic was to make their own shaky constructions central to the protest and, out of the junk, create a moral architecture which could effectively seal off the corruption of the airport itself, and transform it into an island. The strategy was a qualified success. In the years since the airport opened, the government has apologized to the families and officially given up the effort to take their land by force. It has paid compensation to residents for the removal of 567 homes, and purchased more than 1,200 acres of land. It has paid to have neighbouring homes, schools and other facilities soundproofed; more than 7,000 buildings have been treated at a cost of $43 million. It has even installed more than 26,000 special television antennas and seven relay towers to suppress the interference of TV programmes by incoming jets. Some locals are satisfied, but others cannot forgive the damage done to the ecosystem by the airport's drainage ditches, sewage systems, fuel pipelines and cable ducts. Over the last 20 years, water levels have dropped, wells have turned foul or dried up altogether, and the ancient irrigation system so crucial to rice production and wet farming has largely been destroyed.

In August 1997, the airport moved closer to completion as several families finally agreed to talk to the government about selling and renting their land to permit the construction of the second runway, strips of which had already been laid so that one day, when the remaining fields were available, the final tarmac could be put in place quickly. (Even now, as one lands at Narita, one sees 100 or so feet of the new runway parallel to the original and then, at the point at which planes might be rotating, the tarmac runs out to be replaced by clumps of vegetables.) Only two farmers are still holding out, maintaining two crucial plots covering about 40 acres. One of them, Koju Kitahara, is a mild, grey-haired man, whose age has not dimmed the passion he harbours to destroy the airport. By way of explanation, he told a reporter: 'I mean stopping the airplanes, tearing down the buildings and removing the runways.' It is too late; the pact has been signed. One can never recreate lands destroyed in the name of creation.

In Arthur Hailey's *Airport*, a reporter presses the general manager of Lincoln International, and asks: 'What *should* we do about airports? What *can* we do?' Mel Bakersfield responds with passion:

> A few airports are being built as circles – like doughnuts; with car parking inside, instead of somewhere out beyond; with minimum distances for people to walk; with aids like high-speed horizontal elevators; with aeroplanes brought close to passengers instead of the other way around. What it means is that airports are finally being thought of as special and distinct; also as units instead of separate components. Creative ideas, even outlandish ones, are being listened to. Los Angeles is proposing a big offshore sea-drome; Chicago, a man-made airport island in Lake Michigan.[34]

Hailey was writing in 1968. In 1974, a doughnut landed at Roissy, in the form of Terminal 1 of CDG, which subsequently became known locally as *'le grand fromage'*.[35] But the audacious plans for the 'sea-drome' in Los Angeles and the 'man-made airport island' in Chicago came to nothing. That particular concept would find its niche in the Far East, in countries highly populated but short of space, and prepared to spend prodigiously to avoid the kinds of civil unrest seen at Narita.[36]

Kansai Aiport, intended to serve the central Japanese cities of Osaka, Kobe and Kyoto, opened in 1994. So that the environmental impacts of noise and pollution might be diminished, the facility was erected on a man-made island, what Smithson would have described as 'a firmament of statistics'.[37] Measuring 3 by 1 miles, and covering 1,250 acres, the island was built in Osaka Bay on a sheltered stretch of water about 60 feet deep, and is one of the largest offshore landfill sites on earth. The sea bed here consisted of 50 feet of soft, yielding clay which, before creation of the artificial island, had to be compacted and stabilized by having the water forced out of it. To do this, a million 'sand piles', each 2 feet in diameter and 6 feet apart, were driven into the clay, over which was then laid several feet of sand. Layers of earth were dumped on top, its weight expelling the water from the clay into the piles, and then upwards and outwards through the sand. Steel caissons, large watertight chambers open at the base, were sunk to create the perimeter of the island; two nearby mountains were destroyed and an adjacent island quarried for the infill of crushed rock. To create the airport's land height of 130 feet above the seabed, about 6.4 billion cubic feet of sand and earth were used, roughly the volume of 73 Great Pyramids.[38] Unfortunately, the clay compacted more than original quantity surveys had predicted, and a third mountain had to be demolished to provide extra aggregate, adding a year's extra work to the project. When construction finally began, the island was still subsiding, and it will continue to move for some time; the mile-long terminal building was hard-wired with subsidence monitors, and all its pillars can be adjusted vertically on hydraulic jacks to compensate for uneven settlement.

In some respects, Kansai is exactly the kind of 'low and unnatural ... chimera shape' William Faulkner imagined he saw in New Orleans in 1934, a strange, monstrous hybrid of 'reclaimed and tortured earth dragged with slow mechanical violence into air'.[39] But it is also an attempt to be a hybrid of technology and ecology; or rather, as the architect of the terminal building, Renzo Piano, has claimed, 'technology emulating, and in harmony, with nature'. Hence, its basic shape derives

Osaka-Kansai International Airport: the island airport, 1994.

Osaka-Kansai: the terminal (designed by Renzo Piano), 1994.

from nature's own profiling of sand-dunes at the ocean's edge. At the heart of the Kansai terminal's design is a large, lofty public concourse nearly 300 yards long, which serves, ostensibly, as a means of orientation for passengers, but which is clearly meant to remind them, nostalgically, of landscapes. This space, decorated in shades of terracotta and ochre, the colours of clay and crushed rock, is known as the 'Canyon'; across the aqua floor of this deep gorge, a stream of passengers flows incessantly. Since the island's surface is capable of sustaining vegetation, at the entrance to the terminal, Piano's plans (for aesthetic reasons as much as to supplement the supply of oxygen or control erosion) envisage a small wood rather than rows of cultivated trees.

What is remarkable about Kansai is the degree to which it seeks to pre-empt the destruction of the natural world for which airports have been renowned. The 20-foot-high seawall which surrounds the island was built up as a naturally sloped rubble-work mound which would support the ecology of existing

Osaka-Kansai: the 'Canyon', 1994.

marine life in the area. With the exception of the airport's concrete and asphalt working surfaces and an armour-stone shell at water level, the entire land reclamation was undertaken using locally occurring materials. In fact, apart from the hydraulically controlled piles which support the terminal building and those of the bridge piers, there is almost no direct contact between the ecostructure and anything artificial. With its highly effective incinerators and sewage treatment plants, Kansai is like the most modern of aircraft carriers in that it produces little waste and discharges only fully treated water back into the bay.

That the airport, arguably the least sustainable and most destructive of all modern urban structures, should try to emulate natural systems of creation is perhaps Kansai's main claim to be an originator of modern terminals; but then it is simply echoing Faust's dying sentiments: 'A paradise our closed-inland provides, / Though to its margin rage the blustering tides' ['*Im Innern hier ein paradiesisch Land, / Da rase draussen Flut bis auf zum Rand*']. And yet, through all the feats of engineering and technology, surviving here is what Smithson called the 'idea of the airport'. Kansai may justifiably announce itself as an island, but it is nothing other than an airport.[40]

III Splendours of Space

'The beauty of an airport lies in the splendour of its space!'[1] So Le Corbusier proclaimed in early 1946 at a symposium concerned with 'Infrastructure', staged under the auspices of the Congrès de l'Aviation Français, the first to be held since the end of the war. Le Corbusier had spent much of the enforced break in his career brooding on problems of utilizing public space in urban planning. Now that much of Europe, through a combination of Allied offensives and Axis scorched-earth policies, had been flattened, and its new governments were demanding fresh architectural ideas, he had the opportunity to air some of his thinking about the infrastructure that would be required to serve the technologically advanced machines that war had spawned.

Though his interest in aviation was long-standing, Le Corbusier had frequently been exasperated by the airports he visited. In *Aircraft* (1935) he recalled:

> In 1928, before setting out for Moscow, I thought I would shorten the journey by taking an airplane. I discovered the airports at Le Bourget, Cologne, and Berlin. I perceived that persons by dint of faith and determination had little by little, higgledy-piggledy, equipped hangars, instruments, buildings, and staff. And that the airports were stations like railway stations. One set off at a given time and, lo! one arrived with chronometric exactitude.[2]

The fact that these airports succeeded 'by dint of faith' in receiving and despatching bodies and cargo, and did so while maintaining 'chronometric exactitude', meant that they resembled the kind of railway infrastructures celebrated by Théophile Gautier: 'These cathedrals of the new humanity are the meeting points of nations, the centre where all converges, the nucleus of the huge stars whose iron rays stretch out to the ends of the earth.'[3] Henry Petroski has observed:

> Such contexts, which develop along with inventions and in which inventions develop into innovations, involve systems and infrastructure which shape technology and its use. Indeed, after a while the individual artifacts and the supporting infrastructures become so interdependent that the one no longer can be considered without the other.[4]

One might be left unsatisfied by the vagueness of 'involve' and imprecision of 'after a while', but – stretching comparison a little further – neither railways nor aviation could have developed at the speed they did without adequate groundwork. Besides the locomotive, an equally pressing prerequisite to railway transport was the track itself, and all the attendant 'infrastructure': embankments and cuttings, bridges and tunnels, sidings, signal boxes and engine sheds, and, of course, stations. The early engines and rolling stock were soon obsolete, and by the time Gautier was writing, new types were replacing old at frequent intervals; however, the 'iron rays' and most of the 'cathedrals' were still extant, and, with many patches and extensions, continued to be serviceable well into the next century.

By that time, airports, the new 'cathedrals' of transport, were demanding the construction of facilities quite as complex and radical as those seen at railway stations. However, airports were even more necessary; their location and efficiency were crucial to the service and safety of the aircraft making use of them. Given the limitations of suitable ground space and the heavy capital outlay involved, airports might have been expected to have a long life, and should therefore have been designed for relative permanence. Flying to Moscow in 1928, Le Corbusier was annoyed to find that the same planning errors made in the early days of rail were being repeated; airports were being established gradually, expediently, and 'higgledy-piggledy' without giving thought to their spatial identities or geographical situations. As examples of this haphazardness he cited Le Bourget, Paris' main airport until World War II, and Butzweilerhof, serving Cologne. Both were built some way from the cities they served, as they had originally been established as aerodromes during World War I, and then passed into the hands of the local authorities.

Consider the case of Berlin's Tempelhof. Owing to its location in the middle of the continent, this airport had become known as 'the crossroads of Europe' by the time Le Corbusier was travelling. Having opened in 1923, it had quickly expanded to become a model for other airports, mainly because the construction of a continuous concrete apron stretched along the entire front of the terminal buildings allowed passengers to embark or alight without getting muddy feet, while an advanced underground fuelling system allowed the simultaneous servicing of six aircraft. Enormous hangars whose combined floor space of 7 square miles was sufficient in 1926 to house over half of the entire German civil aircraft fleet – flanked the terminal; it was as though the arriving machines were formally received by the buildings themselves, lined up in a guard of honour. The lighting equipment also added to the sense of drama. When an aircraft took off at night from Tempelhof, heading for Moscow, the factory chimneys around the airport were illuminated by floodlights. Masts and church spires were

Berlin-Tempelhof terminal (since demolished), 1932.

lit by red lamps as a means of warning pilots, and from then on, a trail of lights, visible even in Prussian weather, marked out the route east. The airport and the vicinity became a veritable *son et lumière* show for the locals.

Tempelhof was unrivalled, too, for its proximity to the residential centre of the German capital. Originally laid out on part of a huge parade ground, the aerodrome was surrounded by public parks, a pleasure garden and suchlike, its position securing for the city – at least until the airport's redevelopment in 1936 – a central breathing space. Le Corbusier appreciated this location, writing in 1930:

> ... the city of Berlin has an airport inside town, whereas the airports of other cities are at such a distance from the center that the time saved by plane is simply lost by the time needed to go from the airport to the center. At Berlin, at the Tempelhof airport, they were satisfied with a central core 300 meters in diameter; on the perimeter of this core, a regulation covers all the surrounding constructions; it generates a cone, rising from zero at the perimeter at an angle of 15°; it is forbidden to build higher than the conical surface thus produced; simple, absolute, but also flexible.[5]

Certainly, traffic connections were excellent: roads, new and old, led from the airport to the shopping, administrative and business centres. A main canal dock was within reach in the north of the city, and stations on the main ring railway, the underground and the trams were all within a few hundred yards of the main entrance. But because of its central location, and the general prohibition on building, the airport was constrained; even in the 1920s there was nowhere to expand. Adjacent to the flight path was a 400-foot-high chimney, erected in the late nineteenth century and belonging to a local brewery; flanking the station itself were two huge wireless masts, necessary for communication and navigation but situated in such a way as to cause several operational incidents, such as the gashing of the *Graf Zeppelin* in 1931.

Another architect, Erich Mendelsohn, flew from Charlotten-

burg to Berlin in July 1928: 'We flew with a tail wind unbeliev-
ably quickly and were at Tempelhof shortly after one. Here at
once into the vortex which still does not know where it is going.'[6]
He obviously meant Berlin, not its airport, but Tempelhof was
experiencing serious problems. Space was tight, requiring much
'higgledy-piggledy' improvisation on the part of its managers,
and there was not sufficient money or vision to rectify matters.

It would take the Nazis to materialize a transport interchange for Berlin such as Le Corbusier had been propounding
since *Urbanisme*, his visionary account of modern town-planning, had been published in 1925. Assuming an 'ideal site' to
begin with, he inscribed a pattern with major and minor axes,
star intersections of orthogonal and diagonal roads, and sites
for the remaining infrastructure. Industry was consigned to the
outskirts; the city centre consisted of nothing other than a transport interchange surrounded by skyscrapers: 'Everything is
concentrated in them: apparatus for abolishing time and space,
telephones, cables and wireless; the banks, business affairs and

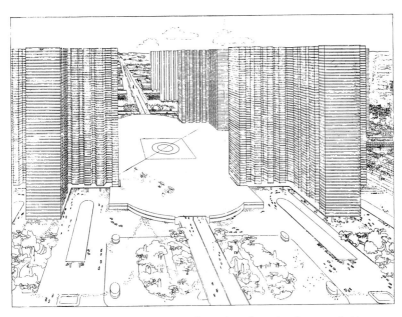

Le Corbusier's drawing of an airport under an 'autodrome' and surrounded by
skyscrapers, from his 1925 book *Urbanisme*.

117

the control of industry; finance, commerce, specialization. The station is in the midst of the skyscrapers, the tubes run below them and the tracks for fast traffic are at their base.'[7] The 'station' was a massive seven-storey complex serving, as one might expect, trains and automobiles; but its uppermost level formed an aircraft landing space flanked by towers. As Reyner Banham later suggested, such a compact solution to questions of transport infrastructure was by no means revolutionary; in spirit, and in many of its design principles, Le Corbusier's project was indebted to the visions of Antonio Sant'Elia, an Italian Futurist architect who between 1912 and 1914 made several hundred drawings of building and town-planning ideas, a group of which were exhibited 3 months before the outbreak of World War I under the title *Citta Nuova*. A railway terminus was to be constructed in the gorge between slab-sided buildings; above

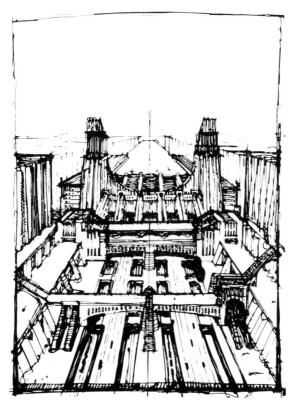

Antonio Sant'Elia's drawing of the 'Future City', 1914.

the rails, tubular walkways funnelled passengers from platform to pavement, and then, if need be, to the airport on top, whose runway drew the eye into the empty distance of the Futurist world. In Sant'Elia's vision of the future city, residential and transport systems would be combined; every part of urban existence was to be concentrated into vast edifices built over a massive network of communications, in which mechanized and pedestrian traffic were to share space but function separately. As Banham noted, the original impetus behind these sketches seems to have been the proposal to rebuild Milan's Central Station; Sant'Elia's flourish was his plan to cover the wide avenue of the Viale Vittor Pisani with a platform in order to provide a landing area for aircraft between its two rows of skyscrapers. Unfortunately, he died before his plans could become anything more than flights of fancy.[8]

Like such visions of future transport systems, in Le Corbusier's city the flat space at the centre of the urban space must be seen as the generator of its kinetic energy, a machine which sends out physical communications through the body of the metropolis and out to the nation, helping to maintain it as a viable political entity: 'The aircraft arrive at the centre, on the station; who is to say that they would not arrive exactly on the raised platforms of the skyscrapers themselves, in order to set off without wasting a minute towards the provinces and beyond the state's borders.'[9] Nevertheless, the array of 50-storey skyscrapers, standing about 300 yards apart, directly on the edge of the flight platform, would have presented insurmountable problems for aviation operations; given the unpredictable winds and pressure vortices created in the canyons between the towers, each landing and take-off would have been a journey into the realms of impossibility. A mischief-making footnote to Le Corbusier's account shrugs at the possible technical difficulties:

At this time, the space ['aéroport'] envisaged on the terrace is only a rank for aerotaxis which shuttle to the larger airport ['aérodrome'] situated in the outskirts of the city. The techniques of landing are not yet sufficently well-developed to permit large international aircraft to set down on the central station. The issue of landing on the terraces of individual buildings remains equally in the balance; it is impossible to say when and how we will achieve a private, domestic aviation.[10]

Ignoring the heavy-handed pun on 'in the balance', which imagines the outcome of a pilot misjudging the tricky procedure of landing an aircraft on a roof, it is not entirely clear what Le Corbusier meant by 'domestic aviation'. Presumably, he was suggesting that at some point in the future, aircraft ownership would be sufficently universal that one might fly from one's dwelling to one's workplace; the verandah or garden might double as a landing strip. By 1930, however, Le Corbusier had found a solution to this question, and was entertaining the idea of air taxis capable of short take-offs and landings. He predicted that 'in two years, not the big international planes but taxiplanes, will be able to land vertically in city centers.'[11] This idea was being developed simultaneously by Frank Lloyd Wright in his designs for Broadacre City; there, small aircraft – autogyros and 'aerators', a kind of 'self-contained mechanical unit that is sure to come' – would be 'capable of rising straight up and by reversible rotors able to travel in any given direction under radio control at a maximum speed say of 200 miles an hour, and able to descend safely into the hexacomb'. Such would be their manoeuvreability that they could land 'by a doorstep if desired', thus permitting citizens to live in widely scattered settlements and forestalling the need for large central airports.[12] By the time he published *La Ville Radieuse* in 1933, Le Corbusier was able to announce that atop the skyscrapers of the business centre would be 'runway platforms available 25 metres wide by 150 to 100 meters in length'. Once again, such structures would have been dangerous, presenting a tiny margin for pilot error if an aircraft was landing at speed; but for Le Corbusier, any objection was irrelevant since 'the problems involved have already been largely solved by naval aircraft carriers,'[13] a type of vessel which he later described as 'the shifting airport'.[14] It has been suggested that since 'it was not [Le Corbusier] who had proposed an unusable airport, but rather the airplane builders who had not yet done their work', his commentary was deliberately 'naive, even arrogant'.[15] Perhaps; but it also showed his mistaken belief that the aircraft industry would accommodate the needs of aggressively visionary architects such as himself.

Nevertheless, Le Corbusier was also beginning to think more practically, placing his airport in the city centre but now on flat land on the periphery of the skyscraper quarter of the *ville radieuse*, a modified version of his urban utopia. His 1933 competition design for the development of the left bank of the Schelde in Antwerp, developed from his theories of the radiant city, envisaged a large airport situated 'in the city itself and not some distance out of it'. His reasoning was simple: 'In practice, commercial aviation has shown that an airport placed outside the city is a serious mistake, cancelling out the advantages of travel by air.'[16] However, the space occupied by the 'Antwerp Air Terminal' is roughly triangular, abutting the river, so as to accommodate both sea and air planes, and creating a transport node for three elements. In terms of lay-out, it is entirely conventional. The terminal building sits on the periphery of a field 800 yards in diameter, on which are laid out, along several bearings, the 'omnidirectional' grass 'runways' to allow aircraft to take off into the eye of the wind.

Throughout the 1930s, Le Corbusier continued to push his ideas of an integrated transport system, the airport as a machine situated at the heart of the city and designed to dispatch the traveller. Yet in *Les 4 Routes* originally published in French in 1941, he claimed that he had only ever had two truly encouraging impressions that the immense potentiality of air travel might be fulfilled. One of these had taken place in 1929, when he had conceived the ideal situation for the airport at Buenos Aires; the other had occurred in 1936, when he had spent 6 weeks in an office building in Rio de Janeiro overlooking the new aerodrome, Santos Dumont.

This facility, still operational today, lies hard against the high buildings of Rio's central area and has the waters of Guanabara Bay on its three sides. In March 1934, the city signed a contract for the levelling of ground on the Ponta do Calabouco, a point of land jutting into the bay and measuring about 900 by 500 yards, for the construction of a municipal land and marine airport; it was intended that the Ponta should be joined to the island of Villegagnon, lying about 500 yards offshore, in order to permit the construction of a 1,500-yard main runway. Even though the project also involved construction of a sea wall and some land reclamation, Le Corbusier's account of the work involved was typically exaggerated:

> An engineer devised it; originally, old-fashioned planning of a type which it seems to us offers no solution of modern problems had intended this spot for the erection of a capitol ... the engineer intervened; this is the place for an aerodrome. A mountain was removed – a 'moro' – and thrown into the sea.

When the new airport was eventually opened by the President of Brazil on 1 November 1938, the space it occupied was almost square; the runway was a little under 3,280 feet in length and 150 feet wide, while near the north-west corner was a large hangar and flying-boat slipway. Even on its completion, the

Le Corbusier, Sketch plan of Rio de Janeiro development (including the airport), 1936.

facility was severely restricted; the Pão de Açúcar, better known as the Sugar Loaf mountain, lay only a couple of miles and loomed over the runway. But because of the fact that it was at an intersection of elements, of *voies*, Le Corbusier overlooked such technical shortcomings and instead announced the setting of a precedent: 'a triumph of wings is well worth the loss of a capitol. We have suffered long enough that sordid exile in the suburbs of Bourget or Croydon; at Rio, the planes come out of the sky to land direct at the waterfront.'[17] Here, then, is a recapitulation of charges he had made some years earlier in *Aircraft*: in their haphazard development on the edge of cities, airports were effectively suburban rather than urban. To situate them in the middle of the city, sacrifices such as the 'loss of a capitol' would of course, have to be made, but they would be for the sake of the larger urban plan.

Similarly, on his visit to Buenos Aires in 1929, Le Corbusier had been informally approached by the Argentinian government to advise them on the best site for the capital's new airport:

> I began to think in terms of geography and world and finally arrived by means of that thought and the lines which expressed it at a prophetic point of convergence: at a given precise spot where the lines would best achieve their end. I had drawn the Atlantic with its ships from Europe, the Cordillères of the Andes – gate to the Pacific – the tablelands, the pampa, and that place where the waters cut though the barranca. Planes in the air, boats on the water, rails running through the grassses, and the highroads which had helped to colonise. The sweeping circular line crossed in one precise American zone, which was Buenos Aires and not Buenos Aires itself, their course automatically determined the future lay-out which the city's urbanization would have to take.

The site he identified was near the Palermo Gardens on the bank of the Rio de la Plata, only a few minutes by taxi from the city centre, where the trans-Andean railway terminated, and close to the then popular marine-air terminal, from which domestic and international flying boat services operated.

However, after he had suggested this 'point of convergence' between the natural terrain of central South America and the demands of urbanism, there was a delay of almost a decade before Le Corbusier, in collaboration with two Argentinian architects, was finally commissioned to complete a 'key plan' for Buenos Aires. By which time, he later claimed, such all-encompassing transport systems were regarded, in Europe at least, as *passé*: '… so much sniggering, so much shrugging of shoulders had greeted such methods in Europe, that in 1938, having been asked to I had dropped this matter of the aerostation and allowed a far more conservative installation to the south of the city, on the border of the delta.' However, when the Argentinian Ambassador to France saw the 'conservative' plans Le Corbusier was now proposing, he acted quickly: 'He was courteously categorical: I was to have no fear and to put the aerodrome back on the propitious spot which had virtually been ordained by the gods! Happy country, able to remain abashed at the impact of a daring idea.' Consequently, the Aeroparque de la Ciudad de Buenos Aires, named after Jorgé Newberry, began operations in January 1947; it is still in use today, and is the busiest such facility in South America.

TOTAL RUNWAY

After World War II, there occurred what has commonly been regarded as a major shift in Le Corbusier's architecture. Charles Jencks describes it in the following terms: 'Instead of being the epitome of a Machine Age it was now thought to be almost primitive: instead of being made up of right angles and straight lines, it was thought to be arbitrarily made up of curves and whimsical shapes.'[18] Henri Lefebvre, in his magisterial account of 'the production of space', perhaps came closest to identifying the processes lying behind this shift when he observed that, although Le Corbusier eventually claimed to be working 'towards a technicist, scientific and intellectualised representation of space', what in fact had been originally involved was simply 'a fracturing of space':

> ... the homogeneity of an architectural ensemble conceived of as a 'machine for living in', and as the appropriate habitat for a man-machine, corresponds to a disordering of elements wrenched from each other in such a way that the urban fabric itself – the street, the city – is torn apart. Le Corbusier ideologises as he rationalizes – unless perhaps it is the other way round.[19]

Under the aegis of 'unless', that fascinated and speculative conjunction, Lefebvre was suggesting that Le Corbusier's desired process of rationalization – that is, the creation of the new urban space – had been driven by a fundamental ideological violence whose meaning remained unknown to him, until, 'perhaps', he finally transposed the terms of his original approach; once 'the other way round', he immediately understood that space was being fractured for the sake of a *theory*, rather than a practical need. By 1945, it seems that Le Corbusier appreciated that, in respect of the compound of 'man-machine', neither element was static; the former evolves through biology, the latter through technology, and both types of progress demanded the concrete solutions known as infrastructures.

Every mode of transport requires infrastructure, facilities and equipment permitting the management of its vehicles. At first glance, the airport exists as the essential infrastructure of air transport, serving to receive aircraft on the ground, service them and return them to their element. Such a function – 'the turnaround' – barely existed in the early years of aviation, when the only imperative was to expedite flight at any cost. This was part of the problem, as Le Corbusier learned on his odyssey across Europe in 1928; airports were so in thrall to the new technology that they would do anything to be part of it, adapting themselves 'higgledy piggledy' to the exigencies of flying machines. At that time, aircraft faced such a myriad of difficulties in simply getting off the ground that it was impossible for airports not to yield to their technical demands, in order to avoid endangering them. As the century continued, the aircraft continued to impose their demands; runway lengths and pavement strengths had to be increased to accommodate quicker and faster planes while taxiways and aprons needed to be expanded to allow for manoeuvreability.

Such investments had serious consequences. By the time he wrote 'Die Frage nach der Technik' in 1954, Heidegger was asserting that the chief characteristic of technology was the fact that 'everywhere everything is ordered to stand by, to be immediately at hand, indeed to stand there just so that it may be on call for a further ordering.'[20] He termed whatever was ordered about this way – the infrastructure, say – the 'standing-reserve', the German word for which, '*Bestand*', implies continuance, stability, vigilance. By way of illustration, Heidegger offered the example of aircraft, about to take off, its cabin full of passengers:

> ... an airliner that stands on the runway is surely an object. We can represent the machine so. But then it conceals itself as to what and how it is. Revealed, it stands on the taxi strip only as standing-reserve, inasmuch as it is ordered to ensure the possibility of transportation. For this it must be in its whole structure and in every one of its constituent parts, on call for duty, i.e., ready for takeoff.

Heidegger argued that no matter how autonomous a great airliner may appear, until it actually flies it only exists as an instance of 'standing-reserve' within, and subject to, the larger structure; the infrastructure. The machine ready for take-off is in fact capable of flying off on its own; the fact that it can become detached from the ground says nothing about its essential embeddedness within the technological system which one might term 'airport', an embeddedness which is also not contingent on the fact that the pilot may experience the aircraft as a means of performing a job. In effect, what the airport has done to the airliner, architects such as Le Corbusier did to humanity and nature, reducing the sublime energies of being to a carefully calculated, pragmatic use and displacing the sense of infinitude and power into their own machinery and facilities, interminable infrastructures in which the subject is 'ready for take-off'.

Such philosophical speculations might explain why, after World War II, Le Corbusier revised his view of airports so radically. In 1946, he must have surprised members of his seminar at the Congrès de l'Aviation Français, when he sketched out a new type of facility, now in flat open country far away from the city, whose terminal building, fed by a link road, sat in the splendid space lying at the centre of rigid cement runways. 'An airport should exist in a denuded area, consisting only of wide-open skies, a wide-open prairie, and wide-open cement runways.'[21] Crucially, Le Corbusier proclaimed that the airport exists as 'architecture in two dimensions', length and breadth, so that 'at take-off and at landing the airport will appear only in the precise shapes of its runways.'[22] Such openness of architectural form would ensure that the airport could never detract from the reason for its existence: the aircraft themselves.

Throughout his career, Le Corbusier had always argued that architects, when drawing up plans for new commissions, should regard the aircraft as a paradigm of their own practice. Most notoriously, in *Toward a New Architecture* he claimed:

> The airplane is indubitably one of the products of the most intense selection in the range of modern industry.
> The War was an insatiable 'client' never satisfied, always demanding better. The orders were to succeed at all costs and death followed a mistake remorselessly. We may then affirm that the airplane mobilized invention and daring: imagination and cold reason. It is the same spirit that built the Parthenon.[23]

Le Corbusier first invoked the Darwinian prerogative and then applied it to Fordist industry to describe the means by which the greatest manifestation of progress of the century – humans taking to the air – was achieved through the challenging commission of the war machine to build 'bombing machines'. Eight years later, his veneration of these new contraptions of wood and canvas, metal and wire, hit fresh heights: his introduction

127

to his picture book *Aircraft* (1935), subtitled 'L'Avion accuse', concluded with this statement: 'The airplane, in the sky, carries our hearts.' That sentence carries an important qualification: 'in the sky'. How should the aircraft be regarded when out of its element, when on the ground? Le Corbusier would not answer this question properly until 1946.

The sketches that accompanied his 'Infrastructure' presentation that year exaggerate certain features. In one, the plane, no longer an air-taxi, but now vastly winged, four-engined, seems to tower precariously over the apron, its unwheeled undercarriage acting as a plinth rooting it in the concrete. In another sketch, the aircraft is depicted with rather more detail, but aloof and circumspect, it turns its back on passengers and terminal building. Apart from the insectoid huddle of passengers, moving either away or towards the long, low building stretching away to the point of infinity, the place is empty, a desert. Again, the machine is pre-eminent, for Le Corbusier felt that the only type of architecture suitable to an airport was that of the aircraft itself:

> Only one kind of architecture seems tolerable and perfectly admissible: it's that of the magnificent aircraft which have carried you, or which you are going to take, and which take up all the visible space in front of you. Their biology and their form are in such harmony that no architecture seems appropriate beside them, no building seems suitable.[24]

Crucially, Le Corbusier resorted to metaphors of the organic to describe these magnificent machines; they manifested a *'biologie'*

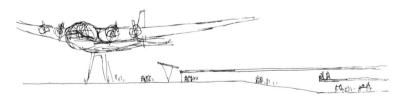

Le Corbusier, 'Coupe sur la gare d'un aéroport', sketch view of an airport with cross-section of a station, 1946.

128

which meant that each generation of machines evolved naturally and technologically, a process to which architecture could never measure up. Hence, 'the beauty of an airport lies in the splendour of its space'; the fact that in its vacuous flatness it existed only in two rather than in three dimensions, laying itself down, in deference, to the inexorable, final approaches of aircraft.

Between 1951 and his death in 1965, Le Corbusier flew frequently and recorded his impressions in notebooks; his impressions of airports at which he found himself stranded are most revealing. In November 1955, he was waiting in the colonial terminal building at Karachi which once served as the terminus for the Britain–India air service, and set down his observations:

> ... art is made by the addition of facts in view of one another // Karachi airport the aircraft of various kinds of artifice // the sky Pass the Shell or Burma Tanks for replenishing fuel. All colours, the graphic quality of the enormous or little inscriptions, full of art. The delicately shaded, oiled runway in front of the building, geometric elsewhere baggage pulled along on wagons, the ladders moved close to arriving aircraft. The men who carry on their business.

Gazing at the array of objects and people working across the wide expanse of the apron, his eye met and moulded an architecture of agglomeration; it was a poetry in motion which

Le Corbusier, 'La beauté d'un aéroport, c'est la splendeur de l'éspace', sketch view of an airport, 1946.

rendered landscape and still life largely irrelevant.

> Question: What the fuck can a Picture painted of a flowering apple tree, or of a package of tobacco mean today? exception made for a Fouquet for a Chardin for an El Greco!
> Air compressors = sky blue red lemon yellow // gasoline red / shot through with yellow // the disciplined flight crews. // the stewardess // the polished aluminum of the airplanes their admirable purity // the burned grass on the horizon // the medley of airplanes according to Iranian Airways // Air France // Air India continental // BOAC. // TWA. // PAA etc.[25]

The history of art ceased to matter when the new masterpieces were the massive, barely decorated intercontinental airliners, framed by tarmac and parched earth, which announced their discipline and purity of form across the open space of the viewing terrace.

Faced with such machines, the only suitable airport structure, Le Corbusier suggested to members of the 1946 seminar, would be building consisting of 'a wall of pretty stones, 2.5 meters high, behind which would be arrayed the reception

Le Corbusier, Sketch of Nice airport, from his Sketchbook H33, June–September 1954.

areas, customs posts etc.; so that the foundation necessary for
such a structure would be the only architectural element visible
above ground'.[26] Rather than a high curtain-walled terminal, he
proposed a long construction, more akin to a shed than a tec-
tonic creation. Presumably, the 'architectural element' of this
simple open-plan building would reside in its natural detailing,
especially the flowers that would only be seen as one descended
from the aircraft: '… the point of disembarkation for its passengers might be the neatest, prettiest flower bed or other such
adornment. Rather disembark into flowers than rocks from
Burgundy … Let Holland furnish fields of tulips and Versailles
the floral designs!'[27]

On 2 April 1955, Le Corbusier spent the morning at Nice
Côte d'Azur International Airport, waiting for a flight. It was a
place he often had passed through in the 4 years or so since he
had built a chalet facing the sea at Roquebrune-Cap Martin. As
he surveyed the scene across the apron, he recalled his 'airport
prediction' of 1946 and, with a sharp eye and lazy hand, sketched
out the vista before him: 'prediction airport 3 m. high + flowers
1946 (this morning in Nice, that's it … // The sea // The total
runway // the flowers // the impeccable airplanes // the

131

macadam // the sea // the flowers.'[28] This is an affecting record of instant perception; the great architect's eye circles around the airport flying a holding pattern, taking in the wide expanse of sea in which he would drown in 1965, moving inland to dwell on the massive runway, the beautiful airliners and the flora growing in strips between, diving into the big blue once more, before coming to rest at last in 'the flowers'. This is the airport he had predicted in 1946: a splendid space, completely bereft of infrastructure.

THE OBSOLESCENCE OF AIRPORTS

Were he alive today, Le Corbusier would not recognize Nice Airport. The international departures hall where he stood in 1955 has been rebuilt several times, and now consists of a vault measuring roughly 50 by 100 yards, designed, seemingly, to make airspace a vacuous place to wait. The contrast with the openness that Le Corbusier tried to capture in his sketches is perverse; here, the brightness of the Midi skies filters through a special grid across the inverted vault of a geometric black roof, composed of a metal fabric covered with thin, almost imperceptible veins. Like a great sheet, it stretches gently over the covered spaces, first dipping down and then suddenly taking off towards the sky to provide a dark foretaste of departure. Flowers are nowhere to be seen in this mausoleum.

The airport Le Corbusier sketched in 1954 was one of the most famous and historic in Europe. Its origins lay in April 1910, when several thousand people attended a flying meeting organized by the town of Nice on a rocky field beside the Mediterranean and alongside the mouth of the Var. At the event, Hubert Latham, astride his Antoinette monoplane, set speed and altitude records. After World War I, a grass strip of 700 yards was laid out adjacent to the Nice racecourse, and this historic flying ground, known as the 'Californie aérodrome', became the home of the Aero Club of Nice and the Côte d'Azur.

View across the car park at Nice airport, 1997.

In 1936, after some local hostility, Potez Aéro-Service instigated a Nice-Toulouse-Bordeaux-Corsica service, and plans were made for the construction of concrete runways, but this project was frustrated by the war. In August 1944, Allied military forces liberated Nice and immediately set to work on the construction of an air-supply base for the Italian campaign, which was still dragging on over the nearby border. A concrete runway 4,400 feet in length was laid, later extended to 5,500 feet, and in 1946 the site was opened to commercial air traffic under the name Aéroport de Nice-le Var.

Le Corbusier was sketching an airport about to undergo 40 years of perpetual change, because in 1956 the Chamber of Commerce and Industry of Nice and Alpes-Maritimes obtained a 50-year concession to operate the facility. Almost immediately, the cartel extended the runway by 500 yards, began construction of a new passenger terminal and freight centre; all these facilities were commissioned in 1957. In 1961, the main runway was extended by another 500 yards, a project which involved reclaiming a small amount of land from the sea. In 1969, the terminal was enlarged again, and in 1973, by reclaiming another 60 acres from the Var and the sea to the west of the airport, the runway was lengthened to nearly 10,000 feet. However, relentless growth in traffic meant that the airport

133

needed yet another runway, even though hills blocked northward expansion, the Var prevented expansion to the west, and Nice and its environs prohibited eastward development. A survey had revealed an alluvial plateau at a depth of between 35 and 50 feet just offshore; this would bear reclamation of about 750 acres of which two-thirds could be used to satisfy airport needs, bringing the total airport area to about 1,000 acres. Some 30 million tons of aggregate and infill were required, and this was hewn at the rate of 60,000 tons a day from the Le Collet de Cremat quarry about 7 miles north of the site. Eight years in the making, the second runway was opened in late 1983; shortly afterwards, a second terminal, dedicated to the handling of domestic flights, was begun, and then in the early 1990s, the French airport specialist Paul Andreu was commissioned to rebuild the older terminal, a task that was completed in 1994, by which time Nice was France's second largest airport.

The post-war development of Nice Airport bears out the thesis of Reyner Banham's influential and prophetic article 'The Obsolescent Airport', first published in 1962. Banham's argument arose out of the observation that 'Air transportation began as an army-surplus operation and – in ways both subtle and obvious – has remained one ever since'; more concretely, airports were 'never up to date, never completed, always inadequate, always sprawling slummily into their surroundings in a manner that reveals, only too clearly, the standards of hostilities-only expediency carried over into peace-time operations'.[29] At the time Banham was writing, most of the major airports in Europe were converted military aerodromes, and he felt it was this, as much as more obvious causes such as 'inadequate finances or incompetent planning', that was to blame for their 'functional and aesthetic inadequacies'. The 'war-surplus' mentality had, he claimed, 'moulded the minds and prejudices of the traffic-managers and others operating, and commissioning airports'. His article provides a uniquely perverse history of airports, beginning with their 'pastoral phase' in which light and slow-moving aircraft 'had to take off and land into the eye of the wind'; such machines were nevertheless not reliant on hard runways and 'were capable of rolling comfortably over well-kept and well compacted grass-land'. Originally, Banham argued, flight operations demanded that only two permanent structures – 'the hangar and the petrol pump' – be located at the edge of the field; then, separate buildings were erected for passengers and officials. The increase in traffic meant that it was necessary to provide 'a control-tower tall enough, and well-windowed enough, to permit continuous supervision of the hemisphere of sky as well as the pool of grass'. All the same, the buildings remained in 'a companionable cluster', and so this 'yacht-basin approach' monumentalized itself in the 1930s, at Croydon, Le Bourget and Tempelhof.

Within a few years, however, 'like all monuments in a technological culture', pioneering airports such as those Le Corbusier visited on his trip to Moscow in 1928 were 'superseded before they were designed'. By the middle of the following decade, aircraft were crossing into the first of a succession of dark new eras. 'Only a little while before the aeroplanes come' moaned Gordon Comstock, keeping his head down in Orwell's *Keep the Aspidistra Flying* (1936); 'Zoom-bang! A few tons of TNT to send our civilisation back to the hell where it belongs.'[30] For Banham, however, such heavily laden aircraft also carried the implementation of mass air travel: 'With a few happy exceptions, airliners have been converted bombers, unsuccessful bombers, prototypes of bombers, or by-products of bomber-development programmes.' Hence, the introduction of a new generation of airliners with stressed-steel skins, such as the Boeing 247D, Lockheed Delta and Douglas DC2, all of which were 'close cousins and direct descendants of bomber projects', swiftly brought 'new concepts of speed, comfort and reliability'. When the war finally came, however, aircraft became still faster and heavier; because they were so swift, they could afford to ignore wind direction, but their great weight made them intolerant of grass surfaces, especially when wet, and so landing and take-off operations soon became concentrated on cement runways specially created by military engineers.

As soon as this development occurred,

> ... the marginal location of the buildings ceased to be logical or necessary. With flight-paths forcibly concentrated into a few narrow funnels, broad segments of the sky were no longer needed by the aircraft, and large buildings could be tolerated in many locations – even the very centre of the field – where they could not have been considered before. Like a demented amoeba, the airport turned itself inside out and the original compact cluster of buildings disintegrated.

Banham's article, though dated and idiosyncratically expressed, is exemplary in the emphasis it places on the role of those airliners such as the Lockheed Constellation which were allowed to develop according to the 'logic and logistics of airline operation'. The key to this aircraft's appeal lay in properly sealing the fuselage, so that it could hold a comfortable internal pressure which would enable the aircraft to cruise at 20,000 feet, placing it high above the weather where the air would be smooth. Moving through airspace might now be fast and comfortable.

During its heyday in the 1950s, the Constellation was popularly known as 'The Queen of the Skies'; more grandly, Banham suggested that its form was so perfect that it was a 'kind of absolute Platonic ideal of an airliner'. The fuselage was certainly distinctive. Rather than a simple straight tube that tapered at the back, as was usual for contemporary aircraft, the Constellation and its subsequent variants – the Super Constellation and Starliner – resembled a dolphin. Le Corbusier, a regular passenger on the type, wrote in his notebook: '... the Super Constellation is beautiful: it is like a fish; it might have been like a bird.'[31] Its curvature was particularly elegant, cambering downwards at the front in order to reduce the length of the nose landing gear, which was very long owing to the large diameter of the triple bladed propellers. To reduce the airframe's drag, a slight downward curvature was also employed behind the wing, sweeping upwards at the rear to flow into the *empannage*. The Constel-

Lockheed Constellation prototype, 1944.

lation's triple tail was highly distinctive, too, offering good stability and making the plane easier to steer and to control, particularly with an engine shut down.

However, it was the interior appointments that struck passengers such as Le Corbusier, who spent much time during the 1950s in such machines, usually occupying 'seat Number 5' and revelling in the 'huge space'. Each time he travelled, he marvelled not simply at the smooth ride, high above the clouds, but also at the furniture around him. His most famous post-war building, the Unité d'habitation in Marseille, was completed in 1952; the interiors, designed with Charlotte Perriand, were particularly praised for their compact rooms and deft use of storage space. It is possible that much of the ethos behind this miniaturization of fittings emerged the year before, when Le Corbusier travelled on a Constellation for the first time: 'Constellation October 27, 1951 // the toilet + sink are astonishingly comfortable with their small dimensions lighting // the sink basins of stainless steel / 16 x 28 cm (?) // hot + drain + cold. I must at all costs get drawings of this equipment.'[32] In 1955, en route to Chandigarh, his enthusiam for the next gener-

137

Saarinen's TWA building at JFK, with a Boeing 707 tailplane, 1962.

ation of the aircraft was stated more simply: 'This Super Constellation is astoundingly chic.' As Banham pointed out, the consequence of the plane's popularity was that 'Constellation standards were imposed on every airline in the world, traffic increased by geometrical progression, aircraft were stretched to become heavier, bigger, faster, and there was drastically less air between them.' The Constellation began to demand airports with more than 'army-surplus' facilities; its passengers expected new standards in luxury and design.

'Idlewild is the first airport fit for Constellations,' claimed Banham. Certainly, the architecture of the TWA Terminal approached ideas of flight with unprecedented boldness. Saarinen's dream was that the building would have no facades, that these would be replaced by glass curtains to suggest that the infinite possibilities of flight in fact began on the ground, at the airport. Yet even as it was being completed, airliner design was running far in advance of Saarinen's spatially generous conception; as soon as it was opened, the terminal was already being used by Boeing jets. Banham observed: 'Already the air-side faces of its buildings are being crusted over with giant louvres to deflect the jet-blasts – the first harbingers of a transportation revolution that may prove as drastic as that of the thirties.' Saarinen had underestimated the forces that would be expelled by the newly developed jetliners; as Michael Brawne reflected in 1962:

> Wind speeds 150 ft behind the exit nozzles of a Boeing 707 can be 80 m.p.h., and noise levels 200 ft. away around 120 decibels, with a good deal of the sound energy in the uncomfortable high pitched zone above 500 cycles/second. Winds over 75 m.p.h. are seldom experienced inland, and a comparably high-pitched wood saw produces only 100 decibels at a distance of three feet; these are formidable figures with serious architectural implications which must also cast doubt on current solutions.[33]

It was certainly true that for the passenger inside the 707's luxuriously appointed, sound-proofed cabin, the experience of flight was much quieter than in the piston-powered airliners. But for those who stood on the terraces at Idlewild, the sound was deafening. These first jet airliners, spun off, as ever, from military projects, were, indeed, infernal; as Lewis Mumford observed, 'The jet plane … as befits a machine originally designed for strictly military purposes, produces the maximum amount of environmental injury and social disruption.'[34] Unlike

A Boeing 707, 1964.

A Boeing 747, 1994.

propellers, which were visible, the jet, which operated on the principle of ingesting large volumes of air in the forward intake, compressing it, adding fuel in a combustion chamber and passing the rapidly expanding burning gases out of the tailpipe to produce thrust, provided an invisible propulsion, a strange kind of fire. Military jets had been flying in considerable numbers for more than 10 years before the Boeing 707 made its debut, but military air bases generally were located far away from populated areas, and their defence missions often seemed to be of such top priority that such aircraft never evoked much public protest. With the advent of commercial jets and the desire to locate airports closer to cities, the authorities needed to act quickly to forestall criticism; hence, grotesque-looking constructions – fences, baffles and the 'giant louvres' which Banham mentioned – appeared on aprons and runway thresholds to contain the sound when it was loudest.

Le Corbusier was intensely discomfited by the arrival of these structures, claiming that 'since "jet engines" another cape has been rounded: it's the projectile = a perforator and no longer a glider'; and what it perforated most often was his ear-drum.[35] As he visited airports, he made repeated complaints about their acoustics, the fact that they were inadequately soundproofed against the new machines, and the increasing numbers of passengers making use of them. Of the new Brussels National terminal at Zaventem, opened in 1958, he remarked: 'The new Airport looks good at a glance. But the acoustics are catastrophic: Loudspeaker unintelligible ... This racket is abominable ... In ¾ of an hour, I have gotten a frightful migraine.'[36] Similarly, at Cairo Airport, even above 'the horns + the calls' of the loudspeaker could be heard 'the stridencies of the Boeings', while inside such aircraft it was an 'asylum of salvation'.[37] Only at the new Orly terminal, designed for jets, did he find that '... everything is "acoustic", silent clean and vast. It's a very handsome building.' But nowhere was perfect: 'I will write a note to the architectural engineer of Orly. Some bastards have installed in the Main Hall 14 horrid gilded crown-shaped light fixtures.'[38]

Ultimately, the problem lay with the jets. In 1961, for a flight to India, Le Corbusier was offered seats on a Constellation and a Boeing 707; after choosing the older plane, he justifed his decision: 'I refused the Boeing because it's American taste, even when run by the Indians!! Constellation = 550 Km instead of 1,1oo. But here I am at home, in airborne India, the hostess and the steward = nice Air India Constellation is very well kept (Tata) Indians and French agree with each other naturally, But the USA floods the world with its stupidity and human mediocrity.'[39] The new American jets drilled holes into previously impenetrable places, and then filled them with mediocrity, or worse.[40] The world was shrinking; and because of the jet, cultures which had been isolated from each other now found themselves coming together in airspace.

Such uniformity would accelerate with the introduction in 1969 of the Boeing 747, an aircraft which, originally conceived as a cargo plane, has since carried 2.2 billion people, around 40 percent of the world's population. With a wing span of nearly 200 feet, a take-off weight of over 400 tons, and a seating capacity of up to 550 passengers, the 747 was the first of a new generation of big jets that would not only bring about a general rethinking of terminal design at airports throughout the world, but would also seem to bring parts of the airport itself with it

141

into the sky. While on the ground, noted Clive James, '... the 747 is perhaps a bit fussy underneath, like a house being moved around on a lot of roller skates, but when it gets into the air ... there is nothing less awkward or lovelier aloft.'[41] For Saul Bellow, the 'great 747', is 'an illuminated cavern, a theater, a cafeteria'on 'bowed eagle legs';[42] for the poet Les Murray, it is a 'five-hundred seat theatre'.[43] The key to the plane's success was the potential of its splendid spaces. Most distinctive about the jet's shape was the 'whale's anterior hump' behind the cockpit and above the cabin.[44] A practical reason existed for this quirk, since the space had originally been allocated for air conditioning and other systems. However, the President of Pan Am, Juan Trippe, who had placed an initial order for the aircraft, had other ideas: 'This space is reserved for passengers. Couldn't we install a bar there?'[45] From its inception, the aircraft was large enough to no longer be regarded as such; its very form veered away from the aeronautical, and approached the architectonic. The idea travels to its furthest extreme in Thomas Pynchon's *Vineland*: 'Each 747 in the Kahuna Airlines fleet had been gutted and refitted as a huge Hawaiian restaurant and bar, full of hanging island vegetation, nightclub chairs and tables instead of airplane seats, even a miniature waterfall.'[46]

In 1991, the British architect Norman Foster was commissioned by the BBC to make a programme about his favourite 'Building Sight'. No doubt his producers were surprised when they read the opening sentences of his presentation:

> This design has a place in time that is without doubt fixed in the last half of the twentieth century. It exudes confidence, style, technology, and friendliness in a way that few others have managed. Most buildings are specialized, but this one is very specialized indeed. It is a jumbo jet.[47]

Before beginning a detailed analysis of the great plane, Foster expressed strong objections to what seemed to him to be the general hostility of architectural critics towards manifestations of engineering: 'The fact that we call this an aeroplane rather than a building – or engineering rather than architecture – is really an historical hangover, because for me much of what we have here is genuinely architectural both in its design and thinking.' He then described the architectural aspect of the aircraft:

> With about three thousand feet of floor space, fifteen lavatories, three kitchens, and a capacity for up to 367 guests, this is surely a true building. But at the same time, this machine blurs the distinction between technology and building, and what's more it flies. It has an extraordinary presence. The tail is higher than a six-storey building. I suppose it's the grandeur, the scale; it's heroic, it's also pure sculpture – it doesn't really need to fly. It could sit on the ground, it could be in a museum.

This piece of 'industrial architecture' is in its element in the sky, obviously; but equally, its singular form makes it perfectly suited to installation in an exhibition space:

> Once you are inside there are many parallels with modern buildings. Like many offices, it is a fixed shell and a moveable interior but there's a certain anticlimax. It's really rather bland in many ways. You could say it is in the international hotel style, which I suppose is appropriate – people come and go, it doesn't have a great deal of character and it could be almost anywhere.

Like Le Corbusier on the Constellation, Foster was perhaps vigilant for design detail which he could reuse in his own work:

> The surprisingly tiny but ruthlessly functional flight deck is a twinkling beauty … the layout is ergonomically efficient … the business class toilets are admirably space efficient and highly detailed pieces of industrial architecture. Elsewhere there are elegant touches: recessed snag-free handles on all the doors. The galleys have a marvellous 'American diner style', all stainless steel and black plastic.

Such detailing dated the aircraft, but it had not yet consigned it to obsolescence:

This is a sixties aircraft and it first flew in 1969. Its projected life is maybe another thirty years. We think of buildings as enduring. This aircraft is more enduring than a lot of the sixties buildings which are already coming down. Why are they coming down? Because they can't respond to change. This aircraft's shell is enduring – it responds to change. There is a lot to learn from this building. In one sense you could say that it is the ultimate technological building site.

Because Boeing had continually developed the machine, offering extended versions and different spatial configurations, the 747 would not be 'coming down' just yet. Of course, Foster, a pilot himself, was making mischief with his verb; for this piece of architecture to 'come down' prematurely would be disastrous.

By way of conclusion, Foster claimed that the 747 was a 'monumental achievement'. In fact, when it entered service, this plane, like other revolutionary jets before it, rendered pre-existing airport facilities obsolete, turning them into monuments. Older airports such as Heathrow and even Orly had to construct new facilities to accommodate these aircraft. In 1962, Banham expounded on this phenomenon:

> The grandeurs and miseries of this moment of grotesque fulfilment, in which an airport explodes into a regional planning problem, have been monumentalized in London Airport, Orly, Leonardo da Vinci and, par excellence, at Idlewild with its pointless *Marienbad Allée* in the middle of a spaghetti of roadways and a fairground of competing terminal buildings. Monumentalized … it has happened again.[48]

His article offered the prime example of JFK, which in the late 1950s, to cope with fast new jet aircraft, created a 'terminal city' – in fact, a city within a city – eventually comprising nine passenger-handling facilities, each housing a major airline and with its own unique architectural style, all strung out on a thin necklace of approach roads. For a few years, the concept worked, but with the arrival of ever-increasing passenger numbers travelling on the new wide-bodied aircraft, the whole complex began to swell, causing it to explode in the face of the city which it serves. On bad days, it can now take longer to drive from Manhattan to JFK, than to fly from JFK to Chicago.[49]

During the late 1960s, the planners of the new CDG airport were mindful of such 'impeccable aircraft' as the 747. When the facility came into service in March 1974 passengers considered its terminal to be one of the most efficient in Europe, and pilots recognized that the airside structure successfully responded to the size and handling characteristics of the new generation of wide-bodied aircraft such as the 747 or the DC10, one of which, unfortunately, crashed in nearby Ermenonville the week the airport opened.[50] Like Le Corbusier's earliest urban plans, CDG was designed more as a transportation interchange rather than simply as a passenger terminal; it was intended as an *aérogare* providing links to underground and main line railways and bus services.[51] Following Le Corbusier's *Urbanisme*, the airport's architect, Paul Andreu, sought to make this infrastructure explicit:

> As the airport terminal represents an intersection between cars and aeroplanes, both the aeroplanes and the car park had to be visible. I did not find it embarrassing that, at long range, the terminal could be mistaken for a car park surrounded by aeroplanes. On the contrary, I found it gratifying.[52]

However, in contradiction of Le Corbusier's earlier ideas, and following his later precepts instead, CDG was built far away from the city, in the flat, open area known as Roissy-en-France, famed for its beetroot and wheat, about 20 miles north of the capital, between the Seine and the Marne. Since its opening, it has undergone continuous growth and transformation, and now consists of a series of architecturally distinct complexes, occupying about 12 square miles, more than a third of the area of the city

145

Approach to Roissy-Charles De Gaulle, 1975.

of Paris, within the *Péripherique*. However, it was the original terminal, now known as 'Roissy I', which caused the greatest stir when it opened.[53]

Andreu has claimed that his basic intention in planning it was to create a relaxed facility where travellers would not have far to walk to their flights. Because of various extensions during the 1960s, Orly had acquired the etiolated jetties, which called for passengers to cover great distances simply to board their aircraft. Instead, Andreu sought to create a more comfortable, less physically taxing environment:

> As we wanted to reduce the distances the passengers had to walk, we needed to find a way of arranging the aeroplanes. After a few attempts, we came up with a sort of double wraparound arrangement, whereby aeroplanes were wrapped around the satellites, and these satellites were wrapped around the terminal. This meant that 28 aeroplanes could be arranged at a minimal distance from the centre of the terminal.[54]

Initially, he sought to design a conventional building within this circle of machines – 'a building which would look circular, but would not function like a circle, a building which was highly asymmetrical inside, or even a square building'. However, as soon as the decision had been made to deploy the aircraft in a ring, it became clear that the approach roads and the terminal

146

building would also need to be circular. Following the motto 'let the circle be a circle,' Andreu proposed a hollow-centred, up-ended cylinder in which the airport's functions would be stacked together vertically on five main levels, all similar in plan, with offices or control points ringing the central concourse areas: arrivals on level 5, departures on level 3, shopping on level 2 and (though eventually abandoned for security reasons) car parking on the roof. This central building was connected with the seven smaller 'satellite' terminals by two-storey tunnels, some 800 feet in length. All around, ramps revolve within a perimeter system of great concrete columns, which fork as they rise higher, a lay-out that is complemented by a number of landmarks – the water and air-traffic control towers, and service roads – making the airport as much an intersection of processes as a building. If Orly had resembled a large monumental display window, a beautiful *vitrine* from which one could frame the sky, CDG would be a concrete ring, whose huge scale and geometrical clarity suited the age of the wide-bodied jet.

When Andreu and his team applied this spatial form to the

Roissy-Charles De Gaulle Terminal 1, 1975. Seven satellite terminals, each capable of handling four wide-bodied jets simultaneously, ring Terminal 1. They were designed as triangles so that planes could manoeuvre more easily into the docking areas while remaining close to the terminal.

terminal's interior they soon discovered that, in such a system, the convergence of circles had eventually to come to a halt: 'You cannot go right into the centre, as that is the very place where you lose all sense of direction, like a compass needle spinning at the North Pole.' Hence, in order to prevent passengers collecting at the still centre of the terminal, Andreu's teams proposed that all the airport's installations be arrayed around a void, an empty space intersected by transparent perspex tubes containing belts upon which passengers would be conveyed to the different levels of the airport. By opening up the centre of the concrete cylinder in this way, the team claimed to have created a 'primordial place, a place for breaking off with old traditions, for moving on'.[55] Following this interpretation, Michel Serres has sought to present the great void at the heart of Terminal 1 as the 'focal point of messages in transit':

> In this place of partings and reunions, the architecture echoes the ways in which messages transit and circulate in space; it has diagonals traversing a circular intersection, in the shape of transparent tunnels, travelators and baggage conveyers ... While it mimics the circular form of the world and the universe, this miniature model also seems to represent the flight paths of the aircraft which the passengers are waiting to board.[56]

Such descriptions may strive to suggest that Andreu's terminal complements the drama of the mass air travel it facilitates; in the final analysis, they are unconvincing as the design is to those who use it. Throughout his conception, so brutally rationalistic and utilitarian in its inspiration, Andreu seems to have favoured the abstract, placeless geometries of architectural masterplans. His terminal, rushing to embrace the great jets, seems to have become as prodigious as those great machines themselves, and to have lost sight of more practical dimensions. Arriving baggage, for example, must be elevated six stories to the reclaim areas, a process that requires wasteful expenditure of energy; the electricity consumption for the moving walkways and tubular travelators has always been sky high, and

Roissy-Charles De Gaulle Terminal 1. Passengers move through inclined tubes connected to the transfer level of the main terminal, 1975.

when the power supply to them fails, or they are out of commission for reasons of maintenance, the movement of people and goods around the airport becomes unworkable.

Certainly, Andreu's circular design means that passengers can gain access to their flights more directly than in the previous generation of oblong terminals, such as those at Orly; and the close proximity of the aircraft themselves, which nuzzle around the satellite terminals, eventually offers departing passengers exciting views. However, Andreu's attempt to reconcile the linear progression of ticket controls, security checks and final boarding within a circular form undermines the rationale of the terminal. Furthermore, since each floor is much like the one above or below, it is difficult for passengers to gain a sense of relative level or direction, and, rushing from airside to landside or across the airport to make a tight connection, it is all too easy for them to become disorientated and lost. Moving through the tunnels and tubes at the centre of Terminal 1, the traveller seems to be suspended above a heart of darkness; as Clive James has suggested, the building is, 'alienationsville', a

149

factory to process movement: 'it is every nightmare Jacques Tati had come true.'[57]

Worst still, soon after the opening of the terminal, it became clear that even the passenger collection areas Andreu had provided were inadequate for the arrival of fully laden wide-body jets; crowding was generating chaos at the immigration controls. Above all, his circular concept contradicted the basic precepts of airport building, since it did not allow for future expansion, and in no way expressed the internal function of its space; the fact that its rationale was modern air transport. His terminal, intended as a surrogate for the totality of the jumbo jet, lacked the capacity to uplift those who entered its space. Within a few years of its completion, his building was reviled as a monument of bad design, nothing more than 'a rotary milking machine with pretensions to elegance'.[58]

As a pilot himself, it was clear that when the British architect Norman Foster turned to terminal design, he would not make the same errors of conception. Though he, like Andreu, had recourse to Le Corbusier's ideas of transport infrastructure, rather than being drawn to *Urbanisme*'s descriptions of 'air stations' which lay behind the *aérogare* design of CDG, Foster was attracted by the later post-war conceptions of the airport as 'splendid space': a facility spread low over one level, from which one could watch the impeccable flying machines being readied for take off. However vainly, Foster's plans try to recapture the airports that the French architect had got to know in 1928 – Le Bourget, Cologne and Berlin. His terminal at Stansted, for instance, is a large open space, on one level, transparent and airy, even though as a design ideal, it was quickly compromised by its operator, BAA plc. At a launch party held in the baggage hall a few days before the building opened, Foster complained that the space was already being corrupted, since for 'security reasons', the authorities had installed screens to prevent through vision and erected advertising hoardings; it was only a matter of time, the architect suggested, before the appearance of 'lager-advert umbrellas' on the concourse.[59]

In 1990, Foster was commissioned to design the terminal facilities for Hong Kong Chep Lap Kok Airport. This was the kind of civil engineering project Le Corbusier had undertaken on a much smaller scale in Rio de Janeiro in 1936. The island of Chep Lap Kok and its smaller neighbour island, Lam Chan, were flattened and transformed into a giant runway complex almost 4 miles long and 2 miles across. The remnants of the original islands are only a quarter of the airport's land area – the rest is crushed rock topped with a tough geotextile fabric, and thick layers of sand and tarmac, creating an area as big as the whole Kowloon peninsula. Foster laid his most basic ideas on this platform, as Peter Davey notes: 'Here is the Stansted model resolved on a massive scale. The visual principles of being drawn from ground transport towards the aeroplanes are maintained (and you can here see the tail fins from the departures hall).'[60] Overhead stretches the lightweight roof, which, as one approaches from airside, consists of nine parallel arches, each consisting of a curved steel shell, 40 yards wide, the size and shape of a shed, and each of

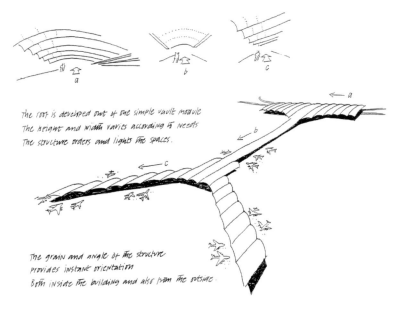

The roof is developed out of one simple vault module
The height and width varies according to needs
The structure orders and lights the spaces.

The grain and angle of the structure
provides instant orientation
Both inside the building and also from the outside.

Norman Foster, Schematic drawing of the 'design principles' of Hong Kong Chep Lap Kok Airport, 1990.

Hong Kong Chep Lap Kok Airport, looking south from the concourse as a United Airlines Boeing 747 lands, 1998.

which pitch upwards slightly, in the direction of travel, so that travellers are constantly drawn forwards to the 747s waiting further along the island. 'An airport must first of all work like a machine. It is a mechanism for processing us between land and air,' observes Davey; at Chep Lap Kok, Foster has taken this eminently fair prescription a stage further, designing an airport which from the air, looks like flying machine complete with a cockpit, two mighty wings, a long, thin fuselage and a tailplane.[61] As if to reinforce the point, a full-size replica of an early Farman II biplane, the first aircraft ever to fly in Hong Kong and one of the machines Le Corbusier saw in the sky over Paris, hangs in the midst of the terminal's vast roof. At least in Foster's version of airspace, this particular impeccable aircraft is (still) in its element.

iv Theatres of War

The poet Stephen Spender travelled around the ruins of Hitler's Reich in 1945. In the closing stages of his trip, he visited Berlin, where he had lived in the early thirties, and whose famous airport, Tempelhof, he had once described as a 'landscape of hysteria'.[1] A decade on, the approach to the city, by road at least, was almost unrecognizable:

> When we got near Berlin, there was a great rainstorm, and the whole of the dull, coarse, flat, grey-green Brandenburgian plain seemed merged into the streaming sky. And this sky seemed to reflect a mass of grey streaks like grass, wet lakes, and smeared views of pine forests. We left the main route because this was marked 'To POTSDAM'. After this all the signs were in Russian, which equally all seemed to lead to Potsdam. Our companion became more and more nervous and in the grey weather on the road which circles round Berlin we had the impression of being in an aeroplane circling above a 'drome in a pouring mist'.[2]

Spender and his companions had this impression because, in the months just after the war, 'the heap of rubble outside Potsdam', as Brecht described it, resembled nothing more than a grey and muddy *Flugplatz*.[3] However, for many others the destruction wrought on the city by the combined force of the USAF, the RAF and the Red Army proved less stirring than the sight of what little remained.

Two years after Spender's visit, on a fine summer morning in July 1947, Albert Speer was woken early in his Nuremberg gaol cell, and taken to the airfield on the outskirts of the Bavarian city. He told Gitta Sereny: 'It was the most beautiful day one can imagine. For the past months we had been allowed an hour's

153

daily walk in the prison courtyard, but somehow at that airport in the countryside near Nuremberg the air smelled different: clean, flowery, alive.'[4] He climbed into the aircraft, a USAF Douglas DC3 'Dakota', which took off for Berlin:

> I was given a window seat in a fast comfortable passenger plane, my guard beside me. After my long imprisonment, this flight in glorious weather was a stirring experience. Villages and small towns lay peacefully beneath us, seemingly intact. The fields were planted, and the forests, in spite of all the rumours, had not been cut down. Because life had stood still around me during the recent past, I had lost awareness of the fact that it was going on outside. A moving train, a tugboat on the Elbe, a smoking factory chimney gave me little thrills.[5]

As they flew north, the continuity of communication and industry seen on the ground below quickened Speer's pulse. Awaiting clearance to land at the airfield at Staaken, from which he would be taken to Spandau prison, where he would spend the next nineteen years, the plane circled over Berlin's broken *Plätze*, and Speer, who at Hitler's request had planned and in part begun a massive reconstruction of that city, caught sight of the edifice of the Reichschancellery:

> We circled for perhaps half an hour over the buildings and ruins of Berlin. While the Dakota flew in great loops, I was able to make out the East West Axis, which I had completed for Hitler's fiftieth birthday. Then I saw the Olympic stadium, with its obviously well-tended green lawns, and finally the Chancellery I had designed. It was still there, although damaged by several direct hits. The trees of the Tiergarten had all been felled, so that at first I thought it was an airfield.[6]

In Hitler's scheme, Berlin was to be rebuilt as the future world capital and, after its completion, renamed Germania on the occasion of a world exposition to be held in 1950. In order to attain this goal, a state planning agency, the *Generalbauinspektor für die Reichhauptstadt Berliner*, was established in 1937, headed

154

Albert Speer's proposed rebuilding of Berlin, with Tempelhof Airport at the top left, and the Kuppelhalle at the centre, 1934.

by Speer.[7] As the Dakota flew over that massively wide avenue which Speer intended as the approach to the largest building in the world, the *Kuppelhalle*, he became ecstatic because, despite the bombardments, something still remained.[8] But then as the plane banked above the squares of grey façades so much less squat than the rubble behind them, Speer glimpsed the Tiergarten, and was stunned. Its trees cut down for firewood in the bitterly cold winter of 1946, the great park in the heart of the city now resembled an airport.

At that moment, Speer might have recalled a famous confrontation in the final weeks of the war, when *Obergruppenführer* Helmuth Reymann, the military commander of Berlin had suggested that a section of the East-West Axis between the

Brandenburg Gate and the Victory Column in the Tiergarten might make a suitable runway for the last-minute evacuation of the *Führer*'s bunker. Hitler himself had agreed to this plan and sanctioned the removal of the ornate bronze lamp standards which bordered the road, but he absolutely refused to allow the trees on either side to be cut down to permit larger aircraft to land. When Speer discovered the plan, he summoned Reymann, who tried to explain but to no avail; Hitler's architect was incandescent. 'You cannot take down my lamp posts!' he exclaimed. 'You don' t seem to realize that I am responsible for the reconstruction of Berlin!'⁹ Even at this late stage, Speer's plans for the city could not countenance the kind of wide open spaces demanded by an airfield in its centre. But this was to dismiss, as he had so often, the unique facility at Tempelhof.

In December 1937, a group of senior Nazi officials assembled at Berlin airport to take part in a 'topping out' ceremony for its new terminal designed to replace that self-consciously modern

A view of a busy Berlin-Tempelhof Airport in 1936, with the 1924 hangar visible in the left background and the Engle brothers' 1929 terminal visible in the right background. Both were demolished in 1938 to make way for Sagebiel's development.

Hermann Göring reviewing a model of the new Tempelhof airport,
December 1937.

facility built in the late 1920s by the Engle brothers. A photograph of the occasion was taken for Goebbels's propaganda
machine.[10] In front of a scale model of the planned airport stand
Hermann Göring, Reichsminister of Aviation, and, to his right,
Eduard Milch, head of the Luftwaffe; behind them lurk various
bureaucrats, bodyguards and Gestapo operatives, coolly surveying the three-dimensional proposal. On Göring's left stands
the man responsible for the huge project, Professor Ernst
Sagebiel, assistant to Erich Mendelsohn until the Jewish architect's emigration to Britain in 1933. He is patiently explaining
his enormous design, intended to build on the success of his
recent Air Ministry HQ on Wilhelmstrasse (1933–6).[11] His eyes
are closed, and though his left hand rests on the edge of the
model, his right fist is clenched, perhaps anticipating the enormous challenge of turning this design into a structure worthy
of Germania; a symbol of the determination of the Third Reich

to rise from the ashes of the Versailles Treaty.

Three years earlier, Hitler had discussed Sagebiel's plans with representatives of the city of Berlin. He had predicted that in the future, every journey over 300 miles in length would be made by air; therefore, any new facility would have to be responsive to developments in air transport as far ahead as 2000. He had then announced that Sagebiel's airport would co-ordinate with the axes of the new city Speer was then designing for him; the terminal's entrance would connect with the eastern approach to his triumphal arch. On its completion, Hitler concluded, Tempelhof would undertake a crucial political role; through its size and appearance, it would 'silence every dissenting critic of Germany'.[12]

As Göring discussed the details of the scale model with his cronies, he may have indicated the resemblance the planned airport bore, from above, to a large bird with great wings outstretched – an eagle landing.[13] Even today, half a century after the terminal's completion, the reach of the massive 3,870-foot-long concave airfield front, forming a continuous crescent in which Sagebiel, for the sake of monumental effect, united all the functions in a broad sweep, is impressive. Its canopy is 40 feet high, and cantilevers out 170 feet for that entire distance. At its centre, the curve joins a large central hall which is, in turn, connected to a complex of entrance buildings at the airport's north-western corner which forms an entire block.

Norman Foster has praised Sagebiel's terminal as 'the mother of all modern airports', yet at first glance, the technology which the British architect's own work celebrates seems absent from the older building.[14] Tempelhof's limestone cladding, massive window frames and monumental entrance, as well as the great stone eagles on the façade, which remain as crisply detailed as the day they were chiselled, seem to proclaim a conservative opposition to radical modernism. Yet behind the façßade, the steel frame incorporated the most advanced structural technology of its time, while the curve of its lay-out and the shape of its roof displayed the influence of Mendelsohn. Back in 1914,

A sketch of Erich Mendelsohn's Aerodrome with workshops, c. 1930.

Sagebiel's old boss had sketched out a design for what he termed an 'Aerodrome', a huge curving building, 1,300 to 1,500 feet long, with a tall central atrium to handle six airships, and at either side low hangars for aircraft and workshops. Though its proportions differ and the style is wholly dissimilar, Tempelhof is Mendelsohn's visionary design in disguise; the wings are present, as is the tall central hall, though now intended for people rather than airships.[15] Within the terminal, the route of passengers arriving from the city is simply staged – they arrive from a broad plaza into the so-called Courtyard of Honour, enter the reception hall and, finally, the departures area; traversed in a straight line, the space narrows gradually to open out again in a very broad arc towards the airfield. Uniquely, the terminal was constructed so that the flow of passenger and freight could move on different levels; on top of the cantilevered roof, Sagebiel envisaged a raised stand for 65,000 spectators, the projected attendance of the annual air shows so popular in Germany at the time.[16]

In addition to its new terminal, Tempelhof now received a larger, elliptical airfield with a ring-shaped, paved runway, which was tripled in size (to 1,333 acres) in the direction of

A model of Ernst Sagebiel's new Tempelhof Airport, 1937.

Construction of Tempelhof Airport, 1937.

Berlin, so that the airport, which had already been unsurpassed in the 1920s because of its proximity to the city, was now only 2 miles from the centre on its north-west side, and linked to Speer's great axes.[17] However, owing to a shortage of labour and building materials, both of which in the late 1930s were being used for military purposes, construction dragged along slowly and the airport was never completely finished. By 1940, work had progressed such that some of the vast spaces could be used for the war effort. The Air Ministry occupied over 9,000 offices, and in 1941 the Weser Aircraft Company moved into several halls, including the main departure lounge, and began the fabrication of aircraft wings. Lufthansa, the state airline, was confined to two small areas of the terminal; nevertheless, it continued to despatch scheduled flights until 22 April 1945, a week before the city fell to the Russians.

During the Battle for Berlin, although it lay only 2 miles south of the Reichschancellery, in the direct line of Zhuikov's main offensive thrust, Tempelhof weathered the Soviet firestorm – a lasting testament to Sagebiel's high construction standards. In the final days, the *Müncheberg* Panzer Division had its command post there, and the field was defended by anti-aircraft batteries, SS troops and tanks, most of them dug in to create near-impregnable positions – but they had no fuel, so were stranded. By 26 April 1945, Soviet troops had broken through the defensive lines and were on Tempelhof airfield itself, attempting to secure the runways and prevent any aircraft from landing or taking off; but it proved a difficult objective. 'We were on one side of the runway', recalled one Red Army infantryman, 'and the German tanks were dug into the ground on the other. They were firing armour-piercing shells, which flopped down in front of us and behind us with a hollow sound, like fat quails in autumn falling on mown grass. We had to use knives and our hands to dig into the ground.'[18] By mid-morning on 28 April, exhausted by relentless attacks from the other side of the airport, the *Müncheberg* Division had no choice but to abandon Tempelhof, finally overwhelmed by Zhuikov's forces. Once they began to explore the huge expanses of the airport, Soviet troops discovered seven levels of catacombs beneath it, a maze of secure accommodation containing, among other secrets, an aircraft factory filled with half completed Focke-Wulf fighters, and a heavily fortified bunker, its doors swinging open, containing thousands of reels of Nazi films, some fragments of which apparently depicted Hitler's private life. In the next few days, the Red Army began using the vast plain of the airport as a central holding point for German prisoners; within a month, its labyrinthine underground corridors had become makeshift prisons for recalcitrant Nazis. By the end of the year, however, the great *Platz* of Tempelhof would be occupied by yet another military power.[19]

Code-named 'Terminal', the final conference between the Western Allies and the Soviet Union began on 17 July 1945 at the Cecilienhof in Potsdam, confirming the treaties made at previous summits at Teheran and Yalta, including vital agreements enshrining Soviet domination in east-central Europe, and also in Berlin.[20] The city was partitioned into sectors occupied by American, British, Soviet and French forces. Later that year, to ensure that civil and military traffic could fly unimpeded across the Soviet zone of Eastern Germany to and from Berlin, three air corridors were defined, linking the city with Hamburg, Hanover and Frankfurt. Tempelhof, situated in the US zone, was transformed into an airbase for the US Air Force. Once the craters covering the airfield had been filled in, the new occupiers set about building a hardened runway consisting of interlocking 'pierced-steel planks' laid over the still relatively unstable grass foundation. On 18 May 1946, the first civil aircraft, an American DC4, landed on this bumpy *Flugplatz*, inaugurating civil air services, initially confined to the relatives of those American soldiers stationed in the city. One of the most pressing tasks was the removal of the Nazi decorations which adorned the building; the head of an enormous stone eagle that Sagebiel had designed for the terminal's façade was dispatched to the military museum at West Point in New York State.[21]

Two years later, ostensibly in reaction to the introduction of the Deutschmark in the Western sectors of Berlin, the Soviet authorities isolated the city, terminating all land communications from the Western sectors (both to West Germany and to the surrounding Soviet zone) and cutting off food, electricity and all other supplies from the areas around the city. The decision made by General Lucius Clay, the Commander of the US sector to break this blockade by air was regarded as a prodigious gamble by the Western powers, and as a bluff by the Soviet command. Nevertheless, an 'Airlift' began on 25 June 1948 when the first Skytrains and Skymasters taxied to a halt at Tempelhof. From the outset, it was unclear if sufficient aircraft could be found and maintained, and, even more importantly, if they could transport the materials the city's population required to subsist: 10,000 tons of supplies each day, including milk, meat, fruit, vegetables and medical supplies, as well as fuel (in the form of coal) and raw materials such as iron ore. In the event, there were more than enough aircraft; the difficulties lay in managing the cramped airspaces around Berlin's airports, as planes took off or landed every 5 minutes, around the clock.

For those living in Berlin, the spectacle of the *Luftbrücke* was constant, as solid a connection as a bridge. Brecht recorded in his journal: 'above the silent streets of ruins the freight planes of the airlift drone in the night / the street-lighting is so faint that the stars in the heavens can be seen from the streets once more'; in the ruined city, only the planes circling overhead and the area around the brightly lit airport seemed truly alive.[22] Twenty-four hours a day, the elevated railway station, which commanded a good view of Tempelhof's runways, was full of enraptured Berliners. A young bank clerk wrote:

> Every two minutes a plane arrives from West Germany, loaded with food for West Berlin! The sound of the engines can be heard constantly in the air, and is the most beautiful music to our ears. One could stand for hours on the Tempelhof elevated station plat- form and watch the silver birds landing and taking off. And at night the brightly illuminated airfield with its countless little col- ored lights is like something out of a phantasm. It is a wonderful sight, which I shall never forget![23]

The blockade lasted until August 1949, by which time the Allies had flown more than 275,000 flights, transporting more than 2,325,000 tons of goods to Berlin, including 782,000 metric tons of coal, 374,000 metric tons of food, 27,000 tons of fuel and 8,000 tons of newsprint.[24] Because of the Airlift, Tempelhof, hitherto associated with the excesses of Hitler's regime, had now become the theatre, the *Schauplatz*, on which the entirety of Berlin's future would be staged; as the *Berliner Stadtblatt* reported: '*Wenn wir Berlin meinen – denn sagen wir Tempelhof*' ['Whenever we think of Berlin, then we say Tempelhof'].[25]

A photograph taken in Berlin on a warm day in the late spring of 1949 illustrates this equivalence. A group of five blond boys, aged between 4 and 7, dressed in shirts and shorts, crouch around a pile of rubble. In the background, behind a tired wire fence, lies a doll's house, façadeless and neglected; the children are more interested in the crescent of bricks they have carefully arranged in a semi-circle. Within this space, the gang have

Children's games during the Berlin Airlift, autumn 1948.

placed a couple of battered pre-war toys (an armoured car, its *Wehrmacht* camouflage chipped, and a small, wheel-less Volkswagen Beetle) between four shiny silver model aircraft (two Lockheed Constellations, and two Douglas DC4s), each mounted on a stand prominently bearing the insignia of the USAF. The eldest child, probably the leader of the gang, looks out over their little theatre and places a protective arm around his little brother; the younger boy looks, equally raptly, at another playmate who, grinning, holds a plane barely above the ground as if it has just taken off again. The game, probably known to these young survivors of Hitler's Berlin as *Luftbrücken*, was deadly serious; and what was being played out in a back-yard was also taking place, at that very moment, in the skies above their heads, and on the airfield at Tempelhof, whose distinctive shape their bricks and toys have so economically reproduced. This photograph, oddly reminiscent of Göring and his

164

staff standing around a model of the new airport in 1937, may represent the beginnings of the German post-war miracle. A Fatherland has been reduced to rubble, but within 20 years, the razed city will be stronger than ever, even though the reconstructive efforts of young people such as these will occasionally be hampered by the terrorists in their midst.

During the Airlift, the Berlin authorities occasionally made use of the empty planes flying west. Once all those Germans who had been stranded in the city by the blockade had been ferried out, space was made available to volunteers for the Ruhr mines, businessmen and politicians in the first instance, and then to anyone who could prove thay they needed to attend a training course or receive medical treatment in the West. Each of these categories paid 16 marks, the equivalent of a second-class rail fare to Hanover. Naturally, there were long waiting-lists for the flights.

On 29 December 1948 Ruth Andreas-Friedrich left her apartment building, and began the 2-hour walk across a wintry Berlin to Tempelhof. During the war, she had been operative in the city's Resistance, and was a founder member of the so-called Ernst Group, a loose, ideologically and politically diverse fusion of liberal, bourgeois and communist members, whose activities had consisted in organizing desertions, and falsifying papers necessary for survival. This time, however, as Andreas-Friedrich entered the airport, her credentials were genuine:

> Everything there is strictly controlled. Luggage inspection, body search, a statutory declaration that one is travelling with no more that 300 Westmarks. Then a cord divides those who are flying and those who stay behind ... Ground mist, I reassure myself; the plane won't fly. But outside, an engine coughed into life. Someone called through a loudhailer 'Passengers travelling to Frankfurt

are kindly requested to take their seats'. Mechanically, I began to move; mechanically, I sat down in my seat and fastened the buckle of my safety belt. 'Into freedom' said the person in the next seat. 'Into freedom', I want to reply. Yet no sound will come from my throat.[26]

Three years after the cessation of the war, the airport seemed a reminder of the rigid policing of Nazi Berlin: inspections, declarations, segregations; night and fog; friends and families left behind; flights to freedom. Nothing, it seems, had changed. As Andreas-Friedrich's plane took off, she saw that Berlin was still a *Schauplatz*: a scene of action, a theatre of war, a political arena:

> The engines roared. We roll over the the runway, slowly at first, then more quickly, until with a jerk, the aircraft lifts off into the air. Grass, lights, the walls of houses, railway lines, streets; they all disappear like scraps in the fog. Somewhere down there stands Heike and weeps like me. Somewhere down there, swimming in the fog, is the theatre of BERLIN.[27]

Indeed, despite its associations with the Airlift, its central role in the preservation of Berlin as an island of freedom, Tempelhof often retained a curious air. In John Le Carré's *The Spy Who Came in from the Cold*, the atmosphere produced by Sagebiel's terminal was almost palpably conspiratorial:

> The airport reminded Leamas of the war: machines, half hidden in the fog, waiting patiently for their masters; the resonant voices and their echoes, the sudden shout and the incongruous clip of a girl's heels on a stone floor; the roar of an engine that might have been at your elbow. Everywhere that air of conspiracy which generates among people who have been up since dawn – of superiority almost, derived from the common experience of having seen the night disappear and the morning come. The staff had that look which is informed by the mystery of dawn and animated by the cold, and they treated the passengers and their baggage with the remoteness of men returned from the front: ordinary mortals had nothing for them that morning.[28]

When Andreas-Friedrich processed through Tempelhof's echoing halls, she found herself moving mechanically; she tried to speak, but no sound emerged from her throat. Effectively, she had ceased to be a person and had become part of the airport's mechanism. As he waited for his flight to London, Leamas too sensed a similar dislocation: the terminal was filled with sudden noises and he felt alienated by the machines lurking outside as well as by the staff. And of course, what Le Carré was mapping out here in Tempelhof's great halls – mastery, superiority, remoteness, an indifference to ordinary mortals – was the almost tangible remnant of Nazi ideology. He was not original in his suspicions. Writers have frequently recognized the extreme politics contained within airports, spaces which could so easily double as parade grounds or rallying points. In Orwell's most famous novel, *Nineteen Eighty Four* (1948), England has surrendered, to be renamed Airstrip One, 'itself the third most popular of the provinces of Oceania'; the whole country it seems has become nothing more than a runway jutting out towards endless world war.[29] (It was perhaps ironic that in 1961 the authorities at Heathrow chose to name the new international terminal 'Oceanic'.)

Such dystopia may have derived much from Rex Warner's novel *The Aerodrome*, published 8 years earlier; in contradistinction to the primacy of 'Airstrip One', the main feature of this airport was its very inconspicuousness: so artfully was it camouflaged in the milieu of hills and woods that it passed almost unnoticed. Much of it lay underground with a railway connecting its various sections; those parts that were not constructed beneath the earth were hardly visible, since they were disguised to resemble older landmarks such as a parish church or a barn. The occupation of the village was undertaken subtly at first. Instead of abolishing prior institutions, the new order, like any far-sighted totalitarian system, set about assimilating them into its own structure; old buildings and houses were adapted to the new purposes and functions, the manor becoming an officers' club, the rectory a gymnasium. Such a slow ingenious absorption of its surrounding environment made the aerodrome less alien and more acceptable to the villagers who at first failed to recognize the full scope of the threat, absorbing it like a slow intoxication. In due course, the facility began to make them aware of changed states, bringing them into the ambit of paranoia, the natural mindset of airspace. Hence, the youthful narrator, Roy, began to see that the natural environment in which he had been brought up as a mess: 'Instead of the older and easy system of relationships with which I had fancied myself to be surrounded, I began to imagine crimes and secrecies on all sides, the results of forces to which previously I had given little or no attention'.[30] Feeling himself lost in 'the intricacies of deception' surrounding his family and friends, Roy decides to enlist in the aerodrome, whose ideology, whose illusion of power, seemed so clean in its determination. Above all, he is seduced by 'the undeviating precision and resolution' of the Air Vice-Marshal, the absolute leader who reveals the true aims of the regime: 'To be freed from time, Roy. From the fast and from the future. From shapelessness.'

An objective of any totalitarian state is the obliteration of the individual and of collective memory; another is the destruction of that sense of identity built up through connections to property and locale. Between the wars, it seemed that the most suitable place to destroy such nostalgia and replace it with a new order was the airport. The most historically acute version of this phenomenon appeared in John Lehmann's *Evil Was Abroad* (1938), a novel set in Austria just before the *Anschluss*. One night, its hero, a young English writer named Peter Rains, has a prophetic dream, its atmosphere 'charged, as a still valley seems charged sometimes on a summer evening with the thunder that is coming, with *conspiracy*'. Finding himself in front of the Chancellery in the Ballhausplatz in Vienna, Peter enters the building and discovers a puppet show in progress in the council chamber; 'and the marionette which was at that moment being manipulated in the tiny illuminated space he recognized to be the Austrian Chancellor himself. But, as he watched, the stage became crowded with the leading political figures of other countries, who began a slow and elaborately ridiculous dance.'[31] Confronted with this scene, Peter is convinced that the source of evil lies behind the stage, but as he tears the curtains down, he is attacked by 'enormous figures, half-dogs, half-men':

> The blows acquired a monotonous unity until he was no longer sensible of them, and the darkness cleared to reveal the road beyond the city leading to the aerodrome at Aspern, along which he was running in a wild attempt to reach it before the morning plane left for Berlin. A passenger in that aeroplane was the chief conspirator, he now knew with bursting certainty. Enormous buses filled with passengers for the aeroplane rolled past him, and out of their windows innumerable handkerchiefs were frantically waved at him. At last he reached the low group of buildings, but just as he plunged through the gates he saw a machine rise from the ground, while the loudspeaker on the aerodrome roof chanted triumphantly 'To Berlin! To Berlin!' The aeroplane disappeared spirally into the clouds.

A restored Junkers 52 at Berlin-Tempelhof, 1985.

The symbolism here is obvious enough; what was so shocking was the sense that, because it facilitated the means to fly quickly over borders, the airport itself was to some extent, complicit in the expedition of such extreme political activity.

Paul Virilio has described the means by which the Nazis took over the German state, 'city by city, or rather street by street, before spreading highway by highway toward the neighbouring territories, as if the German masses, "set in motion" by their leaders' dynamic declarations, could no longer be stopped.'[32] In his brilliant account of the 'dromomania' of Hitler's state, Virilio ought to have stressed the particular use that the Nazi party made of aerodromes to set the *Volk* in motion. Certainly, the plane Lehmann sees spiralling into the clouds above the airport, heading for Berlin, with the 'chief conspirator' on board, was a familiar icon of the time. At the beginning of Leni Riefenstahl's *Triumph des Willens* (1935) we see Hitler's aircraft, a three-engined Junkers 52 (named *Immelmann* in memory of the World War I fighter ace), descending through wispy clouds to appear in a clear sky. The effusive notes issued to accompany early showings of the film announce: '... like a fantastic eagle, an aeroplane glides through the air ... Spreading its wings wide, it plunges forward, its propellers grinding themselves howling into the wind ... Onwards rushes the mighty machine.'[33] Below the aircraft, the medieval city of Nuremberg can be glimpsed, its towers and spires swathed in mist; as the plane comes into focus, the overture to Wagner's *Die Meistersinger* slowly merges into the 'Horst Wessel' song, and the machine lines up to land at the airport from which Albert Speer would depart in 1947:

> There! – as close as the clouds, on the sun-golden firmament, the speeding shadow becomes larger, approaches. Thundering, it circles over the city. An aeroplane. The aeroplane! The Führer is arriving.
>
> As the gigantic bird finally hovers over the airfield, loses altitude, approaches, stops, the tenseness of anticipation of thousands has reached its peak and is released in joyful, enthusiastic shouts. The Führer gets out of the plane. Here and there a brief,

firm handshake, a friendly word, a glance of recognition. On the faces of those who were able to be there is the light of grateful confidence. With roaring cheers from all sides, the Führer rides into the city.[34]

On the occasion of the 1934 Party Day, the apron of the Nuremberg-Marienberg airport amounted to a *Schauplatz* from

Hitler dismembarks from a chartered Lufthansa aircraft during the 1932 Presidential campaign, followed by his pilot, Hans Baur.

which Hitler would begin, in the words of the epigraph to Riefenstahl's film, to 'muster his faithful followers'. It was a display of power that had been perfected during the intense election campaigns of 1932, when he had made the most extensive use of flying by a politician to date. Having hired a plane from Lufthansa, along with one of its pilots, Captain Hans Baur, Hitler justified the expense by arguing that since Heinrich Brüning (against whom he was running) had the advantage of using the radio, there was no better way of competing with his rival's being constantly on air than by his being constantly *in* the air, and able to visit as many different places as possible. This airborne campaign, known as '*Hitler über Deutschland*', impressed the electorate; but then political arguments mattered less than spectacle.

Once, Hitler having informed Baur that he was expected in Munich, his pilot told him the aircraft lacked night-flying equipment: 'So Baur had had an improvised lighting system installed. On arriving at Munich, we wheeled around above the stadium. It was at the time of the Papen elections, when we got our two hundred and ninety seven seats.'[35] This was quite a stunt. Oberwiesenfeld airport, which had just opened, was situated in the vicinity of a 300 feet high gasometer and the large factory complexes of Südbreme and BMW. Flying in the dark with only rudimentary equipment would have represented a considerable test of Baur's skill; on this occasion, according to Hitler, the flaunting of danger may have secured the seats needed to win the election.[36] As Konrad Heiden observed:

> The ear of the masses ... was filled with the roaring noise of Hitler's grey Junkers plane. More than ever these masses regarded the flying voice of thunder as the secret ruling power ... what they saw were the bands of SA men, protected by police, and the Junkers plane descending from the clouds.[37]

Hitler's arrival was always a carefully staged epic scene, a piece of political theatre on the grandest scale in which it became impossible to differentiate the real from its representation, the dictator from his structures of power. Indeed, it has recently been suggested that the Nazi public sphere – that string of captivating scenes in a series of dramas aimed at mobilizing the people and impressing upon them (and the rest of the world) the extent of mass support and the splendour of accumulating power – should be regarded as a 'beautiful illusion' which is, it seems, different from the 'beautiful illusion' of art which serves as a means for private psychic flight from reality: 'The fascist illusion is the factual result of a flight from reality by the petty bourgeois masses, who are socio-economically and socio-psychologically most disposed to such a flight.'[38] Such flights, literal or figurative, necessarily took place on the *Schauplatz*, nothing more than a specular and speculative locus in which politics and theatre converged.

In his essay 'The Sublime and the Avant-Garde', Jean-François Lyotard argues that 'The aesthetics of the sublime ... was able to come and build its architectures of human "formations" on the Zeppelin Feld in Nuremberg,' the great stadium at the heart of the Party Rally Grounds, so named because it was large enough for an airship to land.[39] In such places, Fascism, insists Lyotard, came to depend upon the concept of 'over there', an approaching spectacle whose inexpressibility was firmly grounded at the rallying point by means of expectation and arrival. The questions posed by those gathering on the great open space – 'Is the pure people [*das Volk*] coming? Is the Führer coming? Is Siegfried coming?' – were answered by the staging of the public demonstration itself. As they looked up into the skies and awaited some spectacle of arrival, the previously disordered masses congealed into a coherent *Volksgemeinschaft*.[40] The 'flight from reality' taking place on the great open spaces of the Zeppelinfeld or Tempelhof was one which depended simply on the willingness of the masses to be taken hostage and carried away by the machinery of the totalitarian state.

On 1 May 1933, 3 months after Hitler came to power, a mass rally took place on the assembly grounds at Tempelhof. May Day, the traditional Socialist celebration, had been proclaimed

Hitler addressing troops at Berlin-Tempelhof, 1 May 1934.

by a recent act of the Reichstag as a commemoration of National Labour, an event designed by Goebbels to demonstrate the will that was now motivating the German people. As he wrote in his diary:

> At Tempelhof, massive structures have been erected. They offer a huge image of the National Socialist will to power. The 1 May will become a mass event, the like of which the world has never seen before. The whole people should unify itself with one will and in readiness. In this the first year of our revolution we will give back to the worker his honour and to the proletariat his respect. A complicated mechanism should now be set in motion.[41]

Over the course of the morning, workers from all around Berlin, wearing their overalls, and marching in groups according to factory and occupation, streamed through the streets and

174

converged on the edge of the airport, where they were directed to their designated positions. Later in the day, delegations from around the country, and from German territories lost at Versailles, were flown into the capital as special guests of the Nazi government and invited to tea with *Reichskanzler* Hitler and *Reichspräsident* Hindenburg before being returned to Tempelhof for the climax of the day: Hitler's speech. As Peter Fritzsche has pointed out: 'Even before Hitler mounted the stage, the choreography of May Day had fastened the links between workers and the nation, between machinists and machine-age dreams, between technical mastery and national prowess.'[42] Squadrons of Junkers bombers flew overhead, while on the airfield itself, the popular stunt flyer Ernst Udet performed for the crowd, which was swelling by the minute with excited Germans.[43] In the middle of the afternoon, the nation's newest airship, the *Graf Zeppelin*, hovered in homage, casting a giant shadow across the stage erected for the Führer. Designed by the then little-known architect, Albert Speer, this consisted of a large platform, behind which hung three large banners, each taller than a 10-storey building. Two of these were swastikas, while immediately behind the Führer's podium hung a drape of black, white and red, the colours of Prussia. The structure was illuminated by the airport's huge navigation beacons, and by military searchlights on scaffolds.[44]

Goebbels claimed that by early evening, a million and a half people had assembled at Tempelhof; he and Hitler arrived shortly afterwards, having been driven down from the Reichschancellery:

On the field at Tempelhof, one could not get a proper sense of the immense sea of people standing there. The floodlights moved across, flashing and illuminating. One could see only a grey mass, standing shoulder to shoulder, cheek by jowl. I introduced things briefly, and called for a minute's silence in honour of the unfortunate miners who had died in Essen that day. Now the whole nation stood still; the loudspeakers conveyed the silence across the land.[45]

When Goebbels proclaimed the minute's silence, a radio-link established an exact synchronization with other assemblies taking place throughout Germany; Tempelhof had, in effect, become the centre of the nation. Just before he presented Hitler to his vast audience, Goebbels noticed that the sun was about to break through the clouds, and timed his speech so that light streamed down as the Führer took his place on the rostrum. Hitler spoke for about 45 minutes, praising the dignity of labour and proclaiming that the worker was to be the essential factor in the new Germany, before leading a rendition of the 'Horst Wessel' anthem. Goebbels later gushed:

> The waves of ether transported the voices of the one and a half million people, who were standing as one here on the Tempelhof field in Berlin, across the whole of Germany, through towns and villages ... Now no one can be excluded, here we all belong together, and it is no longer an exaggeration to say that we have become one fellowship of brothers.[46]

Within hours, the unity emanating from Tempelhof would be consolidated further, or broken forever; it all depended on one's political allegiance. The following morning SA and SS units raided trades union offices throughout Germany, ransacked premises and confiscated funds. Leftist officials, who had recently co-operated with Goebbels in staging the nation's May Day celebrations, were arrested and placed in 'protective custody'. This was just the beginning of the terror; by the end of the summer over 100,000 people, mainly party-political opponents, had been robbed of their freedom, with almost 600 murdered. The wave of 'arrests' – little more than kidnappings – brought the victims to a police gaol or to one of the 30 or so 'wild' concentration camps which sprang up to deal with the Nazi state's putative 'enemies'.

Tempelhof would continue to host May Day celebrations for the next 2 years, but in 1936, Sagebiel's enlargement of the airport to the north west of the airfield, swallowed up much of the ground previously used for the great assemblies. This expansion would also efface the most notorious of the ad hoc concentration camps, KZ Columbia Haus, situated on the edge of Tempelhof field. Between 1933 and its closure in 1936, 8,000 detainees passed into it; many never emerged.[47] Originally designed as a military police station for the adjacent barracks, the 'Straf-gefangnis Tempelhofer Feld' contained a guardroom, ten interroga-tion rooms in the basement and 134 cells. By the time it acquired its new name in 1929, it was empty and under the control of the airport authorities. However, the spring and summer of 1933 saw this decrepit military prison fill up quickly; by July, there were 80 detainees, by September 400 and, in February 1934, 9 months after the May Day celebrations, almost 300 prisoners were being held, crammed three to a cell.

It is impossible to state with any certainty how many of those detained in Columbia Haus's first year of operation died; arrest records are necessarily sketchy. But it is known that in late November 1933, SS officers arrested a union activist, Michael Kirzmierczik, tortured him for three days and then conspired to pass off his death at their hands as suicide. His wife travelled to Berlin from the family home in Leipzig a few days later and, after seeing his body in the morgue, testified to the multiple injuries inflicted by the SS gaolers. There was a gaping hole in her husband's neck, his skull was fractured, one of his eyes was missing, an ear had been mutilated, the left arm broken in three places, fingernails removed and fingertips crushed. After requesting Kizmierczik's personal effects from the police, his wife was told to apply, in writing, to Columbia Haus. In July 1934, after even the Nazi government's own inspectors made representations to the Justice Ministry regarding the prison's 'openly sadistic excesses', Columbia Haus was regularized, and placed under the control of Walter Gerlach who ran it as a Gestapo detention centre – in effect, an overflow facility for the notorious HQ on Prinz-Albrecht Strasse. On 8 January 1935 Himmler's deputy, Reynhard Heydrich, announced that hence-forth Columbia Haus at Tempelhof would be officially known as 'Konzentrationslager [KZ] Columbia'.

The true significance of 'KZ Columbia' lies both in its location in the middle of Berlin, next to the airport – those arrested at the terminal often ended up there – and its being the place where many of those who would later thrive in the world of state terror that was the Nazi concentration camp system began their careers. Gerlach, the first commandant, later ran Sachsenburg; his successor, Karl Koch, subsequently became Commandant of Buchenwald before taking charge of the death camp at Lublin-Majdanek. Even those in the lower ranks of the SS garrison at Tempelhof prospered: in due course, Richard Baer and Arthur Liebehenschel would serve as commandants of Auschwitz; Max Kögel would run the women's camp at Ravensbrück, and Albert Sauer would take command of Mauthausen in Austria.[48]

On 18 June 1936, it was announced that from 1 October 'KZ Columbia' would cease to exist; its premises would pass to the Air Ministry, to be disposed of, and any remaining inmates would be transferred to the new purpose-built facility at Sachsenhausen. A telegram dated 16 November 1936 provided the final word on the camp: *'Das Konzentrationslager Columbia in Berlin-Tempelhof is mit 5 November 1936 aufgelost worden.'* Liquidated then, and demolished 18 months later, to make way for Sagebiel's great terminal, 'KZ Columbia' did not disappear completely, however. Its notorious cellars, the SS's torture chambers, form part of the foundations of the northern edge of the current airport. Perhaps it is their presence which accounts for the perpetual chill of Tempelhof. They stand still for the presence of an absence, a conspiracy of terror which, especially at an airport, will not remain underground.

MACHINERY OF THE STATE

At 12.38 am on 18 October 1977, West German state radio carried a news report. A spokesman for the Federal Ministry of the Interior announced that the 86 hostages held by terrorists in a

Lufthansa jet at Mogadishu, in Somalia, had been been freed by *Grenzschützgruppe Neun* (GSG-9), and that three of the four terrorists were dead. It later emerged that the operation's code name was *Feuerzauber*, a Wagnerian allusion to the 'magic fire' surrounding the sleeping Brunnhilde, a barrier penetrated by Siegfried when he claims her as his bride. The German commando team was feted throughout the world; only later did the larger political significance of this intervention become clear.

GSG-9 had been formed in response to the West German police's incompetent handling of the 1972 Munich Olympic crisis, when eight members of the PLO's 'Black September' group broke into the Israeli quarters at the Olympic village, shot two athletes, took nine others hostage and demanded to be flown to freedom. The siege came to a horrific end on the apron of Fürstenfeldbrück airport, near Dachau, when the police operation turned into a prolonged firefight with the terrorists, and cost the lives of all the remaining hostages. Once more, it seemed that Jews were dying on Bavarian soil.[49] Yet, as far as the German state was concerned, there was a another crucial difference between the failure in Munich and the later triumph at Mogadishu. Paul Virilio places it in proper perspective:

> As airports were turned into theaters of necessary regulation of exchange and communication, they also became breeding and testing grounds for high-pressured experiments in control and aerial surveillance performed for and by a new 'air and border patrol,' whose anti-terrorist exploits began to make headlines with the intervention of the German GSG-9 border guards in the Mogadishu hijacking, several thousand miles away from Germany.[50]

Five years after the Munich fiasco, the new unit's action 'several thousand miles away' marked the first time since World War II that German troops had fired shots in anger abroad. The machinery of the German state was now jet propelled; it could land at any foreign airport and, for as long as it took to neutralize dissent, annexe the very apron to its own country's security services.

The hijacking which ended at Mogadishu in 1977 had begun on 13 October, when a Lufthansa Boeing 737, named *Landshut* in honour of a small Bavarian town, took off from Palma bound for Frankfurt. On board were 82 passengers and five crew members, mainly German holidaymakers (including six beauty queens) but also Spaniards, Swedes and Austrians. Almost an hour into the flight, two brunette women who had boarded the aircraft at the last minute, reached into their knee-length boots, withdrew pistols, stood up and, along with two male accomplices further down the aisle, took control and forced the captain to land the plane in Rome for refuelling. On the apron at Leonardo da Vinci airport, the group identified themselves as the Organization of Struggle Against World Imperialism, and demanded a ransom of $15 million, along with the release of eleven terrorists in West German jails and two Palestinian terrorists held in Turkey. Some days later, a letter sent anonymously to *The Times* from Mainz provided more explicit rationale for the taking of the flight. It stated that 'through imperialist interests West Germany was built up in 1945 as a US base'; now, its 'neo-Nazism' was 'getting ever clearer in the machinery of the state':

> Fascist, discriminatory and racist labour laws are enforced; the ugliest methods of psychological and physical torture and murder are applied against fighters for freedom and national liberation; forms of collective punishment are practised; all provisions of international law as to the rights of detainees for humans treatment just trial and defence are completely abolished.[51]

Hence, the Bonn government and the parties of its parliament were 'doing their best to renew Nazism and expansionist racism in West Germany, particularly in the military establishment and other state institutions'.

After refuelling in Larnaca, the jet took off and flew east, until, once more low on fuel, it landed in Dubai to replenish its tanks, before making for Aden. The Yemeni authorities

attempted to prevent its arrival by blocking the main runway
with machinery, but the pilot made a rough landing in a dirt
strip alongside it. Having left the aircraft to inspect damage to
the landing gear, he wandered into an area cordoned off by
security forces. On his return to the cabin, he was forced to
kneel in the aisle, before the leader of the hijackers fired a bullet
through his head, and forced the copilot to fly the plane south
to Somalia. Once the plane had landed at Mogadishu, the
pilot's body, now wrapped in a blanket, was dumped onto the
runway, and the hijackers wired the plane with explosive.

As darkness fell over the small airport, situated on the
shores of the Indian Ocean, a Lufthansa Boeing 707 touched
down and parked on a remote apron a mile away away from
the 737. It contained 30 members of GSG-9 and an equal
number of back-up medical and communications personnel;

they spent the next 2 hours unloading their equipment and weapons. Once this task was complete, a squad of men crept up to the plane, carrying aluminium ladders, guns and highly sensitive sound detectors. Some stationed themselves underneath the plane and fixed the sound detectors in place, to keep track of movements inside the aircraft; others placed stepladders at each of the jet's exits. As a diversion, oil drums were ignited and propelled slowly towards the nose of the aircraft; moments later, its doors were blown open and the commandos, shielding their eyes, tossed in stun grenades which exploded with blinding light and deafening sound. Their faces masked, the troops stormed into the plane, yelling and firing machine pistols. Within seconds, three of the four hijackers were dead; 6 minutes after the beginning of the operation, and 106 hours after the start of the hijacking, all the passengers were safely out of the plane. *Feuerzauber* was over; the force of Siegfried had prevailed.[52]

At 7.15 later that same morning, on the seventh floor of Stuttgart's top-security Stammheim jail, warders collected the keys from the prison's administrative offices, switched off the main alarm system and entered the isolation zone in which four of West Germany's most notorious terrorists were held. It was a zone whose conditions encouraged a comparison of their situation to that of concentration camp inmates: '... the difference between the dead section and isolation', wrote Gudrun Ensslin 'is the difference between Auschwitz and Buchenwald.' As the guards moved into the doorway of Cell 716, they saw the prisoner, Jan-Carl Raspe sitting against the wall on his bed, his head inclined slightly to the right, and hanging down. Behind him, the wall was smeared with blood, and a dark stream ran from the left side of his skull; yet Raspe was still breathing. An ambulance arrived almost immediately and took him to hospital, where he died later that day.[53] Some weeks earlier, it later emerged, he had smuggled a small radio into his cell. Having heard the news from Mogadishu airport on it, he transmitted it to his fellow prisoners over the rudimentary communications system they had set up a couple of weeks before, and, during the next few hours, Raspe, Andreas Baader, Gudrun Ensslin and Irmgard Moller agreed on a suicide pact to remove them from the 'camp' in which they were now held. Raspe had removed a Heckler & Koch pistol from a secret space behind the skirting board of his cell, placed the gun to his right temple and pulled the trigger; the bullet passed through the top of his skull, grazed a wooden shelf and rebounded from the wall. Further along, in Cell 719, Baader took out another pistol from its hiding place in a record deck, crouched down on the floor of the cell and shot himself through the back of his neck. The exit wound of the bullet split his forehead, just above the hairline. Ensslin, opposite Baader in Cell 720, cut a piece of loudspeaker cable with her scissors, tied the insulated two-wire cable to the narrow-mesh grating, placed her head through the noose, and kicked aside the chair on which she was standing. Further along, in Cell 725, Moller took one of the prison-issue table knives, pulled up her sweater and stabbed herself in the chest four times, but did not penetrate her heart sac. She survived to tell the public prosecutor: 'I neither tried nor meant to commit suicide, and there was no suicide pact.' In any event, the heart of the *Rote Armee Fraktion* (*RAF*) had stopped beating once the news came through from its theatre of war, an airport thousands of miles away.

The *RAF* was founded in May 1970, after Ulrike Meinhof and a gang of sympathetic comrades had sprung Baader from captivity when he was carrying out research at a public library on a day release from Berlin's Tegel prison. The abbreviation was deliberate; it reminded West Germans – and Berliners, in particular – of the Royal Air Force. If Bomber Command had flattened Hitler's cities from the sky, the *RAF* would destroy West Germany's post-war machinery from within, attacking everything from military bases to government buildings, from department stores to banks. Before they left for Palestinian training camps in Jordan that summer, they published the 'Concept City Guerilla Manifesto', which outlined how West

German society would be transformed through armed insurrection: 'The urban guerrilla aims to destroy the ruling machinery of state at individual points, to put parts of it out of action, to destroy the myth of the omnipresence of the system and its invulnerability.' The open spaces, the squares and *Plätze* of post-war Berlin, may have encouraged the radical philosophies of the *RAF*; but the movement owes its existence, in the first place, to the events of 2 June 1967, when the city's police decided that the Shah of Iran, visiting the opera house to watch a performance of *Die Zauberflöte*, should not have to witness German youth protesting at his presence. Riot squads charged the demonstrators, but the students would not be moved. The police drew their weapons and within a few minutes, 50 people were seriously injured, and one student, Benno Ohnesorg, had been shot dead. Gudrun Ensslin witnessed the killing, and the following night walked into the headquarters of a German student union, anouncing to those who would listen that the killer of Ohnesorg was one of her parents' generation – 'the Auschwitz generation! You cannot argue with them! Violence must be met with violence!'[54]

A photograph taken earlier that year shows Ensslin at a demonstration in Berlin pushing her baby son, Felix, along in a pram over rigidly ordered cobble stones. The baby's father, Bernward Vesper, son of a well-known Nazi writer, carries a placard on which is scrawled *'was haben ihr gelernt habe? Waffen sind kein spielzeug'* – 'what have you learnt? Weapons are not toys!' In the background stands a large aircraft, a Douglas Liftmaster painted in the colours of the USAF, while on the extreme left, can be seen the edge of one of the grandest façades in Berlin: the terminal building of Tempelhof, still under the control of the American government. Occasionally, the USAF would throw parties and barbecues for the locals; this photograph was taken on the airport apron on one such occasion, and the plane – a relic of the Berlin Airlift – was on permanent public display on the tarmac. The couple seem relaxed and urbane; within a few weeks, things would change radically, and over the next few

Gudrun Ensslin and Bernward Vesper at a protest against the arms trade at Berlin-Tempelhof, 1967.

years, Tempelhof would become a common target in both reality and fiction. Frequently, home-made bombs would be hurled over its perimeter fence, left in the main terminal concourse, or even deposited on the apron itself. In 1972, the 'Movement of 2nd June', a splinter group of the *RAF*, placed a suspect device – a large clay pot containing Czech Semtex – next to the front wheel of the Liftmaster. The US Army's Explosive Ordnance

185

Disposal unit was called in to disarm the bomb; the straightforward task was completed in 20 minutes. However, as they were packing up their equipment, one of the crew peered into the undercarriage bay of the aircraft. Tucked into the wing was a package: another bomb.[55]

In Don DeLillo's novel *Players*, Berlin's oldest airport is once more the scene of a failed urban terrorist attack; Marina Vilar's brother and his associates do 'the rockets at Tempelhof', planning the attack to the last detail, but unfortunately 'they hit the wrong plane. They hit the DC9. They were totally stupid. One plans something to the closest degree of precision. What happens?'[56] Though such a bazooka attack never took place at Tempelhof, it had, however, occurred at Orly in 1975.[57] Clearly, through this transposition, DeLillo was suggesting that in 1977, at the height of political terrorism in Germany, Tempelhof remained a potent symbol. Like Berlin itself, it was a manifestation not simply of the 'machinery' of 'West' Germany, but also of the nation's complicity in global terror. Nor was this airport, built by Hitler's architects and still occupied by some of the very forces which destroyed his Reich, the only symbol; for by the early 1970s, many of the runways, aprons and terminals of Europe, Middle East and North Africa were to become the theatres, the *Schauplätze*, of a new world war fought by those born, for the most part, during the last global conflict.

AERODROMES OF REVOLUTION

On 6 September 1970, hijack teams from the People's Front for the Liberation of Palestine (PFLP) struck simultaneously. The most daring scheme, the seizure of an El Al Boeing 707 in the airspace over the Thames, failed shortly after it was initiated. One of the hijackers, a Nicaraguan, Patrick Arguello, ran toward the flight deck with a pistol drawn, but was shot down by Israeli guards; at the other end of the jet, Leila Khaled pulled hand grenades from her blouse and charged down the aisle, but was tripped up, overpowered and handed over to the authorities at Heathrow by the crew.

However, two other planes were taken that day: a TWA 707 bound for New York out of Frankfurt, and a Swissair DC8, leaving Zurich for JFK, were forced to double back in the direction of the eastern Mediterranean and directed to land at Dawson's Field, an abandoned wartime RAF facility situated in the Jordanian desert, 15 miles to the north of Amman. After touching down, the airliners were surrounded by detachments of the PFLP, who pronounced that henceforth this rough airstrip would be known as 'The Aerodrome of Revolution'.[58] While the 300 passengers aboard both aircraft were being held, detachments of Israeli paratroopers crossed the border and landed near the towns of Irbid and Jerash in an attempt to liberate the hostages, but their effort came too late. Meanwhile, at the 'aerodrome' the PFLP guerillas feared that the Jordanians, who had provided camps for them, but with whom they had been in recent conflict, would attempt a rescue. King Hussein knew, however, that his country was so heavily infiltrated by Palestinian guerrillas that if he attempted an assault, civil war might ensue, and so he held back. Then on 9 September, in order to persuade the British to release Khaled, a BOAC VC10 with over a hundred passengers and ten crew on board was hijacked after taking off in Bahrain; at gunpoint, the captain was forced to fly to Dawson's Field. Representatives of the five nations now involved in the crisis – Britain, Israel, Switzerland, the US and West Germany – met to discuss joint action but, with little bargaining power, moved to succumb to the PFLP demands; only the Israeli delegation chose to ignore them. Hostages were released in batches until, by 12 September, only 56 people, mainly Israeli or dual American-Israeli nationals, were still held at the airfield. On that day, while negotiations for the release of the hostages and return of the aircraft continued, the three shiny airliners sitting on the Aerodrome of Revolution were evacuated, and then blown up.

The public impact of this act lay not just in the syndicated

The 'aerodrome of revolution': the first aircraft is blown up at the disused airfield known as Dawson's Field in Jordan, 12 September 1970.

images of the jets, the pride of their national airlines, broken and burning in the desert; the shock was also felt throughout the world because the fires started here on this remote airfield were sufficiently magical to draw seemingly random acts of violence into the realm of international relations, and even war. In Amman, as the planes still smouldered, battles flared between Palestinian commandos and the Jordanian Army. Four days later, on 17 September, King Hussein finally ordered his men into the Palestinian refugee camps. Over the next few days, bitter and bloody skirmishes took place, and the Jordanians even had to counter a thrust from the north by a Syrian armoured column moving to help the guerrillas. But by the end of the month, the 'Black September' of 1970, the PFLP guerrilla presence had been virtually eradicated from Jordan, only to emerge even more intensely in the airports of Europe and the Middle East.

The PFLP's exploitation of this airspace had, in fact, began on

188

Boxing Day 1968 when its guerrillas attacked an El Al 707 waiting on the runway at Athens to take off for New York.[59] The organization claimed credit for the assault, which killed one passenger and wrote off the plane, alleging that El Al was not 'undertaking innocent civilian transport' since it had operated flights under the supervision of the Israeli Defense Ministry, and had ferried 'air force pilots trained in flying Phantom jets in preparation for a surprise attack, and new aggression, against the Arab states.'[60] In 1970, the group's leader, George Habash, announced that El Al's aircraft

> belong to the enemy; they connect the island of Israel with other shores; and they transport troops and ammunition. They are flown by reserve officers of the Israeli Air Force. In a war, it is fair to strike the enemy wherever he happens to be, and this rule leads us also to the European airfields where El Al planes land or take off.[61]

Two years later, on 30 May 1972, the most notorious of all attacks took place, at the very heart of Israeli airspace. Having

Aftermath of the terrorist attack at Lod International Airport, 30 May 1972.

stopped at Rome *en route* from Paris, an Air France 707 arrived at Tel Aviv's Lod International Airport. Among the 115 passengers who disembarked that afternoon were three young Japanese men, who had boarded the aircraft at Leonardo da Vinci airport looking, for all the world, like keen tourists. Having cleared immigration control, the trio stood at the baggage carousel, and waited for their Samsonite suitcases. Another large jet had just arrived, and, by now, about 300 people were milling around the conveyor belts in the hall. Having retrieved their cases, the Japanese men opened them, removed three VZ-58 automatic rifles and opened fire on the crowds. In less than a minute, the attack was over; the floor was strewn with bags and belongings and awash with blood. Twenty-six people were dead, sixteen of whom were from a party of Puerto Rican Catholic pilgrims on a visit to the Holy Land. Two of the terrorists also died, one killed by a seemingly random burst of bullets from the direction of the other, whose head was subsequently blown off when the grenade he was holding detonated. The surviving member of the squad, by now out of ammunition, ran out of the terminal building and attempted to blow up an Scandinavian DC8 parked on the apron; here he was disarmed by an El Al security guard.

The assailant identified himself as Kozo Okamoto and claimed to be working under the auspices of the Japanese Red Army, a terror group subcontracted by the PFLP to carry out the mission. When tried in Israel later that year, Okamoto set out his philosophy in a rambling oration, and claimed that the massacre at Lod – subsequently renamed Ben Gurion International – was a 'means of propelling ourselves onto the world stage'; yet again, an airport was being used as a political *Schauplatz*. He claimed: 'War involves slaughtering and destruction. We cannot limit warfare to destruction of buildings. We believe slaughtering of human bodies is inevitable. We know it will become more severe than battles between nations.'[62] The old staples of conflict – battlefields, nation states and rules of engagement – were no longer valid. In this new theatre of war, the 'aerodrome of revolution', mass destruction would be carried out in confined areas – on the ramp, in jets, at check-in desks, or in baggage halls – locations with which the international media was entirely familiar. Paul Virilio observed:

> With the Palestinian problem, popular war had suddenly taken on global proportions. Indeed, the tactic that consists in embracing in a diffuse manner the most widespread territories to escape the powerful nuclei of military repression could have no meaning for them, since the very cause of their struggle was the deprivation of geographic territory. They therefore lost no time in literally settling into the time zones of international airports. *The new unknown combatants, come from nowhere and no longer finding a strategic terrain, fight in strategic time, in the relativity of travel time.* Since in the final account there is no road that is not strategic, from this moment on there is no longer a truly civilian aviation.[63]

The ends of this 'strategic time' were not only the victims of the terrorists' actions, or civil aviation itself, but beyond them, other targets, too: 'world opinion', their sworn enemies (in the form of traitors in the ranks, moderates and weaklings), and of course, comrades already incarcerated. In order for the fate of the victims (or, for that matter, of aircraft) to have the desired impact on such targets, there had to exist not simply a means of communication but also a stage that would guarantee awe, outrage, anguish, or horror; that stage, inexorably, became the airport itself, whose anonymous public spaces seemed to be oddly complicit in random acts of terror.

After Lod, where the majority of victims were not even Jewish, the PFLP announced that its targets would no longer simply be Zionists or Arab traitors but anyone remotely connected with Israel; indeed, according to Okamoto, they would 'slay anyone who stands on the side of the bourgeoisie'. The list of potential targets seemed endless – as did the issues of security within airports. The first step the authorities took was to establish a *cordon sanitaire*. In the late 1960s, it was possible to drive a vehicle from landside to airside, across the apron to the airliner, and open fire; or less ambitiously, to attack it with rockets from the perimeter fence on take-off. There were few armed guards, and the only security intervention a passenger might experience was at understaffed customs checkpoints, at which one might simply choose a green channel, and claim to have 'Nothing to Declare'. There were no Special Forces, no Contingency Plans, no anticipation of The Unthinkable. However, as the roster of incidents grew longer, airport defences in most developed countries were greatly tightened: visitors were discouraged; guards were moved in; aircraft were made more inaccessible; the terminal buildings and airports began to share security features with maximum-security prisons. Paul Virilio notes:

> Practically, this meant examining clothing and baggage, which explains the sudden proliferation of cameras, radars, and detectors in all restricted passageways. When the French built 'maximum security cell-blocks' they used the magnetised doorways that airports had had for years. Paradoxically, the equipment that ensured maximal freedom in travel formed part of the core of penitentiary incarceration.[64]

El Al developed elaborate precautions, and even installed its own state-run security facilities within foreign airports. All luggage was inspected, not just carry-on bags, and was not placed on board until it had been identified again on the tarmac; in this way a suitcase bomb could not be loaded into the hold unless the passenger vouched for it. At various control points, cameras were opened; typewriters were dismantled; radios, tape recorders, alarm clocks or shavers were tested out or taken apart; pillboxes were opened; aerosols were squirted; toothpaste tubes were squeezed; books were opened. Passengers processed though metal detectors and sniffer dogs were on hand to identify Semtex. Throughout these examinations, police continued their interrogations, repeatedly requesting passengers' names, dates and places of birth, reasons for visiting Israel and so on. Consistent answers were expected. Security personnel who had memorized photographs of known terrorists mingled in departure lounges along with discreet guards armed with specially developed low-calibre pistols who followed passengers onto jets, with orders to shoot to kill.

Yet until all other airports adopted similar security procedures, Israelis would still be at risk from terrorism. On 27 June 1976, an Air France Airbus A300, flying from Tel Aviv to Paris, landed at Athens Hellenikon to pick up 56 passengers. The plane, now carrying 257 people, including twelve crew, took off shortly afterwards and, while still in Greek airspace, was commandeered by four terrorists, two of whom had flown from Kuwait to Athens. Here they were not subjected to body searches, and simply boarded the Airbus with their weapons concealed in large tins of dates. The hijackers' leader announced over the intercom: 'This is the Che Guevara Brigade of the Popular Front of the Liberation of Palestine. I am your new Commandant. This plane is renamed *Haifa*. You are our prisoners.' Ordered to fly south, the plane first landed in Libya to refuel and allow a pregnant woman to leave. After departing from Benghazi, the Airbus flew on and attempted to land in Sudan, but permission was refused, and so it headed for Uganda's main airport at Entebbe, on the shores of Lake Victoria, south west of the capital, Kampala. After landing, the hostages were taken to a disused terminal building, a long, low, 2-storey structure, infested with termites. Inside was the main hall, lined with wooden benches, its walls crumbling and dusty; leading off to a smaller room was a connecting door, barred with strips of wood nailed across it. For the next four days, this grim space would be their prison.

The terrorists demanded the release of 40 prisoners held in Israel, five in Kenya, one in France, one in Switzerland and six in West Germany, most of whom were involved with the Baader-Meinhof group, including Jan-Carl Raspe, then in Stammheim. Though he negotiated in Arabic, the leader of the terrorists spoke with a strong German accent and was later identified as Wilfred Böse, a long-term *RAF* activist. He was assisted by Gabrielle Kröcher-Tiedemann, a young Austrian woman, who, in 1973, had been convicted of three attempted murders, blackmail and theft. A German court had sentenced her to 8 years in prison for these offences, but within 2 years, the *RAF* managed to secure her freedom after kidnapping Peter Lorenz, a prominent politican and holding him hostage. On her liberation, Kröcher-Tiedemann was flown to freedom in Aden, but would soon re-emerge in Germany's underground groups and behave, according to the hostages on the Airbus, 'like a true Nazi'. One witness later reported that 'the sadistic German female terrorist, who was marching around with a pistol the whole time ... was frank about what she was,' and behaved with open enmity towards many of the passengers from Israel.[65] Böse, a far less volatile personality, handled the situation more calmly, and some of the hostages applauded him when he proclaimed: 'No harm will come to you. The whole history of hijackings proves that we did not kill the passengers. We shall negotiate. We have demands. If they are met, we shall release you and you'll return home.' Others, however, were upset by such an easy tone:

> The German man adopted a pleasant manner. He was a concealed enemy, pretending, tempting his victims to believe in his good intentions. He was so quiet, so pleasant, so affable that, after my conversations with him, I found myself accusing myself: You believed him. He succeeded in deceiving you. If he had said to march in a certain direction where his colleagues were awaiting us with machine guns, ready to mow us down, we would have gone.[66]

On 30 June, the hijackers released almost 50 elderly women, sick people and children, and the following day set free 100 more hostages, who, on their debriefing by the authories, informed them that just prior to their release a selection had taken place. All Israeli passport holders – and, indeed any passenger with a Jewish sounding surname – had been ordered into the side room, which had now been specially opened up to contain them. Böse told the hostages that 'the hall was too crowded and that for the benefit of everyone it had been decided to split us up into two groups. He emphasised that there was no significance in the way the selection had been made.' Nevertheless, among those held at Entebbe were several who had survived Nazi concentration camps; once again they were being ordered about by guards with guns, shouted at and physically abused; and once again they were being identified for 'special treatment'.

The news of the selection procedure confirmed to Israeli intelligence that the real targets on the Airbus had been Jewish. Indeed, Mossad had also learned from the tapped telephone of Wadi Haddad, the PFLP's planner of terrorist operations in Mogadishu, Somalia, that the Jewish hostages would die in any event. Consequently, *Operation Thunderbolt* began. Several Israeli Hercules transport planes left Tel Aviv for Entebbe, and flying low to avoid hostile radar, landed at a deserted section of the airport. A black Mercedes limousine transported the first group of crack commandos to the terminal where the hostages were being held, some reports alleging that a burly Israeli was blacked up to resemble the Ugandan dictator Idi Amin and con-fuse the local soldiers guarding the building. A second team set off bombs in another section of the field, as a diversionary tactic, and, to prevent the Hercules aircraft being intercepted on their escape, destroyed 11 MIGs of Amin's Air Force. A third unit secured the airfield entrance gate, holding off a squad of Ugandan soldiers. In the fierce gun battles which ensued over the next 53 minutes, the terrorists, taken by surprise, were quickly shot dead; also some hostages were killed or wounded when they stood up in the cross-fire, and the leader of the com-mandos was fatally injured. Once the raid was over, all of the planes successfully returned to Israel.

In the letter written over a year later offering justification for the Mogadishu hijack, the *RAF* claimed that it had seized the Lufthansa 737 in reaction to 'the Zionist invasion of Entebbe' which, owing to the 'close cooperation between Mossad and the German intelligence service, together with the CIA and DST', was 'the dirtiest piracy of the imperialist reactionary alliance'.[67] That, of course, is a biased assessment. More precisely, an act of air piracy had brought an equal and opposite reaction from the Israelis who, by intervening without invitation at Entebbe, had made off with the sovereignty of Amin's Uganda. But the *RAF* were right to identify this as an epochal moment in post-war history, since from this point on, airspace would officially become a police state whose electrified borders were crossed as one passed into the *Schauplatz* of the airport.

v Cultures of the Terminal

In his 1967 essay 'Towards the Development of an Air Terminal Site', written during his involvement with the DFW airport project, Robert Smithson reflected on the significance of flight, and related it to larger issues involved in the maintenance of culture:

> Our whole notion of air-flight is casting off the old meaning of speed through space, and developing a new meaning based on instantaneous time. The aircraft no longer 'represents' a bird or animal (the flying tigers) in an organic way, because the movement of air around the craft is no longer visible. The meaning of airflight has for the most part been conditioned by a rationalism that supposes truths – such as nature, progress, and speed.[1]

As a response to this old, increasingly useless concept of velocity, with its outmoded urgency and primitive reliance on the 'movement of air', Smithson suggested a new awareness; one that might countenance the interdependence of time and space, so that '... the stream-lines of *space* are replaced by a crystalline structure of time'. In terms of chemistry, the state to which Smithson was referring is characterized by its permanence, and because it contains little available kinetic energy, it is an appropriate means for categorizing this new human experience of time frozen in immobilized space. Later in his essay, Smithson argued that since the very co-ordinates used by surveyors to measure land and air masses are crystalline, and since even the mapping of the earth, moon and other planets is similar to substantiating the basic axes or coordinates of crystals, it is possible that aircraft themselves may assume crystalline patterns and so become 'pyramidal slabs and flying obelisks'. They may even 'be named after crystals, such as Rhombohedral T.2; Orthorhombic 60; Tetragonal Terror; Hexagonal Star Dust 49'.

As it happens, passenger aircraft built recently by Airbus and Boeing have sought to play it safe with numerical rather than geological sequences: hence, the Airbus A300 has progressed to the A340; the Boeing 707 now arrives at the 777, while aircraft in the Douglas DC series were always counted from 1 to 10. However, over the last 30 years, airport terminals have themselves reflected some of Smithson's ideas about the crystalline order of time, the immobilization of space, and the refutation of worn-out concepts of energizing presences. These ideas found material expression in *Terminal*, a steel sculpture exhibited by Smithson in late 1966 at the Dwan Gallery, New York.

The sculpture is, in effect, a three-dimensional mirror image composed of pentagonal sections on each side of a central core, which, as they radiate outwards, develop an enantiomorph in space. The sculpture turns inwards and outwards, and, as it blandly communicates serial repetitiveness, its equal and opposite structures become indissoluble; as the eye runs over the

Side view of Robert Smithson's 1966 steel *Terminal*.

surface, one has a feeling of the co-existence of beginning and ending, of movement and stasis, or process and closure. The title, of course, carries several connotations: end point; boundary; railway terminus; an electrical relay attached to wire; a cable for making connections; a cathode ray tube linked to a mainframe computer. When he exhibited this sculpture, however, the most likely definition with which Smithson was engaging was that of an airport facility designed to expedite passengers and cargo. Hence, although the work may offer a new image of space-time coordinates – space frozen and time crystallized to a split second – it also provides a sculptural realization of terminal culture; a site where destinations are always approached, never achieved.

Terminal is in many ways emblematic of what Smithson elsewhere termed 'the non-site' or virtual space of late capitalism, and, as such, it prefigures more current concerns with 'placelessness', the persistent mobility and transitoriness of post-industrial life. As a passenger, the subject flows through the terminal, always on the way to some other destination, and simply passing through without registering passage. It seems a modern idea, but from the very beginnings of air transport, architects sought to design transit facilities that, in their attention to 'flow', would hinder as little as possible the sublime experience of flight. In 'Terminals? Transfers?', an influential article published in 1930, Richard Neutra, an Austrian architect newly resident in Southern California, described the airport in his imaginary metropolis, Rush City, as a 'through station', a 'junction', a 'belt-line' and even an 'air-transfer'. In his conception, tubes and ramps link to the arriving and departing aircraft on one side, and to a car park on the other; suspended above the airfield, straddling these two spaces, is an upper-level grand concourse, with 'broad well-illuminated shopping arcades' which run 'in one direction toward the promenade overlooking the field, the café, the amusement park and the hotel, and in the other direction toward the aircraft display hall and the street bridge which connects this concession avenue with the spacious auto park'.[2] Neutra claimed that the optimum turnaround time between landing and take-off, with passengers deplaned and new passengers taken on, was 15 minutes; barely enough time for them to enjoy the facilities. Nevertheless, this prototype airport, a prime instance of theories of 'flow' applied to spatial organization, has emerged in many versions over the last 70 years. As Anthony Vidler argues, this 'ideology of flows, of rush, of transfer, of space opposed to place' lay behind the postwar boom in airport building, and culminated in Saarinen's TWA terminal, which made elegant use of the 'flow of people through the terminal ... to aid and express his flowing forms'.[3] At the time, another architectural critic put it more bluntly: 'However memorable the outside shape, it is but a carapace for the channels of life within'; the composition of the terminal is based upon the 'simple convenience' of the passengers. Hence,

Interior of the TWA Terminal at JFK, 1962.

200

Saarinen had 'succeeded in transmuting the ordinary complex of travel facilities into a festival of ordered movements and exhilarating vistas.'[4] There in the TWA terminal, 'in the broadly flowing steps, in the wide over-arching bridges and balconies, in the integral seating, in the promise of continuing adventures in space and form', exhilaration could be expected to follow order. Four decades later, passengers are still subject to ordered movement within the terminal; but while the activities taking place in this space are still predicated on a single logarithm bounded in space, and applied rigidly to the physical presence of the passenger using the airport – the flow of passengers per hour – the vista which may once have been so exhilarating has been closed off in order to provide room for three main functions pertaining to passenger handling: circulation, process, containment.

Since the passenger must physically pass through the airport terminal, from landside to airside, according to a prescribed pattern of movement – usually reinforced by pictograms and direction signs – the modern terminal is obliged to furnish suitable passenger circulation areas: concourses, corridors and moving walkways. However, in addition to providing these 'through routes', the terminal must also accommodate certain processes associated with mass air travel: ticketing and check-in, customs, immigration control, security checks and, at the final destination, baggage claim. Yet because such 'ordered movements' within circulation areas and processing zones can be undertaken quickly – however large or congested the terminal – the greatest proportion of a passenger's time at the airport is spent in the holding areas of the departure lounges and in the retail concessions. Here, in the midst of news-stands, restaurants, bars, designer outlets, sex shops or even discotheques, the traveller is freed from any duty other than to observe the annunciator board; here, as J. G. Ballard claims, 'we are no longer citizens with civic obligations, but passengers for whom all destinations are theoretically open, our lightness of baggage mandated by the system.'[5]

Despite the material diversions, the cultures of consumption, any freedom within such areas of containment is illusory, and as the traveller waits for a flight to board, it is not difficult to divine the larger implications of terminal space. In Don DeLillo's *The Names* (1982), James, a 'risk analyst' who has spent most of his life 'growing old in planes', waits patiently at the east terminal of Athens Hellenikon airport:

> The terminal at each end is full of categories of inspection to which we must submit, impelling us toward a sense of inwardness, a sense of smallness, a self-exposure we are never prepared for no matter how often we take this journey, the buried journey through categories and definitions and foreign languages, not the other, the sunlit trip to the east which we thought we'd decided to make. The decision we'd unwittingly arrived at is the one that brings us through passport control, through the security check and customs, the one that presents to us the magnetic metal detector, the baggage x-ray machine, the currency declaration, the customs declaration, the cards for embarkation and disembarkation, the flight number, the seat number, the times of departure and arrival.[6]

At the airport, fliers forget that they are undertaking two journeys, one of which is overt, 'the sunlit trip', and the other of which is covert, an odyssey controlled by the authorities through 'categories and definitions and foreign languages'. DeLillo's depiction of the Athens terminal – the last of Saarinen's airport designs to be built – draws attention to the extent to which the systems of modern airspace silently compromise freedom of choice. Hence, the traveller 'unwittingly' comes to a decision, oblivious to the fact that his liberties are being taken, a sense caught at least in 'arrived at', a verb cunningly poised between active participation and passive direction; while 'brings us through' implies a rite of passage as well as a loss of movement, as the individual is assailed by the devices of circulation, process and containment.

In the late 1970s, Martha Rosler, an American artist and writer, began to photograph the countless air terminals through which she moved *en route* to exhibitions and conferences. At first she pursued the project as a hobby, a way of killing time while she waited to board her plane, but in due course, it acquired a greater purpose. Following the rule that she would only ever take photographs while in transit, Rosler sought to record the very phenomenological and textual space of the modern terminal; a space, she soon realized, that was compounded of disorienation and inertia: 'As passengers we lose track of where we are, not only in the air but in the airport. Air terminals, more like each other than like anything else, tell us only of themselves. The airport is where you would rather not be, on the way to somewhere else.'[7]

Two decades later, her ongoing work, recently exhibited around the world under the title *In the Place of the Public*, provides the finest visual meditation on the conditions of the terminal. The terms of her title denote position, her photographic point of view as a member of the public passing through the airport; they also, however imply substitution, the possibility that the very idea of the public – that *sensation* of open space – has been replaced. The concept of her installation is simple enough: each photograph depicts some aspect of an airport, while above and below the print, runs a textual commentary which seems to offer some prospect – or at least some explanation – of what airspace as supplanted, 'in the place of the public'. In autumn 1998, Frankfurt-Main International Airport, in conjunction with the city's Museum für Moderne Kunst, mounted an exhibition of Rosler's work on a mezzanine above Terminal 2's main concourse; it was, she felt, the work's righful home'. In her introduction to the installation, Rosler went on to explain: 'Airplanes and airports are potent symbols of modern life; as a contrast the project reminds us of things and places that otherwise help us locate ourselves in the world.' Hence, the exhibition begins with images of check-in desks, under which runs an elemental word sequence – 'a tree, a rock, a brook' – and then presents the subject's trip through the 'endless corridors', 'blind turns' and 'half-lit tubules' of the terminal. At the heart of this journey are some images shot in the endlessly curving tubes of the TWA terminal's ramps, lit in a weird bloody glow. An adjacent caption asks 'vagina or birth canal'; it is hard to say whether Rosler considers the terminal to represent a principle of entrance or some process of emergence. Some of these pictures show people seated in waiting areas or bustling past, oblivious to the camera, unaware of the 'imperceptible airflow' of passengers of which they are a part, and blissfully ignorant that since they are sited somewhere between 'boulevard or intestine' they 'move in an approximation of peristalsis'. Other photographs present these spaces as strangely bereft 'institutional façades', filled only with 'white noise hiss' and the 'trace odors of stress and hustle'. At the heart of the exhibition, adjacent to an image of the TWA terminal, a stark text announces: 'There are only no fragments where there is no whole'. As the caption carries trace of emendations – 'only' is crossed through, but still legible – one might say that it reflects a paradigm shift. The Industrial Revolution led to a fragmentation of the subject, materialized, for example, in nineteenth-century railway stations, whose massive designs provided a vision of what 'the whole' might do in order to dissipate the masses. Two centuries on, the Information Revolution, symbolized by the 'terminal' of the mainframe or of the airport, again denies the whole, but now creates virtual worlds from the flow of digital fragments, bits and bytes, through systems, and around networks.

A wall poster Rosler photographed at Chicago O'Hare International Airport in 1991 carries the optimistic possibility, 'Maybe there is a substitute for experience'; but in her terminals, substitutes only ever work through advertising, the most basic means of expediting the circulation of capital. The slogan appears in her photograph as part of an advertisement for the *Wall Street Journal*; the frame carrying the poster seems gigantic, and the surrounding area is deserted. If Rosler sees advertising and consumer culture as trying to substitute one kind of experience for another, it is clear in another image that the airport is akin to a lightbox carrying airline posters advertising Germany, Taipei, Korea and England; a container in which destinations

Martha Rosler, *Untitled (JFK)*, 1990.

Martha Rosler, *Madrid*, 1990.

are presented packaged, but not entirely revealed until one leaves the terminal at one's final destination. Thirty or so images later, Rosler's installation concludes with photographs of passengers walking out to their jet, and of a pristine baggage carousel. Above these, imprinted in bold letters, is the caption 'Infinite Deferral', while below runs the commentary: 'flow, transmission, data, bit, byte'. Finally, it seems, the terminal, like a super computer, is simply a means of channelling binary digits so as to forestall the inevitable terrible crash.

INFINITE DEFERRAL

At the check-in area of Terminal 1 at Madrid Barajas Airport, a space through which Rosler has frequently passed, an elderly man with a bushy beard and a flat cap on his head, sits quietly in the heavy summer heat which fills the concourse. (As is usual here, airflow is imperceptible.) Despite the high ambient temperature, he seems to be feeling the cold, wearing thick corduroy trousers and a jacket buttoned tightly over a woollen rollneck. On his feet are heavy boots, down at the heels; it is not clear if he is wearing socks. Behind him, a crowd masses and shuffles at the KLM check-in desk, while passengers at the adjacent Lufthansa and Iberia facilities remain composed. A young couple gaze fixedly at a bank of three television monitors suspended just above their heads, which display information about imminent departures and unforeseen delays; their turn to submit their belongings to the scrutiny of airport staff has not yet come.

The old man remains unmoved by the movements taking place around him and stares straight ahead, his left arm on the metal armrest of the bench on which he sits, his right one placed over a battered, cracked carpetbag. It must be assumed that he has checked in, retaining a small piece of hand luggage, and is gathering his thoughts for the journey ahead, which begins with the crossing from landside to airside. It is odd that he can

Castor Solano's sculpture *Vagamundo* at Madrid Barajas Airport, 1996.

remain so calm, so detached, so 'at home' in the airport; perhaps this is because he will never move. He is, in fact, a permanent fixture, an *objet d'art* named *Vagamundo*, created by the Spanish sculptor Castor Solano. Since its installation in early 1996, this representation of a globetrotter has, according to the airport's enthusiastic press release, become 'a firm favourite'; the firmness, no doubt, derives from the fact that the figure is cast in bronze, the same colour as happy tourists from Northern Europe departing the airport for home. AENA, the airport authority responsible for the commission, chose to place the sculpture on an actual airport seat, 'where other passengers can sit next to him and get a real close-up of one of the most ingenious pieces of three-dimensional art ever seen at an airport'.[8] Yet by looking so closely at this installation, passengers may also find themselves confronting some of the more uncomfortable social and psychological aspects of air travel.

Vagamundo sits within a zone in which travellers are accelerated away to their destinations with the minimum of solicitude. Were he a real passenger, the authorities at Madrid would be less than generous towards his situation; he would become an object of suspicion, like an unattended bag, to be carted away and dealt with. Furthermore, assuming he has checked in, the plane on which he is scheduled to travel cannot depart, since, for reasons of security, each person has to be matched up with baggage already in the plane's hold. In these respects, Vagamundo is a transgressive symbol, a permanent reminder of a breakdown in the passenger-processing system, the failure of the fundamental reason for the airport's existence: the expedition of passengers through a terminal into an aluminium tube waiting beyond a final lounge.

Other aspects of Solano's installation demand investigation. Consider, for instance, the design of the bench on which Vagamundo sits. Constructed out of pressed steel and plastic, it is, one assumes, eminently practical. The polypropylene seat pads mould themselves to the backside of the occupier, and, if need be, can be quickly disinfected; the perforations in the pressed steel frame, clearly designed to reduce the bulk of the unit, also allow dirt and rubbish to fall through, and be easily swept up by cleaning staff. However, the severity of its design serves another, stricter function: it forces people to remain awake. Each bench consists of five seats and four armrests, but there are never more than two seats without an intervening armrest, a design feature intended to discourage passengers from reclining. Terminals need to ensure that delayed travellers remain pacified yet vigilant; to allow them to sleep in concourses might lead to missed flights, or worse. In Martin Amis's *London Fields*, the narrator, Samson Young, a dying novelist, waits at Heathrow to check in for a delayed flight to JFK:

> Heathrow did something to me. I can still feel the burning vinyl on my cheek. What happens, when love-thoughts go out – and just meet vinyl?

Now I've had some bad airport experiences. I've been every-where and long ago stopped getting much pleasure from the planet. In fact I am that lousy thing: a citizen of the world. I've faced utter impossibilities, outright no-can-dos at Delhi, São Paulo, Beijing. But you wait, and the globe turns, and suddenly there's a crevice that fits your shape. Heathrow provided no such fuel for optimism or even for stoicism. Zeno himself would have despaired instantly.[9]

As he drifts off to sleep, Young begins to dream about America, his native land, with its cities like airports and 'life literalized, made concrete, concretized, massively concretized'. He wakes up with a start, still at Heathrow's Terminal 3, with his cheek on a hot vinyl seat. 'For fifteen minutes I watched a middle-aged man chewing gum, the activity all between the teeth and the upper lip, like a rabbit. And then I just thought: Enough.' At which point he catches a cab back into central London.

In early 1993, perhaps in emulation of Heathrow's seating policies, the management at CDG installed new rigid benches throughout the airport, replacing the famous circular seats designed by Joseph Motte and installed in 1974. The rationale was that Motte's seats were too *'confortable'* and were attracting large numbers of individuals *'sans domicile fixe'*.[10] This outra-geous insult to the dispossessed inspired a number of sympa-thetic responses. In 1994, Philippe Lioret, a former film sound engineer, wrote and directed *Les Tombes du ciel*, a strangely off-beat, if not fully realized, comedy about a hapless businessman (Jean Rochefort) who, just before boarding a plane in Montreal for France, is robbed of his passport and shoes. On arrival at CDG, he runs into trouble with immigration control, where sus-picions are further aroused by his status as a dual national – French and Canadian – living in Rome and married to a Spaniard (Marisa Paredes). It is also New Year's Eve, so the sit-uation cannot be resolved until after the weekend. The busi-nessman, condemned to waiting in the transit lounge, encounters a cast of strange characters: a former mercenary, a young Latin, an African boy and an enigmatic black man who

Seating designed by Joseph Motte at Roissy-Charles De Gaulle, 1974.

speaks an obscure language. In a long, sentimental digression, the group break out of the airport to celebrate the new year in Paris.

The chance to escape the clutches of Immigration is a flight of fancy, of course. Without proper accreditation, the subject cannot move, but must remain inert, like Vagamundo, and await the decision of authority. It is in these, acrid, fluorescently lit holding pens, alive with static electricity, sweat and polish, that the traveller comes to understand what it means to have been furnished with the identity of a nation state; and it is here that the implications of statelessness on mental health are fully comprehended.[11]

A searing account of such estrangement emerges in Michel Serres' *Angels*, which places most of its speculations and inquiries within the spaces of CDG. In an episode entitled 'An Archangel', Pia, a young doctor at the airport's medical centre, is called to deal with a casualty who has collapsed at the gate for the Boston flight clutching his boarding pass. Once Pia arrives, she finds an unconscious man aged between 40 and 50, with a dirty black beard and tangled, matted hair, smelling strongly of neglect: 'His feet are wrapped in ragged bandages tied on with string. He wears a tattered old raincoat. His hands are red and swollen marked with the pale scars of chilblains.' She checks him over, but finds no sign of 'accidental injury, visible sickness or shock'. Her friend, Pantope, a travelling inspector for Air France, approaches and inquires after the casualty. Pia offers her diagnosis:

Airports are built on the outskirts of cities, in the suburbs, what we call the *banlieue*: a place of banishment. Excluded and pushed out to the margins, the down-and-outs end up here. It's almost a law of nature. When they arrive, they're amazed to discover they can actually sleep here, in the dry, on benches, like ordinary travellers ... their movement is like the movement of passengers arriving and departing – it never ceases. They stay for a while and then they move on, like everyone else.[12]

Unlike the vagrant, however, 'everyone else' is transitory, not permanent, and clutches the validation of the state that sponsors him or her. No larger than a packet of cigarettes, a passport is just as comforting to the nervous; no thicker than a folded map, it is just as orientating to the lost. As DeLillo explains:

> Air travel reminds us who we are. It's the means by which we recognize ourselves as modern. The process removes us from the world and sets us apart from each other. We wander in the ambient noise, checking one more time for the flight coupon, the boarding pass, the visa. The process convinces us that at any moment we may have to submit to the force that is implied in all this, the unknown authority behind it, behind the categories, the languages we don't understand.[13]

Pia claims that whereas city authorities would once have provided the homeless with single tickets to other towns, they are now sent abroad, for other terminals to deal with. Vagrants are identified 'by the fact that they're not wearing socks'; ejected from the airport, they return almost immediately: 'Sometimes we even get to know them by their first names.' Serres' account is based in fact. The most famous of the vagrant residents of CDG was Karim Nasser Merhan, better known as Alfred, an Iranian-born refugee who spent 11 years living on a red plastic bench between Burger King and Pizza Grill in the basement of Terminal 1, telling his life story to anyone who would listen. Frail, with long, thinning hair, sunken eyes and hollow cheeks, Alfred was 29 when he left Iran in 1974 in search of his mother, whom he believed to be British or possibly Danish. Having failed to locate her in Britain, and having dropped out of University in Bradford, he returned to Iran, only to be stripped of his citizenship for having participated in demonstrations against the Shah. His subsequent travels took him to airport holding cells at Frankfurt, Moscow-Sheremetyevo, Schiphol and finally Brussels-Zaventem, where in 1981 he was given documents attesting that he was a stateless person, and allowed to leave the immgration area. He lived in Belgium and France for several years, until after all his papers were stolen in a Paris train station in 1988, he decided to re-enter Britain at Heathrow, from where he was sent back to France. Since he was subsequently unable to produce the necessary credentials at CDG, the police arrested him, only to discover that his statelessness made it impossible to deport him. So he remained at Terminal 1 until 1999, when the Belgian authorities reissued his refugee certificate. During his incarceration at Terminal 1, Alfred subsisted on contributions from airport and airline staff, and items discarded by passengers. He rose at 5.30 each morning, showered in the airport washrooms, which he also used as a laundry facility, breakfasted at the burger bar (always bacon and eggs) read the papers (the *International Herald Tribune* and sometimes *The Guardian* or *The Times*), before beginning work on assignments for the several correspondence courses on history, economics, and business management to which he signed up, courses delivered to him – along with numerous letters of support – care of the airport post office. The medical service treated his

Check-in and baggage trolley at Frankfurt-Main International Airport, 1995.

occasional illnesses, and the police left him alone. When the end came, he was reluctant to leave the sanctuary of the terminal.[14]

This feeling has its precedents in modern British fiction. Late in his career, Anthony Burgess, that great chronicler of the psychiatric effects of deracination, produced a short story about an elderly man who, taking advantage of the immigration procedures in operation at international airports, chose the easy passivity of statelessness. Mr Paxton, a retired widower with grown-up children, checks in at Heathrow, and, determined to spend the rest of his life in the comfortable emptiness of airport transit lounges, places his passport 'in one of the deep rubbish bins, burying it under an accumulation of discarded duty-free bags, chocolate wrappers and cigarette packets'. A fellow passenger, the narrator, tries to talk him out of this act of abandon, to no avail. Having ordered a stiff drink, he sits in the windowless terminal bar with Paxton who shows him the contents of one of his bags:

> 'God almighty,' I said. What he showed me was a large yellow plastic folder crammed with air tickets. He said, riffling through them:
> 'Going everywhere. Rio de Janeiro, Valparaiso, wherever that is, Mozambique, Sydney, Christchurch, Honolulu, Moscow.'
> 'If there's one place where you'll need a visa, it's certainly Moscow,' I said. 'But, damn it, how do you propose to go anywhere without a passport?'
> 'There's going and going,' he said. 'When I get to one place then I start off right away for another. Well, in some cases not right away. There's a fair amount of waiting in some of the places. But they have what they call transit lounges. Get a wash and a brush-up. Perhaps a bath. Throw a dirty shirt away and buy a new one. Ditto for socks and underpants. No trouble, really.'
> 'In effect,' I said, astonished, 'you'll be travelling without arriving.'[15]

Travelling without arriving is the peculiar expression of modernity which Burgess shows to be fatally flawed; six weeks after Paxton has dumped his travel documents, the narrator encounters him again, and remarks to an airport employee: 'His only mistake is thinking he's a free man. Nobody's free these days.

He's abandoned a structure and now the demons of chaos are getting at him.' Individuals have been transformed into numbered 'pax', a term used thoughout the airline industry as an abbreviation for 'passenger'; this word also reminds the airport that individuals need constantly to be pacified, the flow of their progress from check-in to take-off continually smoothed. Paxton travels on through the world's airspace, but, having lost sight of his cultural identity, his statehood, the only means left for him to assert himself are prejudice and bigotry. At the conclusion of the story, he is seen in a state of agitation, having arrived at Berlin on a flight from Munich:

> He was in a wheel chair and apparently strapped to it. He had two white-coated attendants and a couple of uniformed officials of Lufthansa to accompany him. He was shrieking something about always knowing it would come to this, the bleeding Nazis had got him at last and he was a free British citizen, got a passport to prove it but the bastards have taken it away. He was gently wheeled towards the exit, with no nonsense about immigration formalities. For his presumed destination no passport was required.[16]

DAMNED DIGITS

In Brigid Brophy's novel *In Transit*, the central character and occasional narrator, having 'nowhere to reside' and having chosen to remain in the transit lounge of an international airport rather than fly somewhere, is relieved to see that

> (besides the archipelagos of individual armchairs which stippled the Lounge, each an islanded mosque with its own slim, free-standing muezzin-tower ashtray) there was, backing up against the farthest wall, a classical terrace of soft chairs. Undivided by arm-rests, they could be made to yield me rest.

Hectored by the public address system, uncertain of his/her sex, native language or personal history, the narrator explains why s/he will 'sit on and just let my flight be called'.[17] From this neutral vantage point, the observer, while offering a transcendent and simultaneous view of the airport, is trapped outside the possibility of its lived reality, since in the first place, the lounge's form is manipulated by individual fantasy rather than by physical circumstance: 'Airport: airpocket. Dwell here in a droplet of the twentieth century; pure, isolated, rare twentieth century.' In such a crystalline form, the airport is a world of arrested time; its stillness emphasizes the activity that is beyond its threshold: 'Here, at the airport, you are already within the ambience of the exciting architecture of getting somewhere, but your nose is not yet pointed towards your destination and held hard to it.'[18]

The architecture of 'getting somewhere' had sufficiently perplexed Robert Smithson for him to suggest that the air terminal casts off the old meaning of speed through space and develops a new meaning based on instantaneous time; for Brophy's narrator, this means resolving to 'perpetually or for a simulacrum of perpetuity remain in the present moment, in at least *semi*-sempiternal transit between departure from the past and arrival at the future'. And this effect is reciprocal, for once one attends to the world of the terminal, the outside world stops and is lost to us. In this it resembles other mythical structures, even sleep. But where a Vagamundo, say, was petrified by the airport's atmosphere, Brophy's narrator is 'Relaxed but not to the extent of sleep or anaesthesia, whetted enough to enjoy but not cut yourself on your own ambition or anxiety, not so intent on the future as to be tensed-up, you could inhabit *this* tense'.[19] Above all, in taking over 'this multi-winged building', in resolving 'to live in in-transit', the narrator is able to 'move into and occupy my own century'. Effectively, such a move announces the distinction of utility, since 'an airport is functional – is a function.' In this peculiar space, where access to speed might mean access to certainty, any function that was once fixed now becomes a matter of transformation – a gesture of narrative, and of art.

Between 1996 and 1998, travellers moving along on one of the linkbridges at Heathrow's Terminal 1 became part of an installation by a young Irish artist, Andrew Kearney. *A Long Thin Thread*, commissioned by BAA plc, consisted of a series of 60 red or green digital counters which continuously recorded the movements of passengers on the walkway, all of whom were in transit between the UK and Ireland. At first sight, the title of the installation may playfully have invoked the cord used by Theseus to navigate the labyrinth of the Minotaur; after all, Terminal 1 is a notorious entanglement, especially if flight connections are tight.[20] But the installation had a more persuasive power. While walking or gliding along this tube, everybody's eyes were caught by the digital display; they began to look more closely, to compare, to become aware of themselves as the 'thread', the single file of passengers flowing in transit. Kearney explained the concept of the piece: 'People are being recorded. A mark is being made. A visible fragment is being left. A shadow remains. Shadows counted on the wall, one by one, pulse by pulse. A mark they leave behind.'[21]

Kearney was secretly staging in Heathrow one of the key moments in the late writings of Plato: the parable of the cave in Book VII of *The Republic*. A group of men have been imprisoned for many years in an underground tunnel, some distance from the entrance, into which light filters. These 'strange prisoners' are horribly confined: their legs and necks are chained tight so that they can move neither their bodies nor their heads, and are only able to see what happens directly in front of them. Above and behind them a fire blazes continuously, giving off artificial light and casting their shadows onto the cave wall opposite; as time passes, they come to regard these virtual images as reality. After a lifetime of captivity, the men are released and, moving out of the cave to the world of dazzling light, they are instructed about their confusion of the real and the represented. However, the distinction between the two states is futile. Even freed of their fetters, such people remain in a kind of epistemological transit between reality and representation.

The wit of Kearney's installation lies in the way he applied this Platonic debate to the dimly lit corridor in Terminal 1; in

Heathrow's airspace, the number that represents each passenger, that poor soul caught between departure and arrival, assumes greater reality than the passenger himself. 'People are being recorded' may simply connote registration; but in the context of the surveyed spaces of the terminal building, it also implies that form of representation which freezes appearance and identity to create a virtual trace on magnetic media. Once transit passengers, moving along the walkway, realize their number is up, the link-bridge becomes a void; no longer wholly in life yet somehow present in the figures counted on the wall, travellers fade away, leaving nothing but a digital trace.

At crucial points in mid-career, the poet W. H. Auden seemed to have been attracted to airports as places frequented only by the inhuman or the inanimate. For instance, in the opening lines of his most famous poem, 'Elegy in Memory of W. B. Yeats', first published in March 1939, he claimed that the Irish poet 'disappeared in the dead of winter: / The brooks were frozen, the airports almost deserted, / And snow disfigured the public statues.'[22] The 'air-port', in Auden's conception, exists forlornly between a crystallized nature, where 'brooks' are 'frozen', and an equally static form of culture, the 'public statues'; yet his hyphenated spelling of 'air-port' asserts the transitional aspect of its space, simply defined as a conjunction of nature and culture, element and compound. In 'Air Port', first published in 1950, Auden, by now a seasoned long-distance flier, elaborated on this view.[23] Having just crossed the Atlantic in a Constellation, he described the stopover at Shannon International Airport, constructed in the late 1930s, 11 miles west of Limerick, on a point jutting into the Shannon River estuary:

> Let out where two fears intersect, a point selected
> Jointly by general staffs and engineers,
> In a wet land, facing rough oceans, never invaded
> By Caesars or a cartesian doubt, I stand,
> Pale, half asleep.[24]

The 'two fears' may be the two flights connected here, or the common concern for safety shared by airport designers and by pilots. In any event, Auden is standing at the closest point to North America (where he had lived since 1939) within Europe. At the time, Shannon was one of the busiest facilities in the world, even though it functioned almost entirely as a transit point; transatlantic airliners headed east or west stopped here so that fuel tanks could be replenished, and passengers diverted into the famous duty-free facilities, established just after the war.[25] James Bond, en route for New York, ate well, but was less impressed with the local merchandise:

> Steak and champagne for dinner, and the wonderful goblet of hot coffee laced with Irish whisky and topped with half an inch of thick cream. A glance at the junk in the airport shops, the 'Irish Horn Rosaries', the 'Bog Oak Irish Harp', and the 'Brass Leprechauns', all at $1.50, and the ghastly 'Irish Musical Cottage' at $4, the furry, unwearable tweeds and the dainty Irish linen doilies and cocktail napkins.[26]

Auden's fellow travellers are strictly 'in transit' and in due course,

> a professional friend is at hand
> Who smiling leads us indoors; we follow in file,
>
> Obeying that fond peremptory tone reserved for those
> Nervously sick and children one cannot trust.

This 'professional friend' is the air stewardess who has been trained to be as amenable as possible; but, as ever with Auden, there is a hint that that adjective might carry greater weight so that we might be dealing with a smiling psychiatrist, or gentle but firm teacher. There is a high cost to allowing oneself to be treated in this way, and in such a non-place as this transit lounge, whose very vacuity is a reminder of the distinctness of other places. In the transitional zone of the airport, 'we are nowhere, unrelated to day or to Mother / Earth in love or in

The duty-free shop at Shannon International Airport, Éire, 1951.

hate; our occupation / Leaves no trace on this place or each other.' Auden's deliberate line break after 'Mother' is meant perhaps to snub Freud's famous account, in 'The Uncanny', of that persistent male dream of travelling that reveals both the repression of the mother's body and its unexpected reappearance:

> There is a joking saying, 'Love is home-sickness'; and whenever a man dreams of a place or a country and says to himself, while he is still dreaming: 'this place is familiar to me, I've been here before,' we may interpret the place as being his mother's genitals or her body. In this case too, then, the *unheimlich* [unfamiliar] is what was once *heimisch*, familiar; the prefix 'un' is the token of repression.[27]

The uncanny, for Freud, is the sudden involuntary awareness of the appearance of the familiar in the unfamiliar; it is not the new or the foreign but something 'old-established in the mind [that] has become alienated from it only through the process of repression'.[28] For Auden, however, an airport could never be regarded as a zone of the uncanny precisely because it is a 'nowhere'; as such, it would be impossible ever to know if one had, in fact, returned to it.

Furthermore, Auden and his fellow passengers are unable to leave any trace on the airport at Shannon, which is nothing but an 'enclosure' in which they are penned. Once 'aggressive' in their desires and consumption, they are now resigned to their journey, and are being controlled by a disembodied voice from above, which 'from time to time calls / Some class of souls to foregather at the gate'. The tannoy, it seems, does not simply function sporadically, but calls across time zones, or even from one epoch to the next; and while 'class' in the context of an airport may announce a level of service, it is also a useful concept if one is seeking to create a taxonomy of transgression. John Fuller has suggested that in this poem the 'unreality of the airport waiting-room' is 'more of a Purgatory than a community', but it is clear that the zone Auden had in mind was more *Inferno* than limbo. Indeed, it is contained in the words spoken by Charon, the ferryman in Canto IV of the first part of Dante's epic:

'Woe to you, wicked souls! Do not hope to see Heaven ever! I come to carry you to the other shore, into eternal darkness, into fire and cold. And you there, living soul, stand by from these that are dead.' But when he saw that I did not do so, he said, 'By another way, by other ports, not here, you shall cross to shore. A lighter bark must carry you.'[29]

Charon, the functionary from Hell, is an animated version of those who stand at the numbered gate collecting identities before allowing passengers to board the aircraft. This may sound whimsical, but it is a recurring motif. In Virginia Woolf's late essay 'Flying over London', her imaginary pilot assumes the form of Dante's boatman: 'Charon ... carry me on; thrust me deep, deep; till every glimmer of light in me, of heat of knowledge, even the tingling I feel in my toes is dulled.'[30] More recently, Martha Rosler has suggested that 'invoking the crossing of Charon, a plane flight becomes an encounter with death'; it is therefore not surprising that Don DeLillo can claim of Athens airport: 'This vast terminal has been erected to examine souls.'[31]

His Constellation having taken off once more, Auden looks down and sees below him a locale where nature and choice both leave traces: 'an ancient / Feud re-opens with the debacle of a river', 'debacle' being used in its original sense to signify the thawing of frozen water after the 'dead of winter'. In the elegy on Yeats, Auden had described how 'The brooks were frozen, the air-ports almost deserted'; now, after his experience in transit, he realizes that airspace itself, rather than being a place of flow, is instead the site of psychological blockage, a zone where the individual is crystallized into blocks of time, losing sight of his personal and aesthetic identity.[32]

Half a century later, the facilities known in Auden's day as 'air ports' or 'stopovers' are now termed 'hubs'. According to the Canadian writer Douglas Coupland, a hub should be regarded as

> ... a pit stop, an in-between place, a 'nowhere,' a technicality, an anti-experience born of technological necessity and the imperatives of petroleum, flight schedules, the curvature of the planet and geographic accident. Hubs are nowheres, with their security apparatuses, landing and fuelling infrastructures, and pictograms both patronising and incomprehensible.[33]

As a concept, the hub grew in utility and popularity after the US government deregulated routes, flights and fares in stages between 1978 and 1981. Quite simply, the rationale of the system revolved around the practice of bringing flights into a single airport – the hub – and sending them out again to their ultimate destinations along spokes which radiated outwards. Before the hub, every air route involved an origin and a destination – a pair of cities – and carriers usually served these places by flying point to point with the occasional refuelling stop *en route*.[34] But another great difference between the 'nowhere' of Auden's 'Air Port' and the 'nowheres' of Coupland's 'Hubs' is that between singular and plural, the individual and the manifold:

The hub is where we experience the horrific torpor of Extreme Progress, where Modernism is fully integrated into a universe of Smarte Kartes, nubbly maroon fabric chairs, non-specific accents squawking across grand halls that flights with numbers four digits long are currently boarding. The hub is a dead-number office for damned digits, where numbers like 1388, 1490, 1218 are abandoned and thrown away, only to reappear with Sysyphean regularity.[35]

In the name of 'Progress', the hub airport engineers an exquisite collision between personal mobility and commodity, then picks up and recycles the pieces into digits. In this pixellated zone, the traveller is defined, practically, by a 'smart' luggage trolley hired with a credit card; graphically, by barcodes attached to luggage; vocally, by computer-generated flight announce-ments; and numerically, by the four-digit PIN which, as the moment of flight approaches, is overlaid by smaller ones, often attached to a letter. So finally, as the hub spins passengers deeper into airspace, the only version they have of themselves is a seat number in an aluminium tube.

INSTITUTIONAL FAÇADES

In early 1999, Don DeLillo's second play *Valparaiso* premiered at the American Repertory Theatre in Cambridge, Massachusetts. Its main character, Michael Majeski, is an 'analyst' who sets out on a business trip to Valparaiso (sometimes known as Valpo) a town in north-western Indiana. As he leaves his apartment that morning, his itinerary seems clear enough: 'I'm headed to the airport where I intend to catch my flight to what I think will be Chicago. They'll meet me in Chicago, a car and driver, and we'll proceed to Valparaiso.'[36] Sitting in the departure lounge prior to boarding his flight, he hears a woman's voice on the tannoy, asking that he present himself 'at the podium'. When he obeys, and submits his ticket for scrutiny, he is told that although his 'routing' to the hub at Chicago is entered correctly, the itinerary stapled to the ticket by his company's travel agent is anomalous. Michael later recalls his feelings at the ticket desk:

> She doesn't look at me. They never look at us. How can they? There are long lines of people all the time. She has her console and her random access memory. I have my nitwit piece of paper. But I want something to pass between us. Some nuance of human sharing. Some milky nipply nuance. I look at her face for a sign. A gesture that might echo through our day. But the moment does not whisper the usual things.[37]

Instead, the attendant asks: 'Why are you going to Chicago if your itinerary says Miami?' Michael does not know whether the ticket or the itinerary is incorrect; the former, since it is 'magnetically printed and coded' and 'computer processed', has more 'authority', whereas the latter is 'a simple piece of paper typed by an ordinary human being'. In the meantime, the attendant has consulted 'the system' and found him a seat on the Miami flight, which is about to leave: 'She has found a seat for me. I don't want to disappoint her.' Like Paxton in Burgess's 'The Endless Voyager', Michael has a ticket to 'Valparaiso, wherever that is' – not now Valparaiso, Indiana, but Valparaiso, Florida.[38] The Miami flight, about to close, will wait for him if he runs for the gate; alternatively, he can wait in the departure lounge for the Chicago plane, 'in a relaxed and civilised manner'.

Michael is shocked. Extraordinarily, an airport is giving him a choice between containment and motion. So he sprints, for the sake of his professional life and also to exercise his free will: 'I run for the gate at the far end of the terminal. I run senselessly and breathlessly … past people with carry-on and people with baggage carts and I run past shuttle buggies filled with people and carry-on and bulging baggage and interracial babies.'[39] Having 'made' the flight, he realizes that he has 'no idea how to get from Miami, Florida to Valparaiso, Florida, and asks himself 'Where is this place?' Someone tells him that 'Valparaiso is way up on the panhandle part of Florida. Just above the Gulf', which means that Michael will need to catch 'a little commuter plane' to get there.

Oddly enough, on his arrival at Miami he finds a *jet* headed for Valparaiso: 'It was strange. The aircraft seemed too big, too wide-bodied for an intrastate flight'; nonetheless, he boards it:

> I was intimidated by the systems. The enormous sense of power all around me. Heaving and breathing. How could I impose myself against this force? The electrical systems. The revving engines. I was substituting for a colleague in the hospital. The sense of life support. The oxygen in the oxygen masks ... I felt submissive. I had to submit to the systems. They were all-powerful and all-knowing. If I was sitting in this assigned seat. Think about it. If the computers and metal detectors and uniformed personnel and bomb-sniffing dogs had allowed me to reach this assigned seat and given me this airline blanket that I could not rip out of its plastic shroud, then I must belong here.

Eight and a half hours later, the jet descends from the sky 'with the seasons reversed', and lands in Santiago, Chile, where Michael is convinced by airport officials to continue, by helicopter, to Valparaiso, the chief port of Chile and the terminus of the trans-Andean railway: 'To make the mistake complete. For the human interest. For the beauty and balance. The formal resolution.'

On his arrival back in the US, Michael is feted by the media, and in the course of a televised interview, comes to understand that he has been spun round in some 'sad nameless nowhere' (the same space familiar to Auden and Coupland) and, instead of being expelled, he is about to 'run out of airspace and landscape'.[40] On the flight to Chile, Michael had gone to the lavatory with his airline blanket and shaving kit. Using his razor blade to slit open the plastic shrink-wrapping of the blanket, he places it over his head, draws it 'snug' around his neck and fastens it with a long strand of dental floss. A light begins to flash and the pilot comes onto the intercom: 'Looks like we're experiencing some real heavy air at this particular point in time.' Michael dutifully unwinds the floss, lifts off the makeshift shroud, and returns to his seat: 'I became a docile traveller once again. I had to submit to the systems. They were designed to save my life.

And I complied gratefully.'[41] In 'heavy' airspace, the technologically neutral concept of authority seeks to replace the notion of the individual subject with the institutional façade of 'systems'.

In the strange new geography created by the deregulation of airspace, an airline, by requiring passengers to change planes at hubs, could vastly increase the possible number of city pairs it served; Valparaiso, Indiana could indeed be linked to Valparaiso, Chile. It all depended on a system of computation: the number of places an airline could serve from a hub increased exponentially as the number of cities reached from the hub increased arithmetically. Using 30 planes, and changing passengers at one central hub, an airline could offer 500 different route patterns; theoretically it would be possible for a large airline such as American or United to fly between almost any two airports in the US. That is, 48,860 pairs of cities with only one change of aircraft. This calculation presupposed, however, that every passenger on every arriving flight had the opportunity to board any departing flight, and so the need arose for carriers to schedule arrivals and departures as closely together as possible; to gain the full geometrical advantages of a hub, flights needed to be precisely timed to arrive and depart in 'complexes' or 'banks'. Aircraft landed in platoons, passengers deplaned by the hundreds, making split-second connections and computerized baggage-handling necessary. Transit no longer seemed to be a 'crystalline' affair, but was instead predicated on confluence, the precisely timed pumping of passengers into and out of an airport's chambers. As a consequence, airlines constructed specially designed terminals to control and direct the masses of travellers periodically flooding into hubs.

Chicago O' Hare, the world's busiest airport, is also the largest hub. It serves almost 70 million passengers a year, of whom only a fraction have the city as their final destination. Intended to resemble a glassy nineteenth-century railway station, United Airlines' $515 million 'Terminal for Tomorrow' opened on 4 August 1987. The complex was designed by Helmut Jahn, and contains 1,200,000 square feet of facilities covering 85 acres. The two 1,600-foot-long parallel concourses feature soaring barrel-vaulted ceilings and provide over 40 gates to accommodate the 50,000 travellers passing through the facility each day. Possibly because its ceilings are covered with nearly 15 acres of curved glass, the terminal has been described as 'the realization of technology's secret goal of placing Plexiglas sheeting between ourselves and the world'; but that goal has also led to serious functional deficiencies.[42] Owing to substantial differences in their coefficients of expansion, the horizontal glass panes are virtually impossible to seal in a steel-and-aluminium structure, and so on rainy days the concourse aisles are littered with buckets to catch the water dripping through the leaking roof. Fine days create their own set of discomforts. A design feature was an energy-efficient cooling system that manufactures ice at night when electricity is cheapest and then uses it to cool the terminal during the day. It is grossly inadequate; the ice melts too quickly, and the enormous amount of untinted glass makes the building nearly impossible to dehumidify. Passengers passing through

A concourse at Helmut Jahn's United terminal, Chicago O'Hare International Airport, 1987.

the concourses absorb the radiant heat of this glazed inferno, while the sunlight streaming through the roof creates the further problem of glare on the flight information monitors, making them difficult to divine.

Since O'Hare is a major hub for United Airlines, scores of flights are scheduled to arrive at approximately the same time; an hour or so later, these depart along 'the spokes', and a new round of arrivals follows. Such scheduling yields minimal connecting times for most passengers who, nevertheless, have basic needs during their short stay: to use a lavatory, grab something to eat, make a phone call on a land line, buy reading material or a gift. It also creates heavy concentrated demands on the facilities. Unfortunately, the 'mausoleum' design of the terminal interferes with its ability to handle these peak loads; indeed, as Martha Rosler suggests, the architectural ensemble of Jahn's terminal functions as nothing more than a 'reminder of individual insignificance'.[43]

The 'food court', essentially a storage area for vacuum packed, cellophane-sealed sustenance, is a perfect example of such deficiencies, since the very concept of 'passenger flow' seems to have been forgotten here. The entrance to the area has retail concessions on both sides of the aisle, but since the corridor is only 16 feet wide, five or six people queueing on each side nearly block it. After proceeding to the table area in the rear, diners must struggle back out using the same route. Furthermore, staff use this same corridor to both supply the concession stands and remove rubbish. The men's toilets suffer from similar problems. The urinals are located on both sides of a long narrow corridor, forcing people with bulky bags to pass beyond those using the facilities to get to a vacant one. Since there is much bumping both on the way in and on the way out, the floor – the only place to set down one's hand luggage – is usually awash with urine.

Perhaps such complaints about terminal design are irrelevant, since any connection to the concerns and solutions of the real world can only ever take place at one's final destination. As Coupland observes:

O'Hare is like what happens to you just after you die and before
you get shipped off to wherever you're going, what happens to
you while your final destination is being determined. It is not
judgment; it is transit distilled – like crack – pure neutrality made
concrete – extreme.[44]

But elsewhere, this 'concrete' materialization of 'transit' and
'neutrality' has assumed even more distinct forms. Consider the
kind of space mapped out by the Theme Building at Los Angeles
International Airport, which opened in August 1961. The structure is made up of two 135-foot-tall arches, which cross to form
an ugly white quadruped in whose innards sit, 70 feet up, a circular restaurant and an observation deck from which the main
view is of 23,000 thousand parking places. Occupying a large
area at the centre of the 'Jet Age' terminal complex, the Theme
Building is nothing more than a perfect waste of space; a monument only to the vacuity with which it was conceived. On early
sketches of the terminal, the building was labelled a 'theme'
structure; the provisional description remained even once the
edifice was completed. Now, 40 years on, it seems to embody
design without function, a distillation of terminal culture in
which the travelling public have never figured.[45]

Cerain art seems made for airports. In his review of Julian
Opie's retrospective at the Hayward Gallery in November 1993,
Andrew Graham Dixon commented:

Opie's work ... knows the blend of pleasure and alienation that
somewhere like Heathrow (certainly the greatest single influence
on Opie) can provide. Moving through an installation of Opie's is
like moving through a modern airport: it is to feel both pleasantly
and unpleasantly removed from reality, in a zone of transit where
what you do or who you are has become both threateningly and
relievingly unimportant.[46]

Such an assessment echoes John Berger – 'Airports are too
polite; reality is always at one remove in an airport' – but goes
further to suggest that Opie's work is at home in a zone hostile

The Theme Building, LAX, 1997.

to personality, and indifferent to aesthetics.[47] So it was appropriate that when BAA plc opened Heathrow's Flight Connections Centre, a secure enclosure next to Terminal 1, designed by the Richard Rogers Partnership to cater specifically for transit passengers making connections with international flights, it commissioned Opie to create an installation. In the resulting work, *Imagine That You're Moving*, the concept was clear enough: to present a version of the British landscape that travellers passing through the airport without visiting the country, would miss. His topographical representation consists of gently intersecting hills and valleys, rolling from foreground to the distant horizon; trees in full leaf follow the shape of swollen clouds in the summer sky. Yet it is a landscape of extreme contrivance and naivety, fabricated out of perspex and poster paint, and consisting of flat, silhouetted shapes and bright acrylic colours, fluorescently backlit. In its entirety, this installation consists of two contrasting but complementary aspects, which are intended to reflect different aspects of terminal experience. Four massive light-boxes run almost continuously along the full length of the two atria dominating the new building, and are viewed by connecting passengers as they ascend or descend the escalators to the waiting areas. Such movements up from, or down into, Opie's plastic-fronted scenery are perhaps intended to complement the passenger's experience of taking off and landing; certainly, the viewer is being transported over a landscape, but the destination announced by the light-boxes amounts to just one more manifestation of consumed culture, a hoarding for something one can never have, or might never desire. This encounter with Britain is inverted in the second part of Opie's installation. Dispersed around the transfer lounge waiting area, hanging from the ceiling are a number of closed-circuit monitors, like those that provide flight information. These terminals show the same stylized landscape as seen in the light-boxes, but now it appears to traverse the screen

Julian Opie, *Imagine That You're Moving*, 1997. Flight Connections Centre, Heathrow; BAA Art Programme.

231

slowly; the viewer is static but the landscape moves on. The title, *Imagine That You're Moving*, attempts to be soothing, but is scant compensation to the passengers who after several hours, find still themselves detained in this place of distilled transit.

A yet more extreme version of this *topos* is to be found at O'Hare. Linking the B and C concourses in United Terminal 1 is an underground pedestrian corridor, 815 feet long, 50 feet wide, through which moving walkways shift tired travellers from one concourse to the other. The passage features the largest light sculpture in the world, a 744-foot neon sculpture by California artist Michael Hayden, entitled *The Sky's the Limit*. The piece is composed of 466 sequentially programmed coloured neon tubes running the length of the ceiling, which cast overhead reflections against the back-lit pastel walls of moulded plastic curves. The first and last sections of the three-section computer-generated sculpture begin with white neon tubes, while the centre section starts with indigo and proceeds through the spectrum from shades of blue to green to yellow to orange to bright red. To complement the multiplicity of the passengers flowing through the tunnel, the pattern of light pulses, synchronized with original music by William Kraft, supposedly never repeats itself. As the traveller approaches the end of the walkway, the ambient soundtrack fades, and a female voice, growing ever more urgent, issues warnings in that 'fond peremptory tone' familiar even from Auden's era: 'Attention … the moving sidewalk is now ending … please look down.' Clearly, for such promptings to be made, the authorities at O'Hare must have realized that this *son et lumière* was liable to stupefy passengers, to the extent that they would be oblivious of their location, their feelings, their identities and the ability to walk. When Martha Rosler stood at the foot of the great escalators that lead to the underpass, and registered the endless passage of those entering and leaving the tunnel, all bearing the same demeanour, she clearly felt that here was an art in the place of the public; that is, the only sense of possibility that *The Sky's the Limit* bespeaks is one intended to supplant rather than create a public space.

232

Michael Hayden, *The Sky's the Limit*, United Terminal, Chicago O'Hare, 1989.

The same cannot be said of Washington National Airport, the smaller of the two airports which serve the US capital, situated at Gravelly Point, on the south-west side of the Potomac River, only 4 miles from the centre of the city. It was opened in 1941, and its original curved terminal building, 'Southern Colonial' in style, and landscaped into a slope, drew its inspiration from the pillared home of George Washington in nearby Mount Vernon. It was constructed of reinforced concrete and steel, and boasted a striking wall of glass looking out over the runways, and further beyond, to the Lincoln Memorial and Capitol Hill.[48] Over 50 years later, the airport was finally extended and the 'New Terminal', designed by Cesar Pelli, and comprising approximately 1 million square feet, 35 gates, and a 1,600-foot-long concourse, was built on to the old facility. In his 'Statement' for the building, Pelli claims its design is 'sympathetic with the context of the historic 1941 terminal'; as in the earlier structure, the functional elements are placed towards the landside, and large expanses of glass allow travellers to see the Federal monuments beyond. Indeed, the airside of the new building is mostly a glazed curtain wall bringing abundant light into the concourse during the day; but in order to contain this effect, Pelli's design abandons the pillar and offers a series of 54 structural steel 'domes', each with a central glass oculus allowing still more light to filter into the concourse. While the dome is one of the most ancient symbols of shelter, it also serves to establish yet another connection with the earlier civic architecture of Washington, DC, just across the river. Hence, Pelli claims that both terminals 'have their own character, appropriate to their time and to the nature of air travel in each period.'

Since it contains the familar retail concessions and restaurant franchises, the airy concourse is described as the 'Main Street' of the building. At first glance, one might be reminded of the United Airlines terminal at O'Hare, with its high ceilings, glazed roof and transit amenities; but here the similarities stop. Jahn's design at Chicago seems unable to countenance the possibility of a view, other than the vanishing point at the end of the concourse, or the 'authoritarian black-and-white-checkerboard floor' along which the traveller moves towards his gate.[49]

The old terminal at Washington National Airport, 1994.

Cesar Pelli's concourse with mosaic by Valerie Jaudon, Washington National Airport, 1997.

By contrast, the concourse at Washington is, in effect, a gallery consisting of 30 commissioned artworks – murals, sculptures, stained-glass friezes and balustrade decorations – executed in a great variety of materials. Pelli claimed that each piece is 'organic to the building', since specific locations and dimensions for the artworks followed the conceptual design for the building. Furthermore, the selection was made by curators mindful that this was not an exhibition in a museum, but art in a public place. Most striking, in this respect, are the ten glass and marbles mosaics, 18 feet in diameter, on the floor of the concourse, the work of among others Frank Stella, Valerie Jaudon and Sol LeWitt. Such resolute geometries lend beautiful effects, and recall the crystalline structures announced in Smithson's essay. Yet who would be so downcast as to be enthralled by the floor of this building, when beyond the great windows beckons the finest of democratic vistas? In any terminal, even one as finely conceived as this, those in transit only ever aspire to be beyond, to be elsewhere and otherwise; and as Rosler's work ultimately suggests, however diverting the culture of the terminal might be, the traveller simply seeks 'to be able to pass without registering passage'.

VI Airs of Finality

En route to JFK, and a major movie deal, John Self, the hero of Martin Amis's *Money* (1984), first needs to negotiate a route through Heathrow:

> Terminal Three was in terminal chaos, the air and light suffused with last things, planet panic, money Judgement. We are fleeing Earth for a newer world while there is still hope, while there are still chances. I queued, checked in, climbed the stairs, hit the bar, I got frisked, X-rayed, cleared, I hit the bar, plundered duty-free, walked the chutes, paced the waiting room until we entered the ship, two by two, all types represented, to make our getaway … Aboard the travel tube (a new kind of waiting room) we sat in lines, like an audience, to check out the art therapy on offer: toothache muzak, and, adorning the canvas curtain of the home-movie screen, a harbour view from a bracingly talentless brush. Next, the death-defying act from the stewardesses, those bashful girls and their oxygen mime. But the stalls gave the bird to this dance of doom. Unhooked from London, we boiled and shuddered and raced. Away! I thought, as we climbed through the air with the greatest of ease.[1]

The oddity here is that the airport, rather than being comfortably numbing, is a fearful place, while the aircraft itself has become a sanctuary, a blessed relief from the chaotic deluge. Lying behind the passage is the short order of Exodus, the precisely organized boarding of the Ark; once aboard this fragile vessel, Self wishfully thinks himself safe and sound, as he is offered 'therapy' in the forms of muzak, murals and pre-flight demonstrations of the safety procedures to be used 'in the unlikely event' of a crash.

For those left behind in the terminal, watching the daring

young men and women on their flying trapeze as they climb through the air 'with the greatest of ease', thoughts quite naturally turn towards mortality. Sitting in the departure lounge of Miami Airport, two double bourbons inside him, James Bond, a frequent flier, thinks about life and death:

> Below the indigo sky the flare paths twinkled green and yellow and threw tiny reflections off the oily skin of the tarmac. With a shattering roar a DC 7 hurtled down the main green lane. The windows in the transit lounge rattled softly. People got up to watch. Bond tried to read their expressions. Did they hope the plane would crash – give them something to watch, something to talk about, something to fill their empty lives? or did they wish it well? Which way were they willing the sixty passengers? To live or die?[2]

This perverse speculation orbits around the possibility that the spectacle of a disaster might in some way assuage the boredom of those waiting for their own flights to depart. Already in 1959, Ian Fleming was anticipating more recents shifts of sensibility, such as the manner in which late twentieth century culture has sought out 'the spectacular public representation of violated bodies, across a burgeoning range of official, academic and media accounts, in fiction and in film, [which] has come to function as a way of imagining and situating our notions of public, social, and collective identity'.[3] Inherent in the experience of viewing such images is a kind of ambivalent process of identification, a 'mass-imaginary transitivism' marked by both resignation and vigilance.[4]

Disaster footage of an air crash, say, provides images of a passive, collective victimization, yet what needs to be remembered is that it involves the very same generalized subject as that which processed though the terminal to board any flight. Since the contemporary disaster always seems to entail the malfunctioning of technological systems, in seeing the victims of an accident, or imagining their fate, we, the viewing public, or the crowd watching from the terminal, envisage ourselves as a

The French Air Union plane 'Vendée' at Croydon Aerodrome for a new London–Paris night airmail service, 1929.

mass exposed to the threat of failure.[5] If such scenes force us to see ourselves as being powerless, they also appear to offer the reassurance that the victim is always someone else, and somewhere else. However, in offering such certitude, these displacements and identifications transform the nature of individuality itself; henceforth, the space of the private self is increasingly shaped and determined by the anonymous 'victims' strewn around the packed departure lounge and, inexorably beyond that, the crash site.

In the autumn of 1933, Quentin Bell, the 23-year-old nephew of Virginia Woolf, was seriously ill. His pleurisy had been diagnosed as tubercular, and his specialist had prescribed for him a period of treatment at a Swiss sanatorium. Early on 3 November, he and his mother, Vanessa Bell, drove across a deserted London to Croydon aerodrome, accompanied by the Woolfs, and there boarded a plane bound for Geneva. The flight would take 7 hours. Over a week after bidding them goodbye, Woolf belatedly recorded her impressions of their departure:

We took them there at 7. Had to be up by moonlight at 6.30. drove across an empty delicately tinted London; lines all much marked; Croydon a great space like a green race course. We stood on top of the roof; saw the aeroplane whirl, till the propellors were lost to sight – simply evaporated: then the aeroplane takes a slow run, circles & rises.[6]

The memory of this take-off would materialize some years later in Woolf's last novel, *Between the Acts* (1941), whose very title announces an attempt to mediate for the age. The novel takes place on a mid-June afternoon in 1939; the Second World War will begin 6 weeks later, but nemesis, 'the doom of sudden death hanging over us', is already familiar in the skies over the picturesque Sussex village in which the story is set, in the form of aircraft taking off from Gatwick, the new 'aerodrome in the neighbourhood'.[7] The peace of the idyll is periodically broken by the sound of pistons and propellers, a squadron heading towards France, in battle formation: 'a zoom severed it. Twelve aeroplanes in perfect formation like a flight of wild duck came over head ... Then zoom became drone. The planes had passed.'[8] At one stage a character says: 'The aeroplanes, I didn't like to say it, made one think'; and for Mrs Isa Oliver, brushing her hair, 'the infinitely quick vibrations of the aeroplane propeller' that she, like Woolf, 'had seen once at dawn at Croydon', make her think of her phantom love, as insubstantial as air:

> Faster, faster, faster it whizzed, buzzed, till all the flails became one flail and up soared the plane away and away ...
> 'Where we know not, where we go not, neither know nor care,' she hummed. 'Flying, rushing through the ambient, incandescent, summer silent ...'
> The rhyme was 'air'. She put down her brush. She took up the telephone.
> 'Three, four, eight, Pyecombe', she said.
> 'Mrs Oliver speaking ... What fish have you this morning? Cod? Halibut? Sole? Plaice?'
> 'There to lose what binds us here', she murmured. 'Soles. Filletted. In time for lunch please', she said aloud. 'With a

feather, a blue feather … flying mounting through the air …
there to lose what bind us here …'[9]

Before a terminal rhyme can be secured, Isa picks up the phone
and rings the fishmonger. As Gillian Beer suggests, the aeroplane here is 'an image of arousal'; in any event, Isa's private
life is such that the last word, 'air', has to be provided by Woolf
explicitly. But then she knew from experience how emotionally
affecting airspace could be.

At Croydon, as Woolf waves off her sister and nephew, and
watches them rise into the dark November morning, it suddenly occurs to her that she might never see them again. The
grass runway, 'a green race course', has, within a few seconds of
their departure, become a space where, rather than jockeying
horses, the lives of one's loved ones are gambled upon and
away. The sense of potential benefit – a magic cure for
Quentin's illness – is co-terminous with the possibility of death:

> This is death I said, feeling how the human contact was com-
> pletely severed. Up they went with a sublime air & disappeared
> like a person dying, the soul going. And we remained. I saw the
> plane become a little mark in the sky. A good funeral could be
> arranged.

Air travel, then as now, was an act of transgression, the denial of
gravity, the assumption of the sublime, all of which amounted
for Woolf to the most basic severing of 'human contact'.

After their departure, the days of waiting for her sister's
restitution were especially difficult for Woolf, as her journal
shows: 'I did not at all enjoy waiting for Nessa to come back
across the Alps: sat making conversation with Lady Simon. So
thats over.'[10] What was 'over' was not simply the anticipation of
news of her sister's fog-bound return flight, but also the threat
initiated at the airport some days earlier and described in a
letter to the composer Ethel Smyth:

Oh I've been in such a twitter – Nessa flying to Geneva and back and circling Paris in an aeroplane in a fog. Here was I sitting forced to make sensible remarks to [Shena] Lady Simon about the education of women – waiting for a telephone. None came. Then the wrong one. Very well I said there's been a crash – went on making sensible remarks.[11]

Here, thankfully, that terrible final call, informing Woolf of a fatal crash, is never received. She simply has to field a wrong number; from the sublime to the ridiculous. Two days later, she writes to her nephew, Quentin, by now safely installed in the Swiss sanitorium:

> … it has been a very agitating week, waiting for aeroplanes to settle. Nessa seems to have flown round Paris in the fog – and then she mounted into the sun, and then she saw the Channel beneath her, and Heaven on top and earth below – oh how I envy her, but never never I hope will she fly again.[12]

To Woolf, such vistas were, naturally, 'more beautiful than any earth scape'. She would aspire to these views but never experience them, even though in a late essay, she imagined how it might feel to be flying over London:[13]

> A thousand pens have described the sensation of leaving earth; 'The earth drops from you', they say; one sits still and the world has fallen. It is true that the earth fell, but what was stranger was the downfall of the sky. One was not prepared within a moment of taking off to be immersed in it, alone with it, to be in the thick of it … trespassing up here in a fine air; repugnant to it, unclean, antipathetic.[14]

This air-mindedness is singularly high-minded; no hoi-polloi on board. As it progresses, however, Woolf's essay, seems to be less about the sociabilities of aviation than the transfiguration of the self in airspace, since at its heart is an encounter with death:

Life ends; life is dowsed in that cloud as lamps are dowsed with a wet sponge. That extinction has become now desirable. For it was odd in this voyage to note how blindly the tide of the soul and its desires rolled this way and that, carrying consciousness like a feather on the top, marking the direction, not controlling it. And so we swept on now up to death.

While Woolf represents the possibility of the sublime, that state of being which, J.-F. Lyotard has suggested, 'is kindled by the threat of nothing further happening', she is also aware that the modern sublime is always accompanied by a fearful, crashing corollary.[15] In early 1937, while walking on the Sussex Downs, she witnessed an aftermath:

> Yesterday at Rodmell we saw a magpie & heard the first spring birds: sharp egotistical, like [illegible]. A hot sun; walked over Caburn home by Horley & saw 3 men dash from a blue car & race, without hats across a field. We saw a silver & blue aeroplane in the middle of a field, apparently unhurt, among trees & cows. This morning the paper says three men were killed – the aeroplane dashing to the earth: But we went on, reminding me of that epitaph in the Greek anthology: when I sank, the other ships sailed on.[16]

The crashed aircraft was an Avro 40K which had just taken off from 'London South (Gatwick)', the aerodrome that had opened the year before.[17] As far as Woolf was concerned, she had witnessed a pastoral scene, a plane where it might be expected, in the middle of a field; only later did she realize that she had seen a disaster, and so the epitaph by Theodoridas came to mind.[18] Eighteen months later, Auden would update this observation, noticing in Brueghel's depictions of an air crash, *The Fall of Icarus*, 'how everything turns away / Quite leisurely from the disaster'.[19]

Indeed, in a situation of radical impotence there is really little else to do other than pass on, and develop the capacity for survival in an environment which, through its narrowing constraints, increasingly makes endurance impossible. According to J. H. Prynne's scheme, the airport is a 'desert', a sterile zone and barren subject familiar from Auden's elegy on the death of W. B. Yeats: 'He disappeared in the dead of winter: / The brooks were frozen, the air-ports almost deserted.' Yet it is also the topos which, in the moments when we are carried away, we so richly deserve: 'the thinning sorrow of flight / the last disjunction, of the heart.' That space between confinement and flight is the 'last disjunction'; in it, the farther we fly the closer we are held to the possibility that there are no limits, and no centre, no determinate places only that indeterminate zone 'in between'. Hence, the return flight only takes us back to previous departures: 'love is, always, the flight back to where we are.' In a sad and self-defeating imitation, Prynne's lines suggest that the airport frames the shapes of our survivals; the wreckage strewn around its spaces is only ever the wreckage of lives held between the thresholds of modernity.

Francis Hope, a noted poet and, until his death in 1974, the Paris correspondent of *The Observer*, had spent a lifetime in airports. Their spaces typically presented to him nothing more than 'the vulgar and wasteful quest for novelty', and compared with such chaotic places, flight was a welcome release, and in an article he wrote in his *New Statesman* column in 1972, he set out his feelings as he leaves the terminal and makes towards the waiting aircraft:[20]

> I should still prefer to let the machine take over, and cultivate my one mystical skill: a firm belief that whenever my life gets nasty, it is happening to someone else. Not only am I not flying the plane, I'm not even travelling in it when the going gets rough. Perhaps the abuse of this slender talent explains my feeling that I'm not there when I've arrived, either. No doubt flying is too fast (as George Orwell thought trains were too fast) for a true flavour of arrival. It merely gives a generalized sense of displacement. But even that is a privilege, and a pleasure. When I'm tired of it, I shall know where they can put me, for keeps.[21]

Those who boarded a Turkish Airlines DC10 along with Francis Hope on 3 March 1974 have felt that they too were escaping the nasty situation which had developed at Orly that weekend. Maintenance engineers employed at Heathrow by British European Airways had decided to strike, and so all of BEA's flights were grounded. Meanwhile, at Orly the other airlines serving London were quickly overwhelmed by the demand for seats. A Five Nations rugby international had taken place the day before – England had drawn with France – and many supporters had been stranded at the airport. As it happened, the Turkish plane, a wide-bodied three-engined jet with a passenger capacity of almost 350, was *en route* to London from Istanbul, less than a third full; BEA ground staff at Orly managed to find seats on it for 216 passengers, who were clamouring to return to the UK.

The DC10 was due to depart at noon, but owing to the crowds of extra travellers boarding at Gate A2 of Orly's west terminal, it did not leave Runway 08 until half an hour later. The weather at the time was near perfect, a crisp spring day with only scattered cumulus clouds at about 3,000 feet. The aircraft headed due east to avoid – as the air traffic regulations demanded – over-flying Paris and then, once over the village of Coulommiers, it turned north-north-westerly for the flight to London. Everything was routine; the jet would touch down at Heathrow by 12.20 local time. Just after 12.40, less than 10 minutes into the flight, at an approximate height of 11,000 feet, the jet's rear cargo door blew open. Air escaped from the rear baggage compartment, and sections of the floor collapsed shearing most, if not all, of the control cables running underneath it to the tail. The last two rows of seats in the left-hand aisle – and the six passengers they contained – were plunged into the cavity and ejected through the gaping hole in the fuselage, to fall the 2½ miles to earth, landing in a turnip field near the village of St Pathus. Meanwhile, the massive jet slowed, banked to the left and began to dive; within a minute, moving at almost 500 mph, the DC10 fell to earth in the forest of Ermenonville, between Senlis and Le Plessis-Belleville,

25 miles north of Paris. The plane bellied into the trees , and even though the angle of impact was shallow, the kinetic energy was such that it instantaneously shattered the whole airframe. Apart from the engines, few pieces of wreckage more than a couple of feet long survived the impact. The DC10's wing tanks were carrying about 10,000 litres of fuel for the short trip to London: as the tanks ruptured this was transformed into a huge cloud of minute droplets which hovered for a fraction of a second before vaporizing in a huge fireball. Trees were scorched and blackened, but the flame was too transient to ignite the surrounding forest still damp from winter snows.

The corollary of Francis Hope's feeling that 'I'm not there when I've arrived' might be that when he never arrived, he would always be there, in spirit anyway. That, at least, is the gist of 'In The Corridor', John Fuller's poem about his old friend, which begins:

> Francis, it was you yesterday, though I knew you were dead,
> Smiling and nodding your head

The Turkish Airline DC10 crash site in the Forest of Ermenonville, near Paris, 3 March 1974.

As though your long-kept secret could wait a little while
To be recounted in style,
Fondly amused at my pain and excitement at seeing you
    here,
At seeing you anywhere
When I thought, when I knew, the historical you that really
    mattered
Had been so cruelly scattered.[22]

Fuller's lines are appropriately awkward in their movement, alternating between fourteen and seven syllables, and the rhyme of 'mattered' with 'scattered' assumes darker proportions, given the crash scene, a great gash in the forest about 500 yards long and up to 100 yards wide. Fuller later explained what he hoped to achieve: 'I tease the reader into wondering how true it might be that it is an experience of a revenant … I'd hope the cautiousness and curiosity would seem matched – a small moment of vision, when something unexpected might be revealed, if we are fit to take it in.' The existence of a revenant might prove that even an air crash may be a round-trip journey, that people could return from flights that went nowhere, or came to nothing but grief. In the end, Fuller decides that he must dismiss the apparition rather than communicate with it:

Only our sorrow for you will come again and again
And goes some way to explain
Why there is fit passage for its evidence of our fears
In a few words and tears.[23]

One might say that, given the reporting of the conditions at the crash scene, Fuller's poem about Hope could only be ultimately hopeless.

A rocky mound had broken the path of the aeroplane, and over this area there were scattered human remains, shattered by impact with disintegrating airframe parts. The policeman in charge, Jacques Lannier, recalled:

On my left, over a distance of four hundred or five hundred meters, the trees were hacked and mangled, most of them charred but not burnt. Pieces of metal, brightly coloured electric wires, and clothes were littered all over the ground. In front of me, in the valley, the trees were even more severely hacked and the wreckage even greater. There were fragments of bodies and pieces of flesh that were hardly recognizable. In front of me, not far from where I stood, there were two hands clasping each other, a man's hand tightly holding a woman's hand, two hands which withstood disintegration.[24]

Two people, scattered and fragmented by death, reaching to each other for a last, brief assurance of existence. As Maurice Blanchot observes in his haunting meditation on the nature of loss and misfortune, *The Writing of the Disaster*: '… whoever falls is not one, but several. Multiple fall. Each one restrains himself, clinging to an other, an other who is himself and is the dissolution – the dispersion – of the self, and the restraint is sheer haste, panicky flight, death outside death.'[25] It quickly became clear to the authorities that the passenger manifest would be of little help in identifying the victims; in the pre-flight chaos at Orly, there had been no time to record the names and addresses of all the passengers clamouring to leave. The emergency services spent over two weeks at the crash site picking up and removing 22 tons of human remains, each fragment of which was ringed and numbered and stored in a plastic bag, and passed on to forensic specialists for reconstruction. At the police station in Senlis, wallets, keys and valuables were laid out on long tables for relatives to inspect and claim; all the watches had stopped at 12.42 pm.

Flight 981 was due into Heathrow just after midday GMT. As its meeters and greeters entered Terminal 2 the flight was shown with an estimated time of arrival of 12.20; as the time came and went, it changed to 12.25 and then to 12.30. Then the ETA vanished altogether, and in its place on the annunciator boards was an instruction to 'Make inquiries at the BEA desk.' The attendants there could say nothing useful to the people who now began to crowd around them, except that the flight was not on the London radar. An airport official arrived at the inquiry desk and bluntly informed the hundred or so people who were waiting of the accident. They were escorted to one of the airport's private lounges, and a large supply of free drinks was brought in. Then, at about 3.30, almost four hours after the crash, a colour television was brought into the room and switched on to channels showing pictures of the crash scene.[26] Martin Amis (a colleague of Hope's at the *New Statesman*) incorporated this heartless treatment of the friends and relatives at Heathrow into *London Fields*, in his account of the orphaning of his heroine, Nicola Six:

Personal possessions recovered from the site of the THY Ermenonville crash, 1974.

After she got the call she drove reflexively to the airport. The car itself was like a tunnel of cold wind. An airline official showed her into the VIP Lounge: it contained a bar, and forty or fifty people in varying degrees of distress. She drank the brandy pressed on her by the steward. 'Free,' he confirmed. A television was wheeled in. And then, incredibly (even Nicola was consternated), they showed live film of the scattered wreckage, and the bodybags lined up on fields of France. In the VIP Lounge there were scenes of protest and violent rejection. One old man kept distractedly offering money to a uniformed PR officer. Coldly Nicola drank more brandy, wondering how death could take people so unprepared. That night she had acrobatic sex with some unforgivable pilot. She was nineteen by this time, and had long left home. Potently, magically, uncontrollably attractive, Nicola was not yet beautiful. But already she was an ill wind, blowing no good.[27]

Already a flighty young woman, Nicola is secured in her future life course by this disaster; henceforth, she will strive to be a 'murderee', a woman actively passive, constantly looking for an opportunity to allow herself to be killed.[28] Ill winds blow across the Ermenonville crash site where her parents die; but then, most events, however unfortunate, will benefit someone, and the shocking blasts generated by air disaster have frequently been exploited by writers and film-makers.

Brigid Brophy, for instance, knew that she ran the risk of unpleasantness by having the genderless narrator of *In Transit* lose both sets of parents in air crashes, the first pair dying when their jet plunges into the Irish Sea, and the second falling victim on a flight to Italy. 'It's grotesque. It verges on a sick joke,' exclaims the narrator, but it's not nearly so nauseating as the novel's denouement, which depicts the collision between two planes in the airspace above the terminal; 'a giant hail of snapped and twisted fragments pelted down', from which only one survivor emerges.[29] In the immediate aftermath of this accident, the transit passengers run from the terminal and literally pick up the pieces, 'fresh, what they wanted, a heart, a lung, a colon'.[30] One traveller stops in his tracks, and looks down: 'It was a penis: very wishily washily pink in the pale light, unimpressively limp in its severed state.' For the duration of the book, the narrator has been in transit between sexes; the recovery of this body part gives Brophy's 'explicit fiction' its final resolution, the narrator having arrived at a point of sufficient certainty to be able to emerge from the terminal in one piece.

FUNCTIONAL SANCTUARIES

Prior to this carnage, Brophy's narrator can do little other than wait and take advantage of the terminal amenities: 'sliding furtively towards' the bookstall, s/he finds 'those vertical take off flights directly out of the present into the never never tense: fictions'.[31] Airports have always supplied reading materials in copious amounts; even in the most primitive of air facilities, travellers can expect to find a branch of W. H. Smith. In the first weeks of Heathrow's existence, passenger facilities consisted of tents containing a telegraph desk, a bar and a news kiosk carrying a good stock of paperback books. Of course, even now, with terminals turned into shopping malls, there's no guarantee that passengers will find what they want. In David Lodge's *Nice Work*, Persse McGarrigle, a lovelorn academic passing through Heathrow, runs 'from terminal to terminal, from bookstall to bookstall, loudly demanding a copy of *The Faerie Queene*', but the shop assistants can only offer him Enid Blyton and the newest issue of *Gay News*.[32] For Brophy's narrator, only pornography and thrillers, the staples of 'airport fiction', are available. The term itself is ambiguous: are such novels designed to be bought at the airport, begun there as the reader sits in the Departure Lounge, and continued in flight; or are they intended to be exported from the dump bins intact, like terminal liquor, and consumed on arrival, before being abandoned, half-finished, on a beach? Perhaps this is why airport fiction is so often regarded as 'junk'. In Martin Amis's *The Information*, the narrator, an unsuccessful writer, meditates on the link between two seemingly separate entities:

Junk novels were sold in airports. People in airports bought and read junk novels. Junk novels were about people in airports, in as much as junk novels needed airports to shift their characters round the planet, and airports served in junk novels, as the backdrop to their partings, chance encounters, reunions and trysts.[33]

This is a dynamic equilibrium, however: junk novels need airports to survive, so airports depend on junk novels to pacify those trapped, from time to time, within their spaces:

Whatever junk novels were, however they worked, they were close to therapy, and airports were close to therapy. They both belonged to the culture of the waiting room. Piped music, the language of calming suasion. Come this way – yes, the flight attendant will see you now. Airports, junk novels: they were taking your mind off mortal fear.

The narrator of *In Transit* doubts that s/he will be able to find any 'aviation fiction': 'Appropriate it would assuredly be, but perhaps also disquieting.'[34] Perhaps Brophy was alluding to a work published in 1968, the year before her novel appeared, which would transform the way in which airports were regarded. As Richard, Martin Amis's protagonist, observes, 'Some junk novels were all about airports. Some junk novels were even called things like *Airport*.'

Arthur Hailey's multi-episodic novel was one of the great publishing successes of the late 1960s. Its plot orbited around the figure of Mel Bakersfield, the general manager of a major Midwestern airport, the infrastructure of which is falling apart: 'Few of the eighty thousand passengers who flew in and out each day were aware of how inadequate and, therefore, hazardous the runway system had become. Even a year previously, runways and taxiways were barely sufficient; now, they were dangerously overtaxed.'[35] Bakersfield's personal life is falling apart, too, but he can do little to save it, as he obsesses first over clearing his snow-bound runways, and then over bringing a big jet crippled by a deranged passenger's bomb down safely. For added piquancy, the stricken 707 is piloted by his brother-in-law, who, just prior to take-off was informed by an air hostess that she was pregnant by him. Yet beyond the sensations of its plot, *Airport*'s accomplishment owes much to its author's emphasis on secondary characters such as airline despatchers, customs officers, mechanics, air-traffic controllers, even snow removers; consequently, certain passages read more like a handbook of airport operations than popular fiction. Consider this account of the mechanics of flight announcements:

> It originated in a machine which in many ways resembled a juke box, except that push buttons instead of coins were required to actuate it. The push buttons were on a console in Flight Information Control – a miniature control tower (each airline had its own FIC or equivalent) – located above the departure con-course. A woman clerk pushed the buttons in appropriate sequence; after that the machinery took over. Almost all flight announcements – the exceptions were those for special situations – were pre-recorded on cartridge tapes. Although, to the ear, each announcement seemed complete in itself, it never was, for it con-sisted of three separate recordings. The first recording named the airline and flight; the second described the loading situation, whether preliminary, boarding, or final; the third recording spec-ified gate number and concourse. Since the three recordings fol-lowed one another without a pause, they sounded – as they were intended to – continuous.[36]

Clearly, this stress on continuity was deliberate. Rather than providing distraction, *Airport* met and guided air travellers through the technological spaces in which they found them-selves reading the novel; rather than providing a route to escapism, it made them feel more secure in their containment; rather than moving them away on a flight of fancy, it brought them face to face with the existential fundamental of airspace, the fear of non-arrival. Like Hailey, recent proponents of avia-tion fiction – Michael Crichton whose *Airframe* concerns a pos-sible design flaw in a fleet of airliners, Dean R. Koontz, whose

Sole Survivor is about a family wiped out in a crash, and Tom Clancy, whose works frequently have recourse to air disasters only just averted – continue to suggest that only through an enlightened sense of airspace can fear ever be conquered. Passengers reading such texts in the departure lounge, and then later strapped in on their flights, seem to believe that the likelihood of a plunge to earth is somehow reduced by clinging to a fictional description of one; hence these fat, unwieldy paperbacks become talismans, 'tangible comforts' which might ward off disaster.[37]

The film rights to Hailey's novel were quickly bought up, and within two years a cinematic version appeared, which necessarily reduced the scale of the book. The entire workings of the international airport were effectively funnelled into the claustrophobic fuselage of a Trans Global Airlines jet, *en route* from Lincoln Airport to Rome and carrying a group of passengers who would become the prototypes for future *Airport* movies: nuns, priests, soldiers, stowaways and deranged terrorists.[38] As the sequels moved further away from the realities, the shapes and the atmospheres of the airport itself, it became clear that when set against aircraft themselves – 707s, 747s and Concorde, vessels of disaster, all – the facility had only ever meant a safe haven. Hence, these films would never provide in-flight entertainment; what Martin Amis ironically calls 'art therapy'.

Yet an aesthetic affinity clearly exists between airspace and cinema, especially with regard to the passivity required of those who remain within the confined expanses of airport or auditorium.[39] Amis's hero, John Self, makes this connection as he sits in the TWA terminal at JFK with a large drink in his fist, and gazes at the 'sky screening a noisy film about the near future – a good film, framed by the porthole and really well lit by the director of photography'.[40] Behind this cinematic conceit, however, in the image of a languid and resigned spectator watching movement, lie distinct traces of Baudelairean and Proustian modernity.

It is a state of mind echoed by the proclamation of Brophy's narrator:

The airport's kernel of wellbeing: – You too can be duty-free.

Flatten your claws, windriven hellions against the outside of the glass.

Furies, conscience, remorse, alarm, slave-driver purpose, super-ego, all that is included in that onomatopoeic of Italian names, smania, word at once smeary and biting, sulphur-fog whose acid drops eat stone and flesh, gnawing the heart and corroding the lungs of monumental statues: you can't get me here. I am super-super-ego, in functional sanctuary. I am the inedible statue in the incorruptible niche.[41]

Since the narrator of *In Transit* is scheduled to fly to Rome, and later stages an opera entitled *Alitalia*, it is not surprising that one of the most notorious scenes of recent European cinema seems to hover behind these words. In 1960, Fellini's *La Dolce Vita* had made use of the same constellation of sanctuary, statuary and *smania* ['frenzy'] to demarcate the limits of the Eternal City's airspace. In the opening frames, a statue of Christ, his arms outstretched in a loving embrace, is carried over Rome by helicopter, a modern version of a *deus ex machina* now seen only by construction workers and off-duty flight crew sunbathing on a penthouse terrace. The machine is not shown landing, so the idea of transcendent flight remains in the air until another scene later in the film when an Alitalia DC6B touches down at Rome's Ciampino airport.[42] The tannoy announces in English and Italian the route it has negotiated to arrive here – 'New York, Shannon, Paris'. As the plane slows to a halt, a large crowd of photographers and officials start running towards it. The turbulence from its propellers, still rotating momentarily, stops them in their tracks, but once they catch sight of its door opening they press forward once again, and, even before the mobile stair has been placed against the fuselage, they are frenziedly leaping around. The media is here to catch sight of the starlet, Sylvia (Anita Ekberg), who is arriving in Rome to make a film. Wearing a black dress of clear silk, which, as it is caught by the breeze, moulds itself to the contours of her statuesque body, and a white cape lined with a leopard print, suggestive of the

'Sylvia's arrival': a still from Federico Fellini's 1960 film *La Dolce Vita*.

jungle into which she has arrived, Sylvia emerges from the aircraft, pauses at the top of the steps. Flashbulbs pop, cine cameras whir and the journalists bombard her with questions and instructions. 'Back', they shout. It is not enough to see her; they want to manipulate the time, and make her 'arrive' once again, in a second coming. So she turns, enters the aircraft once more, and re-emerges, as if she were parading on a different kind of runway, the platform at a fashion show.

The great producer, Toto Scalise, middle-aged, moustached, a pipe in his mouth, runs towards the steps, followed by two waiters carrying a massive aluminium tray in which lies a *pizza al taglio*, piping hot and generously topped. The impresario addresses Sylvia and indicates the deep pan: 'Welcome in Rome … Very happy … Neapolitan pizza. The first wishes of the sunny Italy.' He lifts out a slice and offers it to her; she willingly tears off a piece with her bared teeth and swallows it hungrily as the audience applauds. In its parody of the Eucharist, it is a perplexing scene (though perhaps no more incongruous than Pope John Paul II kneeling to kiss airport tarmac). While Fellini is securing Sylvia's existence as the star, the ultimate object of consumption,

'Sylvia tastes Italy': a still from *La Dolce Vita*.

he also suggests that she has arrived in Italy to consume; no one is safe, even those awaiting her in the sanctuary of the airport. As soon as she descends the stairway Marcello (Marcello Mastroianni), a seasoned gossip columnist, is inexorably drawn to her. Later that day, in a sublime countermovement, he will accompany Sylvia every step of the way as they ascend to the top of the Dome of St Peter's and gaze over the city.

Contemporaneously, in France, directors were also making use of airspace to detail the means by which individuals sought to free themselves from the most basic of personal duties and responsibilities. In effect, the airport represented a functional sanctuary. Jacques Tati's *Mon Oncle* (1958) had ended with Hulot's banishment to the provinces, and although the original script had called for a closing sequence at a railway station, the film concluded with an odd little scene in an airport car park. The crowd of travellers, descending from a coach and rushing straight into the terminal, all bear identical tan leather bags, slung over their shoulders, and move with a collective momentum which carries Hulot away into the building. Who knows if he will be seen again, or even if this location really is an airport:

the winged seahorse symbol of Air France, affixed to a porter's baggage trolley, and the sound of a piston-engined plane taking off, are the only gestures made towards airspace.[43] In fact, Hulot re-emerged 9 years later in *Play Time* (1967), when he crosses the path of a group of American tourists passing through the arrivals area at Orly. In his interview with Bazin and Truffaut, Tati explained the film's basic plot:

> A group of foreign tourists arrive to visit Paris. On landing at Orly they find themselves more or less at the same airport they left in Munich, London, or Chicago. They get into the same bus they'd used in Rome or Hamburg and drive on a road bordered with street lamps and buildings identical to those in their own capital. They find once again the style of architecture that makes living a matter of being constantly on your guard.[44]

However, such architecture was sufficiently on its guard not to permit itself to be filmed, and so Tati embarked on a building project which eventually led to his near bankruptcy: the construction of a modern city, including a replica of Orly, on a stretch of wasteland at Vincennes, north of Paris.

Play Time commences in the clouds, then cuts to a shot of a steel and glass building framed against the sky, an image which proves to be the film's most basic and bewildering spatial motif. Shortly after its release, Tati told an interviewer: 'I don't feel that I have the right to criticise today's architecture … Enormous buildings are being constructed. Glass, nothing but glass. We belong to a culture that feels the need to put itself in a shop window … The world is becoming one vast clinic.'[45] In saying this, he was seeking to suggest that there was little difference between the *vitrine*, the public exhibition space of modernity, and the hospital, the sterile place where private ailments might be displayed. The famous sequence which ensues in *Play Time* supports this convergence, and features a series of moments playing upon paranoias about supposedly neutral spaces.[46] Two nuns, their headdresses flapping to the rhythm of their rubber-soled gait, pass along a glazed corridor, and into a larger space, a hall dominated by a massive window at its far end. In the foreground, a middle-aged couple wait patiently on a plastic bench and watch the nuns as they march past. As the lengthy shot continues, the pair alternate between talking to each other and turning to watch various people who emerge from a set of numbered partitions on the right of the frame. The couple might well be sitting in a hospital waiting area, and their whispered conversation might imply that the man, who looks very nervous, is soon to be admitted for exploratory surgery; this is seemingly confirmed when a man dressed in white passes by, pushing a stainless steel trolley containing vessels and utensils. Once he has disappeared into one cubicle, a portly cleaner in blue overalls emerges from another, carrying a long-handled dustpan and broom, and begins to look for dirt but finds little to sweep up from the spotless floor. A man wearing a military uniform walks the length of the concourse, his jack-boot heels clicking out his agitated progress; he's clearly expecting something, perhaps a baby, as the wife remarks to her husband: 'Look at that man. He looks very important, doesn't he?'[47] The straight-backed woman in uniform who next marches

On the concourse: a still from Jacques Tati's 1967 film *Play Time*.

onto the screen from lower right and exits behind another one of the partitions could easily be a nurse; she is carrying a white bundle or package and as she passes, a baby cries. Moments later, it becomes clear that the woman is, in fact, a chamber-maid, and that she is carrying towels; the baby's cry actually emanates from the carry-cot the couple have with them at lower left of the frame, its shade and texture camouflaging it against the rows of chairs by which it is placed.

Even at this point, the location of Tati's film remains unde-fined. Further back, standing by the great window, are several more uniformed women; only on second or third viewing can it be seen that they are actually full-size cardboard cut-outs, not moving figures. Watching this sequence, an audience has noth-ing to do other than focus on such background detail, even though this spatial indeterminacy is being kept up for longer than most viewers might tolerate. Yet this is precisely the inten-tion since a terminal – for, in fact, that is the location – seeks to maintain its neutrality, so as to insulate the people it contains.

This strange combination of artifice and resignation attracted Tati to airports. In a late interview he claimed:

> But at Roissy [Charles De Gaulle], if ever there's an announce-ment of a delay to my flight, I place myself in a chair and say to myself – this is great – I watch the best film of the week. One day, I was sitting there and I said to myself it's funny: the doors are made out of plexiglass, the chairs are made out of nylon, the floors of plastic, the sandwiches come in cellophane and don't taste of anything. And you are surrounded by all these important people who have deodorised themselves.[48]

But life cannot be 'deodorised' so easily. In *Play Time*, the point of view now shifts, and the space is seen from the opposite angle. Looking down the hall, we now hear a flight announce-ment and the high-frequency shriek of a Caravelle. The jet that the nervous couple presumably will soon be boarding, comes into view, its tailplane moving across the window like a dorsal fin in a swimming pool. After a couple of sequences showing the arrival of a VIP and a group of American tourists, Tati cuts back to the large departure hall, now more crowded, and we see Monsieur Hulot enter from the right, in middle field, where, given the perspective, he only occupies a tiny area of the frame. He drops his umbrella, which clatters on the polished floor, picks it up, and exits again, disappearing into one of the cubicles, leaving barely a trace on this transitory environment. It is not even clear what he is doing there. Indeed, watching Tati choreographing Hulot's movement within it, all that one might say is that this Tati's construction of airspace presents us with a void – a duty-free zone.

FALLING, IN LOVE

A couple of years earlier, François Truffaut's *La Peau douce* (1964) had exploited Orly's vacuous spaces to stage the empty life of a middle-aged writer, Pierre Lachenay (Jean Desailly). Editor of a successful Paris literary magazine, and author of several works of criticism, he is due in Lisbon on a lecturing trip; delayed on his way to Orly he catches his Caravelle with only moments to spare. After an uneventful flight, Pierre

Orly framed in a window: a still from *Play Time*.

checks into his hotel and discovers that Nicole (Françoise Dorléac), one of the hostesses who served him earlier, is a fellow guest. On a whim, he invites her for a drink, and she agrees; the following evening they dine out, and later sleep together. Next day, Pierre returns to Orly on the same flight as Nicole; while queuing at customs on his arrival, he is surprised to discover that his wife, Franca (Nelly Benedetti), has turned up to meet him. Nonchalantly, he blows her a kiss through the screen dividing landside from airside.

After meeting up with Nicole again in Paris a few days later, Pierre drives out to Orly once more; he is in a state of sexual excitement. Inside the terminal, he is about to send her a telegram announcing his devotion to her, when he catches sight of her on the concourse. She is due to leave for Frankfurt, but her flight is late; they have half an hour to kill. As they walk through the terminal, the tannoy, *'la fameuse voix aphrodisiaque des hôtesses de terre'* (the same voice Hailey's novel demystifies) announces the departure of Flight 813. This happens to be the

Pierre blows a kiss to his wife though the plate glass of Orly: a still from François Truffaut's 1964 film *La Peau Douce*.

number of the hotel bedroom where they began their affair, and so Pierre, carried away by the coincidence as he stands at the bookstall, asks the shop assistant for Maurice Leblanc's *813*, the 1910 novel in which Arsène Lupin, the French gentleman-thief, is accused of murder but clears himself by finding the true killer. Unfortunately, it is unavailable in paperback, so instead he buys the first Lupin story, *Arsène Lupin, gentleman-cambrioleur* (1907), and presents it to Nicole as an airport novel. The pair then head towards Le Publicis-Orly, the 300-seat cinema on the fourth floor of the terminal.

Projected on the screen as they sit down is a sequence depicting a pioneer of flight, with a flying machine of his own invention strapped to his back, about to take off from the first floor of the Eiffel Tower. He hesitates and then suddenly throws himself into the void. Seconds later, he is crumpled on the ground, stone dead; his device has failed to function, though it later emerged that during his brief descent a heart attack had killed him. In the darkness Pierre comments: 'Basically, this man is one of the first victims of cinema; you could say that had there been no camera filming him, he probably would not have tried to take off.'[49]

As he says this, Pierre grasps Nicole's hand; her fingers rest for a short time in this tight *entrelacement*, before she disentangles them from his grip and gets up and leaves the auditorium. She must rejoin the rest of the cabin crew. Realizing that she has forgotten to pick up the Lupin novel, Pierre races after Nicole, and hands it to her; they part and he watches her walk away down the great corridor towards her flight. He then returns home and makes love to his wife. The sardonic reflexivity of this *mise en scène* is typical of the 'New Wave', since it emerges that, by abandoning himself to his young lover in the dark heart of the airport, Pierre, like the pioneer of flight he saw on screen, is about to fall.[50] Eventually, this affair will kill him; Nicole will reject his clumsy proposal of marriage, and, when she discovers photographic evidence of his infidelity, his wife, confronting her husband in a restaurant, will throw the incriminating prints at him before

At the book stall, Pierre looks for a Lupin novel; in the background, Hitchcock looks menacing: a still from *La Peau Douce*.

shooting him dead.

Later that year, Jean-Luc Godard released *Une Femme mariée*, a film clearly intended to complement his friend Truffaut's.[51] Charlotte (Macha Méril), a young woman who edits a women's magazine, lives in Paris with her husband, Pierre, a pilot, and her 6-year-old stepson. Since Pierre is frequently absent, moving through airspace, Charlotte has ample opportunities to indulge an affair with Robert (Bernard Noel), an actor. The lovers have arranged to meet up at Orly before his departure for Marseille, where he is due to perform in repertory, but after a consultation with her gynaecologist, at which she discovers that she is pregnant by either Pierre or Robert, Charlotte, now late for her tryst, slips and falls. The frame is then filled with white letters on a black background: 'EVE RÊVES'; the archetypal fallen woman is lost in her dream. She gets up and hails a taxi. Once more the action is replaced with a caption, 'CE QUE SERA', a passive submission to fate. In the next shot the taxi stops, Charlotte gets out quickly, pays and climbs into another cab. Wearing dark glasses, she looks out of the back window; as the taxi heads towards Orly, it passes through a tunnel. The camera hits on a flashing road sign – 'DANGER' – and continues to zoom in until the screen fills with its four central letters 'ANGE'. A fallen angel, Charlotte now seems in danger as she approaches the glass entrance at Orly. Over the whine of departing jets, amplified females voices can be heard making flight announcements, while above the main concourse a massive rotating chandelier, designed to represent the globe, slowly turns and sparkles.[52]

In certain respects, Godard's presentation of Charlotte's journey seems to support that definition of airport space, provided in Brophy's novel, as 'a free-range womb', a place of nourishment and confinement, where one is only ever passing through, and is always being directed outwards, 'in transit' but not independent. For Charlotte, Orly is also seen to function as a vacuum in which she will no longer be subject to certain responsibilities and duties relating to her marriage, and her newly discovered pregnancy. As she moves across the great concourse, she looks

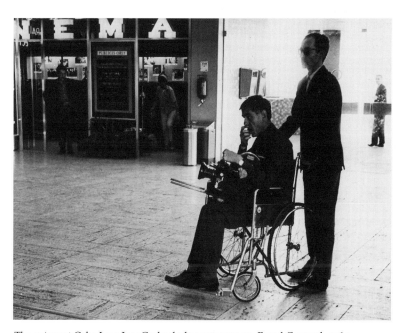

The *auteur* at Orly: Jean-Luc Godard plus cameraman, Raoul Coutard, 1964.

The Cinéma Publicis at Orly: a still from Godard's 1964 film *Une Femme mariée*.

around to make sure she is not being followed; above her head can be seen a large neon sign reading: 'PASSAGE CINEMA'. The camera pans across it, slowly, breaking the first word into 'PAS SAGE', a warning for the audience that the cinema is never wise to affairs of the heart.[53] Charlotte stands on the escalator, and ascends towards the huge bay-window on the first floor, around which are arrayed the bars and *vitrines*, and continues all the way up to the cinema featured in *La Peau douce*. An advertisement for Hitchcock's *Spellbound* stands outside, but without looking at the hoarding, Charlotte hurries towards the box-office, buys a ticket and consults the illuminated seat-plan.[54] Robert is sitting in the middle of the back row, and once her eyes are accustomed to the darkness of the auditorium, she sees him and sits down next to him silently. Shortly after the film has begun, the couple stand up and leave the cinema, and walk across towards the reception desk of the airport hotel. Charlotte sits down behind a pillar, and Robert carrying a small suitcase,

266

drops a key beside her. She picks it up, looks at the number, and hands it back to him. He proceeds towards the bedrooms; she will follow in a few moments.

During the ensuing love-making, the couple are framed in a complex series of jump cuts, and a voice-over commentary breaks in above the roar of jets.[55]

> To find a solution.
> Men are all the same.
> Very blue eyes.
> For the sake of appearances.
> Modern life.
> To forget everything.[56]

It seems that the hard edges of Orly, uniformity and modernity *in extremis*, constitute the ideal place to forget one's life, and one's self. Demurely, Charlotte, her mouth in profile, kisses Robert's forehead, every kiss, followed by a barely audible 'I love you'. Godard's montage works hard here to prevent the audience from participating in an erotic experience, the disruption of continuity fragmenting the lovers' bodies and removing their identities. These scenes in the Orly bedroom emphasize two discrete symbols. As the hands reach towards each other, Charlotte's wedding ring and Robert's wrist-watch are juxtaposed, the symbol of the approved social bond of the 'stable' relationship set against the cipher of a man existing in thrall to time and 'the speed-age' ['*l'époque de la vitesse*']. Indeed, Robert is moving so fast that he lacks the time to undress fully; 'I'm only taking off my trousers. My Caravelle leaves in half an hour' ['*j'enleve que mon pantalon; je prends la Caravelle dans une demi-heure*']. As soon as his imminent departure is mentioned, Charlotte finds it hard to ignore the possiblility of its falling from the sky, and so she asks whether he has taken out insurance. Robert replies that since the flight lasts only an hour, there is no need, but she retorts: 'An hour is quite long enough to have an accident and … die.' He is stoic: 'It's all right to die in a plane crash. It's quick and there are several of you,' a sentiment

'La vie moderne': a still from Godard's *Une femme mariée.*

with which she agrees: 'It's true, it's modern death' ['*C'est vrai, c'est une mort moderne'*].[37] Her phrase now echoes Godard's earlier definition of 'modern life' ['*la vie moderne'*]; in this jet age, living and dying seem to amount to the same form of generalized oblivion.

In Marseille, Robert is due to appear in Jean Racine's deathless tragedy, *Bérénice,* but it seems that within Godard's frame, the airport is already a kind of theatre. Like the stage, it demands that those participating in its spaces question their own existence, and regard themselves as merely playing roles in transit. Within such confines, the traveller, like the actor, must learn the cues and gestures of airspace, and, from time to time, be prompted by lines from the tannoy, an insistent bilingual reminder of the scheduled performance: 'The flight for Marseilles Air-Inter Number 617 is about to depart. Will passengers please go immediately to Gate 17. Départ à destination de Marseille. Vol Air-Inter 617. Embarquement immédiat, port no. 17.' Robert diverts himself with his airport reading, the Larousse Classic version of *Bérénice*, and suggests that Charlotte give him his cues. She, however, is unsure of what Robert expects from her as he intones the lines: 'And if I ever do avoid what I feel, but too late, / These cruel conversations in which I have no part.'[58] He shoots a glance across to Charlotte and reminds her that this is her speech, and so she now recites the lines of the Palestinian Queen, Bérénice: 'I myself wanted to listen to you in this place. / I will listen no more, good-bye for ever!'[59] to which Robert, now fully committing himself to the role of Antiochus, the unrequited lover, responds:

> So how can I put it, finally, I flee from the abstracted glance,
> Which, though always turned in my direction, never sees me.
> Goodbye! I ... [*A pause*].
> Go, my mind is too full of your image,
> To wait for death while loving you
> Above all do not fear ...
> Above all do not fear ... [*A pause*] ... that blind grief
> Will fill the world with sound of my misfortune ...
> The only thing that will remind you I was alive,
> Will be the report of my death, which I hope may come soon.[60]

These verses, spoken by Antiochus just after his confession of love has been rejected by Bérénice, announce his intention to leave Rome because she loves Titus, not him. As he recites these lines, which carry with them the promise of sudden death abroad, rather than a lingering finish in Rome, Robert perhaps realizes that his own situation is approaching that of Antiochus; in these overwhelming silences he understands that Charlotte has no time for him, but he goes on, carried away still further by the airy lines. Charlotte responds, but rather than acting Bérénice's verses, she simply reads them, unfeelingly:

> For ever, oh my lord, think, deep in yourself,
> How terrible this cruel world is when one loves,
> What shall we be suffering in a month, in a year, my lord?

When so many seas separate me from you,
When the day begins, and the day ends
But Titus will never see Bérénice again?[61]

In a brilliant *coup de théâtre*, Godard has made Charlotte recite these lines, out of the context and order in which they occur in Racine's play. There, they are not a rejoinder to Antiochus, but are, in fact, Bérénice's response to Titus, the man she loves, when he informs her that, out of political considerations, he must now banish her from Rome. Her famous speech frames a future of suffering, the infinity of separation.

Unlike Robert, who enters the part fully, forgetting himself for the sake of the role, Charlotte is unable to act. These lines, spoken in the very spaces of Orly which she thought would protect her, represent nothing to her other than the grounding of her flight from reality. As soon as she finishes speaking, the screen is plunged into darkness. Robert withdraws his hand from hers and says: 'Come on, it's over. I must go' ['*Allez! C'est fini. Il faut que je m'en aille*'] to which she replies, in tears: 'Yes … yes … It's over …' ['*Oui … Oui, c'est fini*']. Now the word *FIN* appears on the screen, a brutal reinforcement of the termination of a love affair.

THE END OF THE STORY

Earlier, as Robert and Charlotte sit in the dark of the cinema, we hear a narrated commentary: 'Even a tranquil landscape. Even a meadow with flights of crows, harvests and bonfires.' The first shot of the film is framed upon a colourful field, a flat landscape, as the camera pitches down to reveal lines of barbed wire. Charlotte, in close-up, turns her head towards Robert, and we see him in profile, his eyes narrowing as he listens to the voice over: 'Even a peaceful countryside, even a meadow with flights of crows, harvests and bonfires … Even a road with cars, peasants, couples going along it.' The rest of the sequence follows this pattern: a road is shown, at first directly, then through the wire fence, before a barely-furnished room appears, and the montage shifts back to a landscape criss-crossed with barbed wire. Throughout, the commentary runs inexorably: 'Even a holiday village with a fair, and a steeple, can lead … to a concentration camp.' At this point, Robert and Charlotte avert their eyes, and look at each other. Just as a roll of atrocity is being called – 'Struthof, Oranienburg, Auschwitz, Neuengamme, Belsen, Ravensbrück, Dachau' – they leave the auditorium.[62]

The film showing that afternoon at Orly is *Nuit et brouillard* (1955), Alan Resnais' documentary about the Nazi concentration camp system, its title deriving from a secret order, issued by Adolf Hitler on December 1941, in response to the situation in occupied France, where Resistance operations were steadily growing.[63] The decree provided for the methods to deter the population in all of Nazi-occupied western Europe from engaging in such operations; Resistance activities were now punishable by death, the order allowing military courts to impose sentences without a unanimous decision that had been required previously. Prisoners arrested under this order were meant to disappear in the night and fog (*Nacht und Nebel*), and even their death in camps, detention barracks, or prison was not to be divulged.[64]

At first sight, *Nuit et brouillard* is perhaps a curious feature for a *matinée* at an airport cinema, especially when it forms part of a double bill with Hitchcock's *Spellbound*; but Godard's inclusion of Resnais' documentary is clearly deliberate, since earlier in *Une Femme mariée*, discussion of concentration camps has taken place. When Charlotte meets her husband's passenger, the famous intellectual, Roger Leenhardt, at the airport and he mentions the Auschwitz trials, her mind immediately connects with the thalidomide public inquiry in Liège, a subject of pressing concern to her when she later takes up the subject of childbirth with his doctor. On being reminded of the real meaning of Auschwitz, she says 'Ah oui, Hitler', but cannot comprehend its true significance. Her failure, or dislocation, of sensibility is brought home to us at Orly when she and Robert walk out of the auditorium, just before Resnais' film coolly announces:

> A concentration camp can be constructed in the form of a sta-
> dium, or a hotel, with contractors estimates, competition and no
> set style. That's left up to you. Alpine style. Garage style. Japanese
> style. Without style. Architects calmly invent thresholds that you
> cross once, and once only.[65]

In her clear-eyed account of the trial of Adolf Eichmann, the architect of the Final Solution, Hannah Arendt wrote of 'the banality of evil'. As described here by Resnais' screenwriter, Jean Cayrol, the banal processes involved in the construction and design of the death camps, could equally well apply to the creation of airports, where, occasionally, owing to accidents, those who pass over the threshold into airspace never return.

One needs to exercise tact here; but the connection between airports and concentration camps is surprisingly frequently made. At the beginning of Erica Jong's *Fear of Flying*, the heroine, Isadora Zelda White Stollerman Wing, finds herself on a plane with her second husband, Bennett, a Chinese-American Freudian analyst, and 116 other shrinks (as well as their families) travelling to Vienna to attend a psychoanalytic 'Congress': 'At 6 a.m. we landed at Frankfurt Flughafen and shuffled out into a rubber-floored lounge, which for all its gleaming newness, made me think of death-camps and deportations.'[66] In 1972, two years before his death in Ermenonville, Francis Hope even thought the connection was common enough to be hackneyed:

> The cliche has it that aircraft and airports are characteristic of
> modern alienation: like workers to the factory or undesirables to
> the gas chamber, passengers are herded down Musak-loud corri-
> dors into one set of metal boxes after another, without either
> knowledge or control of their fate.[67]

It is difficult not to dismiss such connections as self-serving; yet these depictions of the existential condition do constitute a final position from which to regard airspaces.

This thesis of extreme passivity is certainly supported in recent critical theory. At the core of Maurice Blanchot's abstract meditations in *The Writing of the Disaster* (1995) lies the Holocaust, which he presents as an instance of 'disaster' (a word, he claims, that can hardly be uttered 'without betrayal, without false aspiration') and the terminal point of human history: 'The holocaust, the *absolute* event of history – which is a date in history – that utter-burn where all history took fire, where the movement of Meaning was swallowed up'.[68] Disaster lies 'beyond the pale of writing' and is, in its 'stress upon minutiae' and the 'sovereignty of the accidental', a matter of oblivion. Modernity is the age of passivity, 'the effacement, the extenuation of the subject' but even for Blanchot that very term, 'passivity', is insufficient since it 'is never passive enough'. Always insufficiently abject, we are ruled and persecuted by larger events we can never grasp. In such a situation, all that is left, all that 'remains to be said' of disaster, is: 'Shining solitude, the void of the sky, a deferred death'.[69]

These three elements lie triumphantly at the heart of Resnais' film *La Guerre est finie*, made ten years after *Nuit et brouillard*. It concerns Diego Mora (Yves Montand), a middle-aged Spaniard living in France who has devoted his life to being a professional revolutionary. Having learned that Franco's secret police have infiltrated their organization, and are about to arrest Juan, one of its leaders, Diego curtails a brief stay in Spain to travel back to France and warn his chief. Once in Paris, he returns to Marianne (Ingrid Thulin), a Swedish woman with whom he has been living in the city for a number of years and who is as much an exile as he. The following day he meets his chief (Jean Daste) who criticizes him for having left Spain so suddenly, and having lost 'all political perspective'; he is ordered to remain in Paris and reflect on his impulsive behaviour. A few hours later, however, Diego receives news of a comrade's sudden death from a heart attack. He volunteers to replace him and leaves by car for

Madrid, to save Juan. In fact, it is Diego, not Juan, whom the Fascist government in Spain regards as the important leader; it plans to apprehend him once he is back in the capital, and imprison him without trial. Consequently, Marianne is enlisted to fly ahead to Barcelona to intercept her lover, and return him to France.

In the closing moments of the film, she stands at an Air France check-in desk on the main concourse at Orly, that vast expanse of glass and steel, whose smooth, polished surfaces echo with the sound of flight announcements, the resonant click of heels on stone. The clerk staples a baggage check onto her ticket, and having done so, wishes her *bon voyage* in a routinely pleasant voice. Marianne hastens through the great terminal and, like Charlotte before her, ascends the escalator, the noise of the tannoy echoing around her. Seeing her flight is about to depart, she almost runs along the interminable corridor which stretches towards the imminently departing Caravelle, towards Diego.[70]

An innovative aspect of *La Guerre est finie* was Resnais' extensive use of the future conditional tense, in the form of anticipatory shots or 'flash-forwards' to illustrate what characters think might take place – the fascinations of possibility. This closing scene on the Orly pier is especially striking in this regard. A superimposed shot of Diego gracefully dissolves into one of Marianne, suggesting an indissoluble union, and despite the fact that the word *FIN* now appears on the screen, it does not obliterate her. Whatever happens beyond the terminal, considerable progress has been made; Marianne, up to this point sympathetic but not active in the cause, has emerged from political seclusion. What happens at Orly represents not so much an end, but a new beginning.

In ending his film in this way, Resnais was clearly mindful of another airport scene, probably the most famous in cinema. Its twin propellers spinning brightly in the night fog, a small airliner bearing the distinctive 'winged horse' livery of Air France, coasts to a stop at a small airport in French Morocco, one of a series

274

Diego and Marianne:
a four-frame sequence
from Alain Resnais' *La
Guerre est finie* (1966).

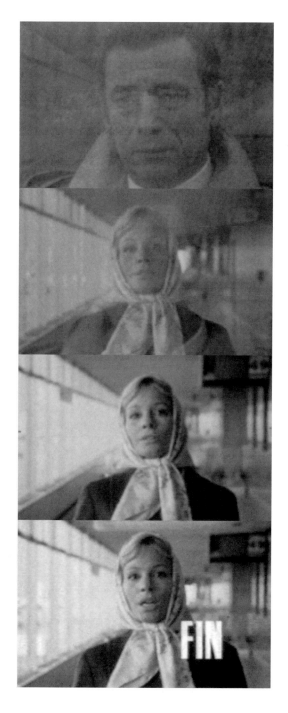

strung out like beads on a necklace stretching across the Sahara between Toulouse and Dakar. It is December 1941, just after the *Nacht und Nebel* decree. A few years earlier, this same airport, 4 miles south of the coastal city of Casablanca, had become synonymous with French colonial bureaucratic officiousness: 'Monsieur de St. Exupéry, I am obliged to advise Paris to take disciplinary action against you, for banking too close to the hangars on take-off from Casablanca.'[71] Now, however, that same 'petty spite' is being directed at those individuals, stateless and in exile, who find themselves in this North African city, awaiting letters of transit which will allow them to leave on the daily flight to Lisbon, now boarding on the dimly lit apron.

The first passengers are already making their way across the oily tarmac towards the plane to supervise the loading of their luggage. One of these, a tall blond man wearing an off-white suit, is Victor Laszlo (Paul Henreid), a French Resistance leader of Czechoslovakian extraction who has succeeded in impressing 'half the world' by escaping from a German concentration camp. As he stands by the Lockheed Electra, he seems preoccu-

The winged horse: a still from Michael Curtis's 1943 film *Casablanca*.

Rick and Ilse: a still from *Casablanca*.

pied, dumbstruck even, and does not look back at the gloomy hangars, which double as terminal buildings, nor at a couple of lovers standing edgily by them, the brims of their hats almost touching. The man is small and pale and his hands are stuffed deep into the pockets of the beige trench coat he wears, fastened tightly. Rick Blaine (Humphrey Bogart) is in his late thirties, though he looks much older; since his arrival in Casablanca, he has clearly spent too many late nights at the club he owns on the edge of the airfield, 'Rick's Café Américain'. No doubt he has often been kept awake by the airport's beacon sweeping across the exterior of his establishment like a prison searchlight, and by the aircraft taking off for the freedom of neutrality. Standing beside Blaine is Ilse Lund (Ingrid Bergman), a striking Scandinavian woman in her late twenties, married to Victor. Eighteen months earlier, just before the Germans marched into the city, she and Rick met in Paris; the affair which began there is ending here, on the threshold of a runway.

This airport scene, from *Casablanca*, was filmed in a studio in Hollywood, on a carefully constructed set and with only a vague idea of a conclusion. Fog-machines generated mist from more than half a million cubic feet of vaporized oil; carpenters had built the interior of the hangar and had also constructed a twin-engined plane, scaled down in size to create the illusion that the studio air-strip was larger than it actually was. Central casting even procured midgets to sit in the dummy plane's windows, to add to the illusion.[72] As scriptwriter Howard Koch recalled, 'The ending of the film was in the air until the very end. We thought of many possibilities and finally decided on the one that was in the film.'[73] The airport was a ghostly theatre of possibility, a stage on which past present and future might converge. Earlier in the film, after hearing Ilse explain that she had abandoned him in Paris because after learning that her husband, Laszlo, whom she thought had died in a concentration camp, was in fact alive, Rick observes: '… it's still a story without an ending.' Now, on the apron of Casablanca airport, with the story about to end, we see that Ilse is on the threshold of tears. A senior Vichy policeman looks away, awkwardly, and enters the names of Mr and Mrs Laszlo on the precious letters of transit, the exit visas which will allow them to leave the colony. Rick is speaking quickly, telling Ilse that she will be boarding the plane with Victor, while he will be staying behind. As she protests, he asks her: 'Do you have any idea what you'd have to look forward to if you stayed here? Nine chances out of ten we'd both wind up in a concentration camp.'

> *Rick*: Inside of us, we both know you belong with Victor. You're part of his work, the thing that keeps him going. If that plane leaves the ground and you're not with him, you'll regret it. Maybe not today. Maybe not tomorrow, but soon and for the rest of your life.
> *Ilse*: But what about us?
> *Rick*: We'll always have Paris. We didn't have, we lost it until you came to Casablanca. We got it back last night.

The dim outline of the present: a still from *Casablanca*.

Here, on the apron, the reality of their lives, the only version of themselves that has ever really mattered, exists at one remove, in the memories of Paris they'll 'always have'. In the life to come, this foggy airport will serve to illuminate only the dim outline of the present. As ever at this ultimate threshold, the past is left behind, so that, at the final call, a future only beckons beyond airspace.

References

All translations are the author's unless otherwise stated.

INTRODUCTION

1 The Chicago Convention on International Civil Aviation of 1944 grants 'complete' and 'exclusive' sovereignty to each state in the airspace above its territory. For future developments, see Chia-Jui Cheng, ed., *The Use of Airspace and Outer Space for All Mankind in the 21st Century* (The Hague, 1995).

2 Allen Curnow, 'Narita', in *Early Days Yet: New and Collected Poems 1941–97* (Manchester, 1997), p. 32. Curnow later explained the background to the poem: 'Narita was Tokyo's very new airport, "small green hills with ginkgo trees", only a week before we flew out, a JAL Boeing 747 on an internal flight crashed, killing 500; only a few weeks earlier, as many died when another 747 went down west of Ireland; Narita was a memento mori for anybody presenting a boarding pass that week.' Quoted in Peter Robinson, 'Allen Curnow's Travels', *English*, 49 (2000), pp. 39–64; p. 60.

3 Brigid Brophy, *In Transit* (London, 1969) p. 24.

4 Michel Serres, *Angels: A Modern Myth*, trans. Philippa Hurd (Paris, 1995), p. 8. For an important reading of this aspect of Serres' philosophy, see Marcel Hénaff, 'Of Stones, Angels and Humans; Serres and the Global City', *Substance*, 83 (1997), pp. 59–80.

5 *Ibid.*, pp. 65–7.

6 *Ibid.*, p. 67.

7 Christopher Ricks, *T.S. Eliot and Prejudice* (London, 1988), pp. 209–10.

8 *Ibid.*, p. 9.

9 Andy Warhol, *From A to B* (London, 1976) p. 145.

10 Brophy, *In Transit*, pp. 22–3.

11 See Sarah Birch, *Christine Brooke-Rose and Contemporary Fiction* (Oxford, 1994) p. 73.

12 Christine Brooke-Rose, *Between* (London, 1968), p. 8.

13 *Ibid.*, p. 29.

14 For a fine account of *Between*, which develops this theme in greater detail, see Karen R. Lawrence, *Penelope Voyages: Women and Travel in the British Literary Tradition* (Ithaca, NY, 1994), chap. 5.

15 J. H. Prynne, 'Airport Poem: Ethics of Survival', in *Poems* (Newcastle upon Tyne, 1999), p. 38.

16 Wolfgang Tillmans, *Concorde* (Cologne, 1997), n.p.

17 My account of the Gonesse crash is derived from the preliminary report by the Bureau d'Enquêtes Accidents, published in August 2000 and available at www.bea-fr.org in French and at www.bea-fr.org/anglaise/index.htm in English translation; and reports in *Le Monde*, 27–9 July 2000.

18 François Maspero, *Roissy Express: A Journey Through the Paris Suburbs*, trans. Paul Jones (London, 1994), p. 26.

19 'Men in white and the bereaved move silently though this graveyard of supersonic aircraft' (*Independent*, 27 July 2000, p. 3).

20 This sentence alludes to ll. 11 and 16 of Stephen Spender's 1933 poem 'The Landscape Near an Aerodrome'; see *Selected Poems* (London, 1965), p. 32.

21 This sentence alludes to the final lines of W. H. Auden's 1938 poem 'Musée des Beaux Arts'; see *Collected Poems* (London, 1976), p. 147.

I THRESHOLDS OF MODERNITY

1 Rigas Doganis, *The Airport Business* (Basingstoke, 1992), p. 1.

2 Steven Bode and Jeremy Millar, *Airport* (London, 1997), p. 54.

3 For accounts of heterotopia, see George Teyssot, 'Heterotopias and the History of Spaces', *Architecture + Urbanism* (October 1980), pp. 80–100; Catherine Ingraham, 'Utopia/Heterotopia', in Andreas Papadakis, ed., *Deconstruction III*, Architectural Design Profile no. 87 (London, 1994); Edward Soja, *Postmodern Geographies: The Reassertion of Space in Critical Social Theory* (London, 1989). On Marc Augé's formulation of the 'non-place', see John Frow, *Time and Commodity Culture: Essays in Cultural Theory and Postmodernity* (Oxford, 1997).

4 J. G. Ballard, *Crash* (London, 1973).

5 J. G. Ballard, 'The Ultimate Departure Lounge', in Bode and Millar, eds, *Airport*, p. 119.

6 Chris Goode, 'The History of Airports', in *Boomer Console* (Cambridge, 2000), n.p. I am grateful to Anthony Paraskeva for bringing this pamphlet to my attention.

7 F. Scott Fitzgerald, *The Last Tycoon* (New York, 1941), p. 10.

8 See Ruth Bowman, *Murals without Walls: Arshile Gorky's Aviation Murals Rediscovered* (Newark, 1978).

9 On Saarinen's building, see Ezra Stoller, ed., *The TWA Terminal* (Princeton, 1999); Toshio Nakamura, ed., *Eero Saarinen: Architecture and Urbanism* (Tokyo, 1984); Eero Saarinen, *Eero Saarinen On His Work* (New Haven, 1968); Allan Temko, *Eero Saarinen* (New York, 1962).

10 Paul Andreu, 'The Airport Town', in *Airport*, p. 76.

11 J. G. Ballard, 'Unlocking the Past', in *A User's Guide to the Millennium* (London, 1996).

12 J. G. Ballard, *Empire of the Sun* (London, 1984), p. 160.

13 J. G. Ballard, 'The Ultimate Departure Lounge', in *Airport*, p. 119.

14 Martin Amis, *London Fields* (London, 1989), p. 2.

15 Brigid Brophy, *In Transit* (London, 1969), p. 20.

16 Marcel Plantevigne, *Avec Marcel Proust* (Paris, 1966), p. 351.

17 Marcel Proust, *À la Recherche du temps perdu*, ed. Jean Yves Tadié (Paris, 1999), p. 535.

18 Marc Augé, *Non-places: Introduction to an Anthropology of Supermodernity*, trans. John Howe (London, 1995), pp. 92–3.

19 *Ibid.*, p. 110.

20 *Baudelaire: Selected Verse*, ed. and trans. Francis Scarfe (Harmondsworth, 1961), p. 125.

21 ['Un port est un séjour charmant pour une âme fatiguée des luttes de la vie. L'ampleur du ciel, l'architecture mobile des nuages, les colorations changeantes de la mer, le scintillement des phares, sont un prisme merveilleusement propre à amuser les yeux sans jamais les lasser. Les formes élancées des navires, au gréement compliqué, auxquels la houle imprime des oscillations

harmonieuses, servent à entretenir dans l'âme le goût du rhythme et de la beauté. Et puis, surtout, il y a une sorte de plaisir mystérieux et aristocratique pour celui qui n'a plus ni curiosité ni ambition, à contempler, couché dans le belvédère ou accoudé sur le môle, tous ces mouvements de ceux qui partent et de ceux qui reviennent, de ceux qui ont encore la force de vouloir, le désir de voyager ou de s'enrichir' (Charles Baudelaire, *Petits Poëmes en Prose*, ed. Robert Kopp [Paris, 1969], p. 121)].

22 *À la Recherche*, p. 1055.

23 *Ibid.*, p. 2093.

24 For an account of angels in Proust, see Marie Miguet-Ollagnier, *La Mythologie de Marcel Proust* (Paris, 1982), pp. 283–6.

25 My account of Agostinelli's death owes much to George D. Painter's magisterial biography *Marcel Proust*, new edn (London, 1989), 2 vols, vol. II, pp. 211–14.

26 *Ibid.*, p. 211.

27 *À la Recherche*, p. 1081.

28 Bibliothèque Nationale, Proust manuscript 16742 NAF, p. 121. Shortly before he died, Proust was revising *La Prisonnière*. As W. C. Carter observes, '… since any ascension is vertical in nature, the inclusion of this word would be redundant, were it not for the thematic importance of the aviator's ascension' (*The Proustian Quest* [New York, 1992], p. 199). I am much indebted to Professor Carter's account of Proust's recourse to metaphors of flight. For another account of the same topic, see Margaret Mein, 'Les Ailes, le vol, et l'aviation dans La Recherche et dans les Cahiers de Proust,' *Etudes Proustiennes IV: Marcel Proust et la critique anglo-saxonne* (Paris, 1982), pp. 161–85.

29 *À la Recherche*, p. 1081.

30 *Ibid.*, p. 2065.

31 *Ibid.*, p. 441.

32 *Ibid.*

33 In a posthumously published article on the music of Reynaldo Hahn, Proust compared the musical score to a runway on which the composer accelerated in order to achieve a flight of higher altitude: 'C'est au contact même du texte, qu'il prend la force de s'elever plus haut que lui, comme ces aviateurs qui courent sur la terre avant de servir de leurs ailes, mais pour mieux s'envoler et plus haut'. See Philip Kolb and Larkin B. Price, eds, *Textes Retrouvés* (Urbana, 1968), p. 196. Kolb dates the piece between June 1909 and July 1914 – that is, it was written before Agostinelli's accident.

34 *À la Recherche*, p. 2282.

35 *Ibid.*, p. 1908.

36 *Ibid.*, p. 2284; p. 57; p. 2256.

37 *Ibid.*, p. 1529.

38 Cited in Painter, *Marcel Proust*, vol. II, p. 210.

39 For a fine account of painters' enthusiasms for aviation, see Robert Wohl, *A Passion for Wings: Aviation and the Western Imagination 1908–1918* (New Haven, 1994), chap. 6.

40 Stefan Zweig, *The World of Yesterday* (Lincoln, NB, 1964), p. 196.

41 Le Corbusier, *Aircraft* (London, 1935), p. 7.

42 *Ibid.*

43 *Ibid.* Le Corbusier offers an alternative version of the escapade in *Sur Les 4*

Routes (Paris, 1941).

44 Cited in Wohl, *A Passion for Wings*, p. 109.

45 ['Vor dem Aerodrom liegt noch ein grosser Platz mit verdachtigen Holzhauschen, für die wir andere Aufschriften erwartet hatten, als: Garage, Grand Bufett International und so weiter' (Franz Kafka, 'Die Aeroplane in Brescia', in *Drucke zu Lebzeiten*, ed. Wolf Kittler, Hans-Gerd Kock and Gerhard Neumann [Frankfurt, 1987], pp. 401-12)]. For a fine account of the meeting, see Wohl, *A Passion for Wings*, pp. 111–14; for an intriguing fictional riff, see Guy Davenport, 'The Aeroplanes at Brescia', in *Tatlin!* (Baltimore, 1974), a short story which imagines a meeting between Kafka and Wittgenstein on the airfield at Brescia.

46 On the connections between aviation and politics in Italy, see Wohl, *A Passion for Wings*, pp. 287–8; Bruno Mantura, Patrizia Rosazza-Ferraris and Livia Velani, eds, *Futurism in Flight: Aeropittura Paintings and Sculptures of Man's Conquest of Space (1913–1945)* (Rome, 1991).

47 François Maspero, *Roissy Express: A Journey Through the Paris Suburbs*, trans. Paul Jones (London, 1994), p. 6.

48 Charles de Gaulle, 'Allocution prononcée à l'inauguration de l'Aérogare d'Orly', *Discours et Message: Avec le renouveau, Mai 1958–Juillet 1962* (Paris, 1964).

49 My account of this accident draws on reports in *The Times*, 4 June 1962, and *Le Monde*, 5 June 1962.

50 Quoted in David Bourdon, *Warhol* (New York, 1989), p. 118. On Warhol's early work, see Thomas Crow, 'Saturday Disasters: Trace and Reference in Early Warhol', in *Reconstructing Modernism*, ed. Serge Guibaut (Cambridge, MA, 1990); Hal Foster, 'Death in America', *October*, 75 (1996), pp. 37–59.

51 And yet this painting was not as final a word as it might have been on the Orly disaster. The report was contingent; 130, not 129, people died. Another person who walked along the terminal pier and boarded the plane should have been remembered but is left behind; he exists as a phantom around this image, a ghost in the machinery.

52 Roland Barthes, *The Eiffel Tower and Other Mythologies*, trans. Richard Howard (New York, 1979), p. 3. 'Le fer donne en effet à la circulation humaine une image nouvelle, celle du jet; comme fondu d'un seul trait (même si, en fait, il est minutieusement assemblé), l'ouvrage métallique semble jeté par-dessus l'obstacle, d'un mouvement rapide, suggérant ainsi que le temps lui-même est vaincu, raccourci d'un tour preste et préfigurant une fois de plus le jet de l'avion par-dessus les continents et les océans' (Roland Barthes, *La Tour Eiffel*, with photographs by A. Martin [Lausanne, 1964], p. 62).

53 Chris Marker, *La Jetée: Ciné-roman* (New York, 1992), n.p.; the French text of the voice-over is also published in *L'Avant-scène cinéma*, no. 38 (June 1964), pp. 23–30. In my reading of Marker's film, I have found the following articles useful: Paul Sandro, 'Singled Out by History: La Jetée, and the Aesthetics of Memory', *French Cultural Studies*, 10 (1999), pp. 107–27; Constance Penley, 'Time Travel, Primal Scene, and the Critical Dystopia', *Camera Obscura*, 15 (1986), pp. 67–84; Bruce Kawin, 'Time and Stasis in *La Jetée*', *Film Quarterly*, 36 (1982), pp. 15–20.

54 Ballard, '*La Jetée*', in *A User's Guide to the Millennium*, pp. 28–9.

55 Jacques Derrida, 'Some Statements and Truisms about Neologism, Newisms, Postism, Parasitisms, and other Small Seismisms', trans. Anne Tomiche, in

David Carroll, *States of Theory: History, Arts and Critical Discourse* (New York, 1990), pp. 63–94; p. 84.

56 Ballard, 'La Jetée', p. 29.

II LANDSCAPES OF PRE-EMPTION

1 Goethe, *Faust*, trans. Philip Wayne (Harmondsworth, 1951), pt II, pp. 252ff.
All further quotations will be taken from this translation.
['Kluger Herren, führe Knechten
Gruben gräben, dämmten ein
Schmälerten des Meeres Rechte
Herrn an seiner Statt zu sein']

2 ['Dort im Fernsten ziehn Segel,
Suchen nachtlich sichern Bort.
Kennen doch ihr Rest di Vogel,
Denn jetzt ist der Hafen dort.']

3 ['Die Sonne sinkt, die letzten Schiffe,
Sie ziehen munter hafenein.
Ein grosser Kahn is im Begriffe,
Auf dem Kanale hier zu sein.
… Wie segelt froh der bunte Kahn
Mits frischem Abendwind heran!
Wie turmt sich sein behender Lauf
In Kisten, Kasten, Sächen auf!']

4 ['Von dieser Stelle ging es aus,
Hier stand das erste Bretterhaus
Ein Gräbchen ward hinabgerißt,
Wo jetzt das Ruder emsig sprißt.']

5 ['Doch sei der Lindewuchs vernichtet
Zu halbverkohlter Stamme Graun.
Ein Luginsland ist bald errichtet
Um ins Unendliche zu schaun.']

6 Marshall Berman, *All That Is Solid Melts Into Air* (New York, 1982), p. 48. See also pp. 66-71 for a fine reading of the 'Baucis and Philemon' episode.

7 On the connections between Faust and aviation, see Robert Wohl, *A Passion for Wings: Aviation and the Western Imagination 1908–1918* (New Haven, 1994), p. 256.

8 The standard history of Schiphol airport is M.L.J. Dierikx and Bram Bouwens, *Building Castles in the Air: Schiphol Amsterdam and the Development of Airport Infrastructure in Europe 1916–1996* (Amsterdam, 1998); but see also Koos Bosma and Martijn Vos, 'The Demise of a Dinosaur', *Archis*, 2 (1998), pp. 8–17.

9 For the history of the estate, see M. Menzel, *De Bijlmer as grensverleggend ideaal* (Delft, 1989).

10 Quoted in Philip Sherwood, *Heathrow: 2000 Years of History* (London, 1999), p. 17. In the account of Heathrow which follows, I am much indebted to Sherwood's research.

11 Don DeLillo, *Players* (London, 1977), p. 88.

12 H. G. Wells, *The War in the Air* (London, 1908), p. 207.

13 H. G. Wells, *The Sleeper Awakes* (London, 1899); see esp. chap. 16, 'The Monoplane'.

14 See Harold Penrose, *British Aviation: The Ominous Skies 1935–39* (London, 1980).

15 Quoted in Sherwood, *Heathrow*, p. 70.

16 W.F.A. Grimes, 'Prehistoric Temple at London Airport', *Archaeology*, I (1948), pp. 74–8.

17 The standard account of this subject is Guy Hartcup, *Camouflage: A History of Concealment and Deception in War* (New York, 1980); for a quirky and concise account, see Hillel Schwartz, *The Culture of the Copy* (New York, 1996), pp. 186–92.

18 David Lodge, 'The World Starts Here', *Observer*, 5 May 1996, p. 6.

19 'Aerial Art' (1969), in *The Writings of Robert Smithson: Essays with Illustrations*, ed. Nancy Holt (New York, 1979), p. 92.

20 'Towards the Development of an Air Terminal Site' (1967), in *The Writings of Robert Smithson*, p. 44.

21 Smithson, 'Aerial Art', p. 92.

22 Smithson, 'Towards the Development...', p. 45.

23 *Ibid.*, p. 45.

24 Henri Lefebvre, *The Production of Space*, trans. Donald Nicholson-Smith (Oxford, 1991), p. 53.

25 *Ibid.*, p. 165.

26 Arthur Hailey, *Airport* (London, 1968), p. 474.

27 *Ibid.*, p. 406.

28 William Faulkner, *Pylon* (New York, 1935), p. 17. For background to the novel, see Joseph Blotner, *Faulkner: A Biography* (London, 1974), vol. 1, pp. 830–87; Richard Gray, *The Life of William Faulkner* (Oxford, 1996), pp. 193–203.

29 Le Corbusier, *Aircraft* (London, 1935), pp. 11–12.

30 Faulkner, *Pylon*, p. 12.

31 Gray, *The Life of William Faulkner*, p. 201.

32 'The Schiphol Equation', *Guardian*, 6 October 1992, p. 18.

33 A good account of the cultural background to the Narita protests can be found in David Apter, *Against the State: Politics and Social Protest in Japan* (Cambridge, MA, 1984).

34 Hailey, *Airport*, p. 450.

35 François Maspero, *Roissy Express: A Journey Through the Paris Suburbs*, trans. Paul Jones (London, 1994), p. 5.

36 After the abortive attempt in the late 1960s to build London's third airport on an enlarged island in the Thames estuary, the airport island is again under consideration in Western Europe. In collaboration with the Dutch government (and perhaps in response to the Bijlmer accident), Rem Koolhaas's Office for Metropolitan Architecture (OMA) has provided a solution for Schiphol's problems. Rather than attempting to shoehorn more airport into the Harlemmemeer, Koolhaas proposes to split off a fragment of the nation itself and build a new city on an artificial island in the North Sea. At its heart would sit a giant airport, a new European hub, walled off by the ocean, connected by a bridge and governed by a charter; it would be both futuristic and medieval. See Gary Wolf, 'The Unmaterial World', *Wired* (June 2000), pp. 308–19.

37 Smithson, 'Towards the Development', p. 45.

38 My account of the construction of Kansai owes much to the detailed assessments of the entire project by Peter Buchanan in *Architectural Review*

(November 1994), pp. 33–71.

39 Faulkner, *Pylon*, p. 12.

40 Smithson, 'Towards the Development…', p. 43.

III SPLENDOURS OF SPACE

1 ['La beauté d'un aéroport, c'est la splendeur de l'éspace!' (Le Corbusier, '1946: L'Architecture et les aéroports modernes', in *Oeuvre Complète: 1938–1946*, ed. Willy Boesiger [Zürich, 1946], pp. 190–91)].

2 Compare also the account of early air travel scribbled in a notebook: 'All of a sudden I recall the airports of London, of Le Bourget, of Ascension, grassy, in the grass. Airplanes going 150 km. per hour, we would be puking for 4 or 6 hours. Pilots Mermoz, Saint-Exupery, killed in action, lost !!! = 1928 arrival in New Delhi 6 o'clock (Paris time) = 1 o'clock New Delhi time' (Le Corbusier, *Sketchbooks* [London, 1981], IV, 690).

3 Cited in Jean Dethier, ed., *All Stations* (London, 1981), p. 6.

4 Henry Petroski, *Invention by Design: How Engineers Get From Thought to Thing* (Cambridge, MA, 1996), p. 104.

5 Le Corbusier, *Precisions*, trans. Edith Schreiber Aujame (Cambridge, MA, 1991), p. 255.

6 Erich Mendelsohn, *Letters of an Architect*, ed. Oskar Beyer, trans. G. Strachan (London, 1967), p. 99.

7 Le Corbusier, *Urbanisme* (Paris, 1925), p. 177.

8 Reyner Banham, *Theory and Design in the First Machine Age* (London, 1960), p. 132. Banham also suggests that Sant'Elia's ideas for the multilevel city may have come from his friend Gustav Kahn, who had drawn his attention to the theories of the communard doctor Tony Moilin, who maintained that Paris' traffic problems could only be solved by the construction of streets at various levels, with overground and underground railways converging at a central station.

9 Le Corbusier, *Urbanisme*, p. 180.

10 *Ibid.*, pp. 180–81.

11 Le Corbusier, 'The Temperature of Paris', in *Precisions* (Cambridge, MA, 1987), p. 255.

12 Wright's visionary scheme was developed over several decades and incorporates several changes. He first published a description in 1932, in *The Disappearing City*, fleshing out the ideas further in a series of articles such as 'Today … Tomorrow, American Tomorrow', *American Architect* (May 1932), pp. 14–17; 'Broadacre City: A New Community Plan', *Architectural Record*, 77 (April 1935), from which the above quotation was taken, and later books such as *When Democracy Builds* (1935) and *The Living City* (1958). The best treatment of the project is Robert Fishman, *Urban Utopias of the Twentieth Century* (Cambridge, MA, 1982).

13 Le Corbusier, *The Radiant City: Elements of a Doctrine of Urbanism to be Used as the Basis of Our Machine-Age Civilization* (London, 1935).

14 Le Corbusier, *Aircraft* (London, 1935), caption 14.

15 Wolfgang Voigt, 'From the Hippodrome to the Aerodrome, from the Air Station to the Terminal: European Airports', in John Zukowsky, ed., *Building for Air Travel* (New York, 1996), pp. 27–51.

16 Le Corbusier, *The Radiant City*, p. 277.

17 Le Corbusier, *The Four Routes*, trans. Dorothy Todd (London, 1947), p. 106.

18 Charles Jencks, *Modern Movements in Architecture* (London, 1973), p. 153.

19 Henri Lefebvre, *The Production of Space*, trans. Donald Nicholson-Smith (Oxford, 1991), pp. 43, 303.

20 Martin Heidegger, *The Question Concerning Technology and Other Essays*, trans. William Lovitt (New York, 1977), p. 17. See Leo Marx, 'On Heidegger's Conception of "Technology" and Its Historical Validity', *Massachussetts Review*, 25 (1984), pp. 638–52.

21 ['Un aéroport semblerait donc devoir être nu, entièrement à plein ciel, à pleine prairie, à pleine piste de ciment' ('L'Architecture et les aéroports modernes', p. 191)].

22 ['Architecture à deux dimensions'; 'A l'envol comme à l'atterrissage, l'aéroport apparaitra dans les dessins précis de ses pistes' (*Ibid.*)].

23 Le Corbusier, *Towards a New Architecture* (London, 1927).

24 ['Une fois au sol, une seule architecture semble tolérable et parfaitement admissible: c'est celle des magnifiques avions qui vous ont amenés ou que vous allez prendre, et qui occupent devant vous l'espace visible. Leur biologie est telle, leur forme est une telle expression d'harmonie, qu'aucune architecture ne devient raisonnable' ('L'Architecture et les aéroports modernes', p. 191)].

25 ['L'art se fait par addition de faits en présence // Karachi air port les avions de divers arts // le ciel Passent les Shell ou Burma Tanks p. ravitaillement d'essence. Toutes couleurs, le graphisme des inscriptions enormes ou petites, pleines de style. La piste nuancée, huilée devant le batiment, géometrique ailleurs les bagages qui sont tirés sur des chariots, les échelles approchées des appareils arrivés. Les hommes qui s'affairent. Une vieille chienne à tetines qui finit ses jours sur le parvis en quête de quoi? etc Question: Qu'est ce qu'un Tableau peint de pommiers en fleurs, ou d'un paquet de tabac peut bien foutre aujourd'hui exception faite d'un Fouquet d'un Chardin d'un Greco! L'aluminium poli des avions leur pureté admirable // L'herbe brulée de l'horizon // le bigarré des avions selon Iranian Air Way // Air France // Air India continental // Boac. // TWA. // PAA etc' (Le Corbusier, *Sketchbooks*, III, 364)].

26 ['Un mur de belles pierres assemblées, de 2m. 50 de haut, derrière lequel s'étendront à volonté les locaux de réception, de douane etc … et le sous-sol nécessaire sera le seul élément architectural debout sur le terrain' ('L'Architecture et les aéroports modernes,' p. 191)].

27 ['le lieu de débarquement des passagers pourrait être le plus coquet ou le plus noble parterre de fleurs ou de broderie que l'on voudra. Autant débarquer dans des fleurs que dans des pierres de Bourgogne! … Que le Hollande apporte des champs de tulipes et Versailles des parterres de broderies!' (*Ibid.*)].

28 ['prédiction aéroport 3 m haut + fleurs 1946 (ce matin à Nice, ça y est … La mer // La piste totale // les fleurs // les avions impeccables // le macadam // la mer // les fleurs' (Le Corbusier, *Sketchbooks*, III, 124)].

29 Reyner Banham, 'The Obsolescent Airport', *Architectural Review*, 132 (1962), p. 252.

30 George Orwell, *Keep the Aspidistra Flying* (London, 1936).

31 ['L-C trouver 1 nom au musée d'Ahmedabad. L-C fournira des idées = des thèmes le Génie des Formes. Ie Super Constellation est beau: il est comme un

poisson il aurait pu être comme un oiseau (Le Corbusier, *Sketchbooks*, III, p. 637)].

32 ['27 oct 51 /l le WC + le lavabo sont étonnants de confort des petites mesures + d'éclairage //les cuvettes des lavabos en acier inoxyd de / 16 x 28 cm(?) // chaud + vidange + froid. il faut à tout prix obtenir plan de ces installations' (Le Corbusier, *Sketchbooks*)].

33 Michael Brawne, 'Airport Passenger Buildings', *Architectural Review*, 132 (1962), p. 341.

34 Lewis Mumford, *The Pentagon of Power* (New York, 1974), p. 180ff.

35 ['... Etc Mais depuis "les réacteurs" un autre cap est passé: c'est le projectile = un perforateur et non plus un glisseur' (Le Corbusier, *Sketchbooks*, III, p. 637)].

36 ['L'Aérogare nouvelle a bon coup d'oeil Mais l'acoustique est a/ catastrophique: Haut parleur inintelligible, vacarme des assiettes et plateaux du Bar. b/ On y étouffe (et pourtant on est à l'ombre! ! !) ... Ce vacarme est abominable ... j'ai en 3/4 d'heure, attrape une migraine effroyable' (*Ibid.*, IV, 136)].

37 ['Par dessus le micro les stridences des Boeings + les claksons + les appels' (*Ibid.*, IV, 789)].

38 ['Ce matin à midi à Orly tout est "acoustique", silencieux propre et vaste. C'est un très beau bâtiment. Et les gens critiquent. J'écrirai une note à l'architecte ingénieur d'Orly Des salauds ont installé dans le Gd hall 14 horribles lustres dorés en couronne' (*Ibid.*, IV, 790)].

39 ['J'ai refusé le Boeing parce que c'est American taste, même tenu par les Indiens! ! Constellation = 550 Km au lieu de 1 100. Mais ici je suis chez moi, aux indes aériennes, l'hôtesse et le stewart = gentils Constellation Air India est très bien tenu (Tata) Indiens et Francais s'entendent naturellement. Mais l'USA inonde le monde de sa bêtise et médiocrite humaine' (*Ibid.*, IV, 688)].

40 François Maspero suggests that jets 'are more sinister, more directly threatening and cruel' than piston aircraft, their 'Great metal bodies devoid of a sense of speed and space-conquering freedom, leaving just the faintest reflection of cold-blooded murder on their grey rivetted forms' (*Roissy Express* [London, 1994], p. 128).

41 Clive James, *Flying Visits: Postcards from the Observer* (London, 1984), p. 8.

42 Saul Bellow, *Humboldt's Gift* (New York, 1975), pp. 404–5.

43 Les Murray, 'The International Terminal', *Collected Poems* (Manchester, 1998), p. 327.

44 Thomas Pynchon, *Vineland* (London, 1990), p. 62.

45 Bellow, *Humboldt's Gift*, p. 406.

46 P. St John Turner, *Pictorial History of Pan American World Airways* (London, 1973), chap. 12.

47 Norman Foster, 'Boeing 747', *Building Sights*, ed. Ruth Rosenthal (London 1994) pp. 110–14.

48 Banham, *The Obsolescent Airport*, p. 252.

49 On the development of JFK, see Dudley Hunt Jr, 'Idlewild: How Idlewild was Planned for the Jet Age', *Architectural Record* (September 1961), pp. 152–6; Geoffrey Arend, *Kennedy International*, rev. edn (New York, 1987); James Kaplan, *The Airport: Terminal Nights and Runway Days at John F. Kennedy International* (New York, 1995).

50 Wood Lockhart, 'A Pilot's Perspective on Airport Design', in Zukowsky, *Building for Air Travel*, pp. 213–25.

51 On the rationale of CDG, see Elliot Feldman, *Concorde and Dissent* (Cambridge, 1985), chap. 2.

52 Paul Andreu, 'The Airport Town', in Bode and Millar, eds, *Airport*, p. 76.

53 In my account of Andreu's work at CDG, I am indebted to Filippo Beltrami Gadola, *Paul Andreu: The Discovery of Universal Space* (Milan, 1997), and Serge Salat and François Labbe, *Paul Andreu: Metamorphosis of the Circle*, trans. Ronald Corlette Theuil (Milan, 1990).

54 *Ibid.*, p. 79.

55 *Ibid.*, p. 78.

56 Michel Serres, *Angels: A Modern Myth* (Paris, 1995), p. 10.

57 Clive James, *Flying Visits: Postcards from The Observer* (London, 1984), p. 108.

58 *Ibid.*

59 Kenneth Powell, *Stansted: Norman Foster and the Architecture of Flight* (London, 1992), p. 51.

60 For entertaining accounts of Foster's airport, see Martin Pawley, 'Hong Kong: Chep Lap Kok – The Airport as Saviour of the City', in Rowan Moore, ed., *Vertigo: The Strange New World of the Contemporary City* (London, 1999), pp. 90–105; Peter Davey, 'Plane Sailing', *Architectural Review*, 203 (September 1998), pp. 50–63.

61 Davey, 'Plane Sailing', p. 50.

IV THEATRES OF WAR

1 Stephen Spender, 'The Landscape near an Aerodrome', l. 27. The poem, first published in 1933, identifies the chimneys and navigation beacons which made the area around Tempelhof airport so distinctive. Between 1930 and 1933, Spender spent about 6 months of each year in Germany. On his first visit to Berlin in 1930, he stayed in Schöneberg, the borough adjacent to Tempelhof, and spent much time acquainting himself with the area. See Stephen Spender, *World Within World* (London, 1951), chap. 3.

2 Stephen Spender, *European Witness* (London, 1946), pp. 228–9.

3 Bertolt Brecht, *Journals 1934–1955*, trans. Hugh Rorrison, ed. John Willett (London, 1993), p. 401.

4 Gitta Sereny, *Albert Speer: His Battle with Truth* (London, 1995), p. 598.

5 Albert Speer, *Spandau: The Secret Diaries*, trans. Richard and Clara Wilson (London, 1977), p. 78 ['In einer schnellen, komfortablen Reisemaschine bekam ich einen Fensterplatz, neben mir mein Guard. Nach meiner langen Gefängniszeit war dieser Flug bei strahlendemWetter ein aufregendes Erlebnis. Dörfer und kleine Städte lagen friedlich und wie unzerstört unter uns, die Äcker waren bestellt und die Wälder trotz aller Gerüchte nicht abgeholzt. Weil das Leben um mich die letzte Zeit stillgestanden hatte, war mir das Bewußtsein verlorengegangen, daß es draußen weiterging. Ein fahrender Zug, ein Schlepper auf der Elbe, ein rauchender Fabrikschornstein waren kleine Gefühlssensationen'].

6 *Ibid.*, p. 79 ['Wir kreuzten wohl eine halbe Stunde über dem Häuser- und Ruinenfeld Berlins. Während die Dakota große Schleifen flog, konnte ich die Ost-West-Achse, die ich zu Hitlers fünfzigstem Geburtstag fertiggestellt hatte, erkennen, dann das Olympiastadion mit seinen offensichtlich gepflegten grünen Rasenflächen und schließlich meinen Bau, die Reichskanzlei. Sie war noch erhalten, wenn auch durch einige Volltreffer beschädigt. Den

abgeholzten Tiergarten hielt ich zunächst für einen Flugplatz. Der Grunewald und die Havelseen waren unberührt in ihrer alten Schönheit'].

7 On the history of the *GBI* and, in particular, its connections with the SS slave-labour programmes, see Paul B. Jaskot, *The Architecture of Oppression* (London, 2000).

8 On Hitler's Chancellery, his plans for Berlin and Nazi architecture in general, see H. Reichhardt and W. Schäche, *Von Berlin nach Germania: Uber die Zerstörungen der Reichhauptstadt durch Albert Speers Neugestaltungsplanungen* (Berlin, 1986); Wolfgang Schäche, *Architektur und Städtebau in Berlin zwischen 1933–1945* (Berlin, 1991); Angela Schönberger, *Die neue Reichskanzlei von Albert Speer* (Berlin, 1981); Stephen D. Helmer, *Hitler's Berlin: The Speer Plans for Reshaping the Central City* (Ann Arbor, 1985); Barbara Miller Lane, *Architecture and Politics in Germany, 1918–1945* (Cambridge, MA, 1968); Brian Ladd, *The Ghosts of Berlin* (Chicago, 1997).

9 Anthony Read and David Fisher, *The Fall of Berlin* (London, 1992), p. 318.

10 The standard work on the history of Tempelhof is Laurenz Demps, *Flughafen Tempelhof. Die Geschichte einer Legende* (Berlin, 1998). On the older Tempelhof buildings, see Helmut Conin, *Gelandet in Berlin: Zur Geschichte der Berliner Flughafen* (Cologne, 1974); John Dower, 'Some Aerodromes in Germany and Holland', *Journal of the Royal Institute of British Architects*, 38 (4 April 1931), p. 351.

11 On the Air Ministry building, see Ladd, *The Ghosts of Berlin*, p. 146; Martin Gilbert, *Holocaust Journey* (London, 1997), p. 27.

12 Cited in Lars Olof Larsson, *Die Neugestaltung der Reichhauptstadt: Albert Speers General Bauungsplane für Berlin* (Stuttgart, 1978), p. 25. On the planning history of Sagebiel's airport, see Hans-Jachim Barun, 'The Airport as Symbol: Air Transport and Politics at Berlin Templehof, 1923–1948', in William M. Leary, ed., *From Airships to Airbus: The History of Civil and Commercial Aviation*, vol. 1 (Washington, DC, 1995), pp. 45–54.

13 To Berliners, because of its shape, the terminal building was known (rather less grandly) by the nickname *der Kleiderbügel*, 'the clothes hanger'.

14 See Demps, *Flughafen Tempelhof*, p. 62.

15 On this connection, see Hugh Pearman, 'Lunch at Tempelhof', *Things Magazine*, issue 10 (Summer 1999); on the exiled architect, see Wolf von Eckardt, *Erich Mendelsohn* (London, 1960), p. 13. The design is reproduced in Erich Mendelsohn, *Das Gesamtschaffen des Architekten – Skizzen, Entwürfe, Bauten* (Berlin, 1930).

16 On the economic and symbolic importance of airshows, see Peter Fritzsche, *A Nation of Fliers: German Aviation and the Popular Imagination* (Cambridge, MA, 1992), p. 135.

17 Yet despite his accommodation of the airport into the Berlin scheme, Speer, it seems, was working to a different plan: the airport, 'situated much too close to the prospective new centre of the city would be turned into an amusement park in the style of Copenhagen's Tivoli' (Albert Speer, *Inside the Third Reich: Memoirs*, trans. Richard and Clara Winston [London, 1970], p. 78).

18 Read and Fisher, *The Fall of Berlin*, p. 394.

19 On the so-called 'Filmbunker', see Dietmar and Ingmar Arnold, *Dunkle Welten: Bunker Tunnel und Gewölbe unter Berlin* (Berlin, 1997); on the immediate post-war history of the airport and the surrounding neighbourhood, see Peter Buchholz, *Tempelhof* (Berlin, 1992).

20 See Anne Deighton, *The Impossible Peace: Britain, the Division of Germany and the Origins of the Cold War* (Oxford, 1990), pp. 28–40.

21 In 1985, the USAF returned the eagle to Tempelhof; it now stands, denuded of its Nazi symbolism, on a plinth in front of the building it previously adorned, accompanied by a plaque identifying the terminal's great entrance quadrangle as Adler Platz, 'Eagle Square'. As Ladd observes: 'The Nazi eagle thus became a symbol of the German–American military alliance' (p. 145). See also Norbert Huse, 'Bauten des Drittes Reiches', in Norbert Huse, ed., *Verloren, gefahrdet, geschutzt: Baudenkmale in Berlin* (Berlin, [1988]), pp. 139, 143.

22 Brecht, *Journals 1934–1955*, p. 401.

23 Quoted in W. Phillips Davison, *The Berlin Blockade: A Study in Cold War Politics* (Princeton, 1958), p. 356.

24 Standard accounts of the Airlift from which much of this information is derived are Ann and John Tusa, *The Berlin Airlift* (London, 1988); Hans-Ludwig Paeffgen, *The Berlin Blockade and Airlift: A Study of American Diplomacy* (Ann Arbor, 1980). See also Alexandra Ritchie, *Faust's Metropolis: A History of Berlin* (London, 1998), chap. 14.

25 Quoted in Buchholz, *Tempelhof*, p. 4.

26 Ruth Andreas-Friedrich, *Schauplatz Berlin: Tagebuchaufzeichnungen 1945 bis 1948* (Frankfurt, 1985) ['Man wird scharf kontrolliert. Gepäckvisitation. Leibesvisitation. Eidesstattliche Versicherung, daß man nicht mehr als dreihundert Westmark ausführt. Dann trennt eine Schnur die Abfliegenden von den Zurückbleibenden … »Bodennebel«, rede ich mir zu. »Die Maschine fliegt nicht.« Draußen knattert ein Motor. »Die Fluggäste Berlin-Frankfurt werden gebeten, ihre Plätze einzunehmen«, ruft jemand durch den Lautsprecher. Mechanisch setze ich mich in Bewegung. Mechanisch sinke ich in einen Sessel und schließe die Schnalle des Sturzgürtels. »In die Freiheit!« sagt mein Platznachbar. In die Freiheit, will ich antworten. Doch aus meiner Kehle dringt kein Laut'].

27 *Ibid.* ['Die Motoren heulen auf. Wir rollen über die Startbahn, erst langsam, dann schneller, bis sich das Flugzeug mit einem Ruck in die Luft hebt. Rasen, Lichter, Häuserwände, S-Bahnschienen, Straßen verschwinden wie Fetzen im Nebel. Irgendwo da unten steht Heike und weint wie ich. Irgendwo da urten liegt verschwimmend im Nebel der Schauplatz BERLIN'].

28 John Le Carré, *The Spy Who Came in from the Cold* (London, 1963), p. 71.

29 George Orwell, *Nineteen Eighty Four* (London, 1948), p. 6.

30 Rex Warner, *The Aerodrome* (Oxford, 1982), p. 43.

31 John Lehmann, *Evil Was Abroad* (London, 1938), p. 74.

32 Paul Virilio, *Speed and Politics: An Essay on Dromology*, trans. M. Polizzoti (New York, 1986), p. 23.

33 Quoted in David Welch, *Propaganda and the German Cinema 1933–45* (Oxford, 1983), pp. 149–50.

34 *Ibid.*

35 *Hitler's Table Talk 1941–1944*, ed. H. R. Trevor-Roper (London, 1953), p. 197. For more of Hitler's views on airspace, see pp. 176–7, 195, 550.

36 For a useful account of Hitler's use of air transport, see Peter Hoffman, *Hitler's Personal Security* (London, 1979), chap. 4.

37 Konrad Heiden, *Der Führer: Hitler's Rise to Power* (London, 1944), p. 375.

38 Rainer Stollman, 'Fascist Politics as Total Work of Art: Tendencies of the Aestheticization of Political Life in National Socialism', *New German Critique*,

14 (1978), pp. 41–60; p. 59.

39 J.-F. Lyotard, 'The Sublime and the Avant Garde', trans. Lisa Liebmann, Geoff Bennington and Brian Massumi, *Paragraph* 6 (1985), pp. 1–18; p. 16. On the Zeppelinfeld, see Miller Lane, *Architecture and Politics in Germany*, p. 190.

40 Lyotard, 'The Sublime and the Avant Garde', p. 16.

41 Joseph Goebbels, *Tagebücher 1924–1945* (Munich, 1992), vol. 2, p. 797 ['In Tempelhof sind gigantische Anlagen gebaut worden. Sie bieten ein grandioses Bild nationalsozialistischen Gestaltungwillens Der 1. Mai wird ein Massenereignis, wie es die Welt noch nicht gesehen hat. Das ganze Volk soll sich vereinen in einem Willen und in einer Bereitschaft. Im ersten Jahre unserer Revolution wird der Arbeit ihre Ehre und dem Arbeitertum seine geltung zurückgegeben. Ein kompliziertes Räderwerk soll nun in Bewegung gesetzt werden'].

42 Peter Fritzsche, *Germans into Nazis* (Cambridge, MA, 1998), p. 225. I am indebted to Professor Fritzsche's account of the May Day celebrations, though I disagree with his conclusions.

43 On Nazi 'airmindedness', see Fritzsche, *A Nation of Fliers*, chap. 5.

44 For the possibility that Speer may have exaggerated his role in the Tempelhof designs, see Sereny, *Albert Speer*, pp. 99–100.

45 Goebbels, *Tagebucher*, p. 798 ['Auf dem Tempelhofer Feld kann man dies ungeheure Menschenmeer gar nicht mehr überschauen. Blitzend und leuchtend fahren die Scheinwerfer darüber hinweg. Man sieht nur Kopf an Kopf die grauen Massen stehen. Ich eröffne kurz und lasse eine Minute Schweigen eintreten für die in Essen amselben Tage verunglückten Bergleute. Nun steht die ganze Nation still. Die Lautsprecher tragen die Stille über Stadt und Land'].

46 *Ibid.*, p. 799 ['Gläubig und stark klingt Horst Wessels Lied in den ewigen Abendhimmel hinauf. Die Ätherwellen tragen die Stimmen der an-derthalb Millionen Menschen, die hier in Berlin auf dem Tempelhofer Feld vereinigt stehen, über ganz Deutschland, durch Städte und Dörfer, und überall stimmen sie nun mit ein … Hier kannkeiner sich ausschließen, hier gehören wir alle zusammen, und es istkeine Phrase mehr: wir sind ein einzig Volk von Brüdern geworden'].

47 My account of the Columbia Haus owes much to Kurt Schilde and Johannes Tuchel, *Columbia-Haus: Berliner Konzentrationslager 1933–1936* (Berlin, 1990). This building, named in honour of the transatlantic fliers Clarence Chamberlain and Charles Levine, who, on 7 June 1927, landed on Tempelhof Feld in their aircraft Columbia, should not be confused with the Columbus-Haus, which Erich Mendelsohn erected between 1930 and 1932 on Potsdamer Platz. In a footnote to her otherwise reliable *Faust's Metropolis*, Alexandra Ritchie's confusion of the two sites gives rise to an unfortunate fiction (p. 964).

48 See Tom Segev, *Soldiers of Evil: The Commandants of the Nazi Concentration Camps* (London, 1990).

49 For a detailed account of the debacle, see Simon Reeve, *One Day In September: The Story of the 1972 Munich Olympics Massacre* (London, 2000).

50 Paul Virilio, *The Lost Dimension* (New York, 1991), p. 10.

51 *The Times*, 19 October 1977.

52 My account of the hijacking draws on details from Barry Davies, *Assault on LH181* (London, 1994).

53 For a full account of the deaths at Stammheim, see Stefan Aust, *The Baader-Meinhof Group: The Inside Story of a Phenomenon* (London, 1987); Michael Müller and Andreas Kanonenberg, *Die RAF-Stasi Connection* (Berlin, 1992). A good overview is provided by Gunther Wagenlehner, 'Motivation for Political Terrorism in Germany', in Marius H. Livingston, ed., *International Terrorism in the Contemporary World* (Westport, 1976). More wayward accounts of West German terrorism include Jillian Becker, *Hitler's Children: The Story of the Baader-Meinhof Terrorist Gang* (London, 1977); Ian Walker, *Adventures in East and West Berlin* (London, 1988), pp. 48–69.

54 Cited in Aust, *The Baader-Meinhof Group*, p. 54.

55 On 28 December 1972, a firebomb was thrown over the fence near a rear gate of the US military air-base portion of Tempelhof; the only damage caused was a small grass fire, quickly extinguished.

56 Later, the event is reprised.
> '… they did the airport in West Germany – West Berlin, I mean. What's it called?'
> 'Shit, I don't know.'
> 'Anyway they hit the wrong plane.'
> 'Must have been hell to pay.'
> 'They hit the DC-9'

(DeLillo, *Players*, p. 156).

57 On 13 January 1975, two men drove a Peugeot 504 onto the apron at Orly and took out a rocket launcher wrapped in an orange cloth. They set it up and fired two RPG-7 rockets at an El Al 707 as it taxied towards the runway scheduled to fly 136 passengers and nine crew, mostly Americans, to Montreal and New York. The first round missed the El Al jet and instead hit the fuselage of a Yugoslav DC9 waiting nearby. The rocket failed to explode but slightly injured a Yugoslav steward, a French security guard and a workman. The second round hit an administration building, causing some damage. The duo, whose rocket launcher had smashed through their Peugeot's windshield, raced off towards Paris, and their car, with the Russian-built bazooka on the back seat, was later found in a cemetery in the nearby suburb of Thiais.

58 On the phenomenon of the hijack, see James A. Arey, *The Sky Pirates* (New York, 1972); Peter Clune, *An Anatomy of Skyjacking* (London, 1973); David G. Hubbard, *The Skyjacker: His Flights of Fantasy* (New York, 1973). For the point of view of the hijacker, see Leila Khaled, *My People Shall Live: The Autobiography of a Revolutionary* (London, 1973).

59 The best introduction to this complex subject remains Edward Weisband and Danir Roguly, 'Palestinian Terrorism: Violence, Verbal Strategy and Legitimacy', in Yonah Alexander, ed., *International Terrorism: National, Regional and Global Perspectives* (New York, 1977).

60 *Middle East Record* (1968), pp. 393–4.

61 Oriana Fallaci, 'A Leader of Fedayeen: "We Want a War Like the Vietnam War": Interview with George Habash', *Life*, 12 June 1970.

62 *The Times*, 14 July 1972.

63 Virilio, *Speed and Politics*, p. 121.

64 Virilio, *Lost Dimension*, p. 11.

65 Christopher Dobson and Ronald Payne, *The Carlos Complex: A Pattern of Violence* (London, 1977), p. 204.

66 *Ibid.*, p. 205.

67 'Anger at "Entebbe Piracy" Motivated Gang's Action', *The Times*, 19 October 1977.

V CULTURES OF THE TERMINAL

1 'Towards the Development of an Air Terminal Site', in *The Writings of Robert Smithson: Essays with Illustrations*, ed. Nancy Holt (New York, 1979), p. 41. In this brief account of Smithson's theory of crystals, I am much indebted to Robert Hobbs, *Robert Smithson: Sculpture* (Ithaca, NY, 1981), pp. 78–9.

2 Richard Neutra, 'Terminals? Transfer?', *Architectural Record*, 68 (August 1930), p. 104. On Neutra, see Thomas S. Hines, *Richard Neutra and the Search for Modern Architecture* (Berkeley, 1994); and Dione Neutra, *Richard Neutra: Promise and Fulfillment*, 1919–1932 (Carbondale, 1986).

3 Anthony Vidler, *Warped Space: Art, Architecture and Anxiety* (Cambridge, MA, 2000) p. 179; 'The Concrete Bird Stands Free', *Architectural Forum*, 113 (December 1960), pp. 114–15.

4 Edgar Kauffmann Jr, *Interiors* (July 1962). For a trenchant critique of Kauffmann's approach, see the anonymous article 'Forget the Bird: TWA Appraised' in *Architectural Review*, 132 (1962), pp. 306–7. For a useful account of the design and construction of Saarinen's terminal, see George Scullin, *International Airport: The Story of Kennedy Airport and U.S. Commercial Aviation* (Boston, 1968), pp. 153–79.

5 J. G. Ballard, 'The Ultimate Departure Lounge', in Steven Bode and Jeremy Millar, eds, *Airport* (London, 1997), p. 121.

6 Don DeLillo, *The Names* (London, 1982), p. 253.

7 Martha Rosler, *In the Place of the Public*, exh. notes, Museum für Moderne Kunst, Frankfurt, 1998.

8 'Silent Traveller Catches the Imagination', *Madrid Airport Yearbook* (1998).

9 Martin Amis, *London Fields* (London, 1989), p. 261.

10 Pascale Blin, 'Aérogares – Le Confort du design', *Atlas* (November 1993).

11 For the sociological implications of this, see Kim Hopper, 'Symptoms, Survival, and the Redefinition of Public Space – A Feasibility Study of Homeless People in a Metropolitan Airport', *Urban Anthropology*, 20 (1991), pp. 155–76.

12 Michel Serres, *Angels: A Modern Myth*, trans. Francis Cowper (New York, 1995), p. 19.

13 DeLillo, *The Names*, p. 254.

14 See 'Six Years of Waiting at Terminal One', *The Observer*, 15 May 1994, p. 15; 'Self-imposed Exile', *The Guardian*, 2 August 1995, p. 13.

15 Anthony Burgess, 'The Endless Voyager', in *The Devil's Mode* (London, 1989), p. 152.

16 *Ibid.*, p. 162.

17 Brigid Brophy, *In Transit* (London, 1969), p. 25; p. 19.

18 *Ibid.*, p. 20.

19 *Ibid.*, p. 24.

20 Kearney was also, perhaps, reflecting on the kind of state-sponsored surveillance that, because of the Ulster Troubles, had become routine on flights across the Irish Sea since the early seventies. For a fine overview of the role of art projects within transport infrastructure, see Malcolm Miles, *Art*

Space and the City (London, 1997), chap. 6. More specifically, see Jean Battersby, 'Art and Airports', *Craft Arts International*, no. 30 (1994), pp. 49–64.

21 BAA, *Art at the Airports* (London, 1997), p. 16.

22 This is the text of the poem as it was first published in *New Republic* on 8 March 1939, and then in *Another Time* (London, 1940), p. 107. In subsequent printings, Auden removed the hyphen in 'air-ports' to create a single word, and revised the fifth line to read 'What instruments we have agree.'

23 'My dear, I'm the first major poet to fly the Atlantic.' So Auden liked to boast after the flight in a USAF DC4 he undertook in 1945, to research, at the behest of the Strategic Bombing Survey, the psychological effects of the Allied air-raids on the German civilian population. Auden seems to have flown for the first time in 1930, and several times during his travels in the course of that decade. He frequently had recourse to the imagery of flight. On this topic, see John Fuller, *W. H. Auden: A Commentary* (London, 1998), pp. 100–112; Edward Mendelson, *Later Auden* (London, 1998), p. 178.

24 W. H. Auden, *Collected Poems*, ed. E. Mendelson (London, 1976), pp. 413–14. When Auden first published the poem in his 1950 collection, *Nones*, it was entitled 'Air Port'; in 1957, when he included it in his *Collected Shorter Poems*, he renamed it 'In Transit'.

25 For the history of the airport, see Joseph P. O'Grady, 'Stopover at Shannon: Origins of the Policy', *Air Power History*, 43 (1996), pp. 34–47. For a fine fictional representation of Shannon, see the closing pages of Elizabeth Bowen, *The World of Love* (London, 1955).

26 Ian Fleming, *Diamonds Are Forever* (London, 1956) p. 44.

27 Sigmund Freud, 'The Uncanny', in *The Standard Edition of the Complete Works of Sigmund Freud*, ed. James Strachey (London, 1955), vol. 17, pp. 217–52. Auden was highly knowledgeable about developments in Freudian theory and frequently applied them to his work. For an account of this, see my 'Auden and the Aesthetics of Detection', *Essays in Criticism*, 43 (1993), pp. 25–45.

28 Freud came to realize that airspaces might contain neurosis. In Lecture 10 of *Introductory Lectures on Psychoanalysis*, he described: 'The remarkable characteristic of the male organ which enables it to rise up in defiance of the laws of gravity, one of the phenomena of erection, leads to its being represented symbolically by balloons, flying-machines and most recently by Zeppelin airships. But dreams can symbolize erection in yet another, far more expressive manner. They can treat the sexual organ as the essence of the dreamer's whole person and make him himself fly. Do not take it to heart if dreams of flying, so familiar and often so delightful, have to be interpreted as dreams of general sexual excitement, as erection-dreams' (*Standard Edition*, vol. 15, p. 188).

29 Dante, *Inferno*, trans. Charles S. Singleton (Princeton, 1970), vol. III, pp. 84–93. My reading of these lines owes much to Robin Kirkpatrick, *Dante's Inferno: Difficulty and Dead Poetry* (Cambridge, 1987), pp. 56–70.

30 Virginia Woolf, *Collected Essays*, ed. Andrew McNeillie (London, 1986–), vol. vi, pp. 186–92.

31 Martha Rosler, 'In the Place of the Public: Observations of a Frequent Flier', in Bode and Millar, eds, *Airport*, pp. 90–109; p. 97; DeLillo, *The Names*, p. 254.

32 An alternative fantastical view of the stopover comes at the conclusion of Saul Bellow's *Henderson The Rain King* as the hero, Eugene Henderson, a

millionaire philanthropist, is flying back to the US from Africa. During his sojourn on that continent, he has been, variously, a plague doctor, a rainmaker and a lion tamer; his favourite lion is stowed in the hold of the Constellation on which he has crossed the Atlantic. In transit, he has befriended a Persian lad whose language he cannot understand; they communicate through gestures. When the plane lands at Gander, Newfoundland, Henderson scoops the child into his arms and descends onto the apron: 'Laps and laps I galloped around the shining and riveted body of the plane, behind the fuel trucks. Dark faces were looking from within. The great, beautiful propellers were still, all four of them. I guess I felt it was my turn to move, and so went running – leaping, leaping, pounding, and tingling over the pure white lining of the grey Arctic silence' (*Henderson the Rain King* [New York, 1959], pp. 340–41). The airport, the 'pure white lining', is here figured either as a form of insulation against the natural world, a means of protection in the wilds or a means of orientation, the lines making out a course to be followed across the flat Arctic expanse. Philip Roth has noted the irony here: 'a man who finds energy and joy in an imagined Africa, and celebrates it on an unpeopled icebound vastness'. But that vastness is entirely the point; from its seeming sterility emerge new beginnings, second chances.

33 Douglas Coupland, 'Hubs', in Bode and Millar, eds, *Airport*, pp. 72–3.
34 On the effects of deregulation on US airports, see Thomas Petzinger Jr, *Hard Landing* (New York, 1996).
35 Coupland, 'Hubs', p. 73.
36 Don DeLillo, *Valparaiso* (New York, 1999), p. 21.
37 *Ibid.*, p. 55.
38 Burgess, 'The Endless Voyager', p. 152.
39 DeLillo, *Valparaiso*, p. 32.
40 *Ibid.*, p. 98.
41 *Ibid.*, p. 103.
42 Coupland, 'Hubs', p. 73.
43 Rosler, 'In the Place of the Public', p. 99.
44 Coupland, 'Hubs', p. 73.
45 On LAX, see Pico Iyer, 'Where Worlds Collide', *Harper's Magazine* (August 1995), pp. 50–57.
46 Andrew Graham-Dixon, *The Independent*, 20 November 1993.
47 John Berger, *And Our Faces, My Heart, Brief as Photos* (London, 1984), p. 93.
48 For background to this and other US airports of the period, see David Brodherson, 'An Airport in Every City: The History of American Airport Design', in Zukowsky, ed., *Building for Air Travel*, pp. 67–95.
49 Rosler, 'In the Place of the Public', p. 99.

VI AIRS OF FINALITY

 1 Martin Amis, *Money* (London, 1984), p. 92.
 2 Ian Fleming, *Goldfinger* (London, 1959), p. 12. Fleming frequently featured air travel and airport scenes in his Bond novels. *Goldfinger*'s denouement takes place on a BOAC airliner over the Atlantic; *Diamonds are Forever* (1956) sees Bond at London Airport pondering the terminology of departure: '"Final Lounge?" Cheerful start to flying the Atlantic, reflected Bond, and then they were all walking across the tarmac and up into the big Boeing and, with a

burst of oil and metanol smoke, the engines fired one by one' (p. 43); *Live and Let Die* (1954) features an extraordinary defence of the fatalism of flight: 'There's nothing to do about it. You start to die the moment you are born. The whole of life is cutting through the pack with death. So take it easy. Light a cigarette and be grateful you are still alive as you suck the smoke deep into your lungs. Your stars have already let you come quite a long way since you left your mother's womb and whimpered at the cold air of the world. Perhaps they'll even let you get to Jamaica tonight. Can't you hear those cheerful voices in the control tower that have said quietly all day long, "Come in B O A C. Come in Panam. Come in KLM"? Can't you hear them calling you down too: "Come in Transcarib. Come in Transcarib?" Don't lose faith in your stars' (p. 172). For some useful insights into the uses thriller writers make of the airport milieu, see Bruce Merry, *Anatomy of the Spy Thriller* (Dublin, 1977) p. 54.

3 Mark Seltzer, *Serial Killers: Death and Life in America's Wound Culture* (New York, 1998), p. 21.

4 Michael Warner, 'The Mass Public and the Mass Subject', in Bruce Robbins, ed., *The Phantom Public Sphere* (Minneapolis, 1993), pp. 234–56; p. 250.

5 Mary Ann Doane, 'Information, Crisis, Catastrophe', in Patricia Mellencamp, ed., *Logics of Television: Essays in Cultural Criticism* (Bloomington, 1990), pp. 222–39.

6 *The Diary of Virginia Woolf*, ed. Anne Olivier Bell (London, 1977), vol. IV, 12 November 1933, p. 187.

7 Virginia Woolf, *Between the Acts*, ed. Gillian Beer (Harmondsworth, 1992), p. 70; p. 47. In the discussion which follows, I am much indebted to Professor Beer's many insights into this novel.

8 *Ibid.*, p. 114.

9 *Ibid.*, p. 117; p. 12.

10 *The Diary of Virginia Woolf*, p. 187.

11 *The Letters of Virginia Woolf*, ed. Nigel Nicolson and Joanne Trautmann (London, 1980), vol. v, 8 November 1933, p. 243.

12 *Ibid.*, 10 November 1933, p. 244.

13 Gillian Beer has pointed out that the 'heady pleasures of air travel probably remained the more intense in Woolf's imagination just because she never flew' ('The Island and the Aeroplane: The Case of Virginia Woolf', in Homi K. Bhabha, ed., *Nation and Narration* [London, 1990], pp. 255–90).

14 Virginia Woolf, *Collected Essays*, ed. Andrew McNeillie (London, 1986–), vol. vi.

15 J.-F. Lyotard, 'The Sublime and the Avant-Garde', in *Paragraph*, 6 (1985) p. 204.

16 *The Diary of Virginia Woolf*, vol. IV, p. 7.

17 Gatwick, connected by underground passageway to a specially built railway station, boasted unheard-of facilities in its cylindrical, two-storey waiting hall (known as the Martello Tower and, later, as the Beehive), the most noteworthy being the telescopic canvas-covered jetties which sheltered passengers as they walked to their aircraft. For a brief history, see Alan J. Wright, *British Airports* (Shepperton, 1999), pp. 41–4; for an account of Gatwick's grand opening, see Harald Penrose, *British Aviation: The Ominous Skies 1935–39* (London, 1980), p. 80.

18 'I am the tomb of the shipwrecked man; but set sail, stranger: for when we were lost, the other ships voyaged on' (*The Greek Anthology*, Bk VII, no. 282).

19 W. H. Auden, 'Musée Des Beaux Arts'. For an account of the background to Auden's poem, see my 'Everything Turns Away': Auden's Surrealism', in N. Jenkins and K. Bucknell, eds, *The Language of Learning and The Language of Love* (Oxford, 1994).

20 Francis Hope, 'Don't Play it Again, Sam', *New Statesman*, 11 January 1974, p. 47.

21 Francis Hope, 'Traveller's Tale', *New Statesman*, 11 August 1972.

22 John Fuller, *Collected Poems* (London, 1996) p. 270.

23 See my 'John Fuller's Lines of Flight', *Essays in Criticism*, 47 (1998), pp. 308–30.

24 Paul Eddy, Elaine Potter and Bruce Page, *Destination Disaster* (London, 1976), p. 4, remains the definitive account of the accident. Other accounts of the crash and its aftermath include John Godson, *The Rise and Fall of the DC-10* (London, 1975); John H. Fielder and Douglas Birsch, eds, *The DC-10 Case: A Study in Applied Ethics, Technology, and Society* (Albany, 1992); Macarthur Job, *Air Disaster*, vol. 1 (Fyshwick, 1996), pp. 127–45.

25 Maurice Blanchot, *The Writing of the Disaster*, trans. Ann Smock (Lincoln, NB, 1986), p. 46.

26 Eddy *et al.*, *Destination Disaster*, p. 12.

27 Martin Amis, *London Fields* (London, 1989), p. 16.

28 It is possible that the motif originated in Muriel Spark's perverse novel *The Driver's Seat* (1974), which uses the rituals of the airport to show the abandonment of a young woman to her own murder. Lise, a 34-year-old office worker, is going on a trip to Rome, during which she intends to have herself murdered: 'She will be found tomorrow morning dead from multiple stab-wounds, her wrists bound with a silk scarf and her ankles bound with a man's necktie in the grounds of an empty villa, in a park of the foreign city to which she is travelling on the flight now boarding at Gate 14' (p. 25).

29 Brigid Brophy, *In Transit* (London, 1969), p. 38.

30 *Ibid.*, p. 232.

31 *Ibid.*, p. 24.

32 David Lodge, *Small World* (London, 1984), p. 257.

33 Martin Amis, *The Information* (London, 1995), p. 318.

34 Brophy, *In Transit*, p. 44.

35 Arthur Hailey, *Airport* (London, 1968), p. 251.

36 *Ibid.*, p. 251.

37 The phrase is Don DeLillo's and features in *Players*, as Lyle Wynant waits at La Guardia for his flight to Toronto: 'He found a cocktail lounge and settled in. The place was absurdly dark, as though to encourage every sort of intimacy, even to strangers groping each other. Airports did this sometimes, gave travelers a purchase on what remained of tangible comforts before their separation from the earth' (p. 191).

38 The ludicrous series consists of *Airport* (1970), *Airport 1975* (1975), *Airport 1977* (1977) and *Airport 79: The Concorde* (1980). As Stephen Pendo has observed, the airport disaster film is the easiest form of aviation film to make. Often all that is needed is a mock-up of a cabin interior and a few stock shots of an airliner in flight (*Aviation in Cinema* [New York, 1985], p. 296).

39 On the relation between aviation and film, see Pendo, *Aviation in Cinema*; Bertil Skogsberg, *Wings on Screen* (San Diego, 1984); Michael Paris, *From the Wright Brothers to Top Gun: Aviation, Nationalism And Popular Cinema*

(Manchester, 1995).

40 Amis, *Money*, p. 230; p. 50.

41 Brophy, *In Transit*, p. 24.

42 For a fine account of 'Second Comings' in *La Dolce Vita*, see Frank Burke, *Federico Fellini: Variety Lights to La Dolce Vita* (Boston, 1984), pp. 85–100.

43 For a useful account of the closing sequence of Tati's film, see Francis Ramirez and Christian Rolot, *Mon Oncle: Etude critique* (Poitiers, 1993), pp. 80–81. On the history of the flying-horse motif, see David Scott, 'Air France's Hippocampe and BOAC's Speedbird: The Semiotic Study of Logos', *French Cultural Studies*, IV (1993), pp. 107–27.

44 *Cahiers du cinéma*, no. 83 (1958).

45 Quoted in James Harding, *Jacques Tati: Frame by Frame* (London, 1984), p. 124.

46 My account of this scene is indebted to Gerald Mast, *The Comic Mind: Comedy and the Movies* (Chicago, 1979), pp. 295–303; Kristin Thompson, 'Play Time: Comedy on the Edge of Perception', in *Breaking The Glass Armor: Neoformalist Film Analysis* (Princeton, 1988), pp. 247–62.

47 These lines are from the English-dubbed version, but the French dialogue is comparable.

48 Serge Delany, 'Eloge de Tati, Entretien no. 2: Propos rompus', *Les Cahiers du cinéma*, no. 239 (1979), p. 23.

49 'Au fond, ce type est l'une des premières victimes du cinéma … car on peut supposer que, s'il n'y avait pas eu la caméra, il aurait probablement renoncé à sauter' (François Truffaut, *La Peau douce*, *L'Avant scène cinéma*, no. 48 [1965], p. 22).

50 On the New Wave, see James Monaco, *The New Wave* (New York, 1976); on Truffaut, see Graham Petrie, *The Cinema of François Truffaut* (New York, 1970); Don Allen, François Truffaut (London, 1974). Pam Cook suggests that *La Peau douce* owes much to Hitchcock (e.g. *Vertigo*) in its portrayal of a man trapped and destroyed by his desires (*The Cinema Book* [London, 1985], p. 136).

51 The film's original title was the definitely articled *La Femme mariée*, but the French censors thought it would generalize about French wives too sweepingly.

52 This was not the first time that Godard had visited Orly. In 1959, before the completion of the new terminal, his first feature film, *A bout de souffle*, contained a scene in which a young American journalist, Patricia (Jean Seberg), attended a press conference on the roof of Orly, given by the great novelist Monsieur Parvulesco (played by director Jean-Pierre Melville), who had just published a pornographic novel. For an account of this scene, see Colin MacCabe, *Godard: Images, Sounds, Politics* (London, 1980), p. 84.

53 I owe this point to John Bragin, 'The Married Woman', *Film Quarterly* (Summer 1966).

54 For Hitchcockian parallels, see Philip French, 'Une Femme Mariée', in Charles Barr, ed., *The Films of Jean-Luc Godard* (London 1967), pp. 72–82.

55 Godard used Orly's bedrooms for some minor scenes in his science-fiction farrago, *Alphaville* (1965), the same airport providing a much more explicit version of dystopia in 'Anticipation, ou l'amour en l'an 2000', Godard's contribution to the omnibus film *Le Plus Vieux Metier du monde, ou l'amour à travers les âges* (1966). In this Orly of the third millennium, the core of human relationships is prostitution, and the airport has expanded into space, as it were, to become a transit facility for passengers arriving from distant

galaxies. John Demetrois (Jacques Charner) is a 'legal' alien who, after a brief examination by the authorities, is conducted to rooms in the airport hotel to meet a ravishing prostitute, Marlene (Marilù Tolo). In this society, prostitutes are only available in two varieties: those who talk (the rhetorical) and those who do (the mechanical). Marlene is the latter, a sex machine incapable of dialogue during love-making. After several sessions with her, John announces that he is bored and requests another lover. Natacha (Anna Karma), a specialist in lovers' discourse, appears, and John teaches her all he knows about *amour*, a technique in which gesture and word combine, in which touch itself becomes language. In a non-stop torrent of words, Natacha and Demetrois manage to communicate, and together, in one of Orly's bedrooms, they 'invent the kiss'. It seems that in 1964, as a spin-off from *Une Femme mariée*, Godard also made a short documentary about the airport, entitled *Reportage sur Orly*. I have been unable to locate a print. See Chris Darke, 'It All Happened in Paris' *Sight & Sound*, no. 4 (July 1994), pp. 10–12.

56 ['Trouver une solution / Les hommes sont tous pareils. / Des yeux très bleus / Sauver les apparences / La vie moderne. / Tout oublier' (Godard, *Une Femme mariée, L'Avant-scène cinéma*, no. 46, p. 30)]. All further quotations are drawn from this text; all translations are my own.

57 ['C: En une heure, on a le temps d'avoir un accident et ... mourir / R: Mourir en avion, c'est bien. On est plusieurs et c'est brusque' (*Ibid.*, p. 30)].

58 ['Et si ce que je fuis, j'évite mais trop tard, / Ces cruels entretiens, où je n'ai point de part' (Racine, *Bérénice*, ll. 273–4)].

59 ['Moi-même, j'ai voulu vous entendre en ce lieu. / Je n'écoute plus rien, et pour jamais adieu!' (*Ibid.*, ll. 1109–10)].

60 ['Que vous dirais je enfin? Je fuis des yeux distraits
Qui, me voyant toujours, ne me voyaient jamais.
Adieu. Je ... (*il hesite.*) vais, le cœur trop plein de votre image,
Attendre, en vous aimant, la mort pour mon partage.
Surtout ne craignez point ...
Surtout ne craignez point ... (*un temps*) ... qu'une aveugle douleur
Remplisse l'univers du bruit de mon malheur...
Madame, le seul bruit d'une mort que j'implore.
Vous fera souvenir que je vivais encore'
(*Ibid.*, ll. 277–84, as quoted in Godard's screenplay)].

61 ['Pour jamais! ... Ah! Seigneur, songez-vous en vous-même
Combien ce mot cruel est affreux quand on aime!
Dans un mois, dans un an, ... comment souffrirons-nous Seigneur,
Que tant de mers me séparent de vous ...
Que le jour recommence et que le jour finisse
Sans que jamais Titus puisse voir Bérénice'
(*Ibid.*, ll. 1111–16, as quoted in Godard's screenplay)].

62 ['Même un paysage tranquille. Même une prairie avec des vols de corbeaux, des moissons et des feux d'herbe. Même une route où passent des voitures, des paysans, des couples. Même un village pour vacances avec une foire et un clocher peuvent conduire tout simplement a un camp de concentration' (Alain Resnais, *Nuit et brouillard, L'Avant-scène cinéma*, no. 1, p. 51)].

63 See Roy Armes, *The Cinema of Alain Resnais* (New York, 1968). For important readings of the film, see Robert Michael, 'A Second Look: Night & Fog, *Cinéaste*, 13 (1984), pp. 35–7; Charles Krantz, 'Alain Resnais' *Nuit et Brouillard*: A

Historical and Cultural Analysis', in Sanford Pinsker, ed., *Literature, the Arts and the Holocaust* (New York, 1987); Leo Bersani and Ulysse Dutoit, *Arts of Impoverishment: Beckett, Rothko, Resnais* (Cambridge, MA, 1993); Andrew Hebard, 'Disruptive Histories: Toward a Radical Politics of Remembrance in Alain Resnais's *Night and Fog'*, *New German Critique*, 71 (1997), pp. 87–113.

64 For an eyewitness account by a Norwegian resistance fighter, see Arne Brun Lie with Robby Robinson, *Night and Fog* (New York, 1990).

65 ['Un camp de concentration se construit comme un stade, ou un grand hôtel, avec des entrepreneurs, des devis, de la concurrence, sans doute des pots de vin. Pas de style imposé. C'est laissé à l'imagination. Style alpin, style garage, style japonais, sans style. Des architectes inventent calmement ces porches destinés â n'être franchis qu'une seule fois' (Resnais, *Nuit et brouillard*, *L'Avant scène cinéma*, no. 1, p. 51)].

66 Erica Jong, *Fear of Flying* (London, 1973), p. 23.

67 Hope, 'Traveller's Tale', p. 193.

68 Blanchot, *Writing of the Disaster*, p. 47. My understanding of Blanchot's work has been greatly helped by Roy Boyne, 'Crash Theory: The Ubiquity of the Fetish at the End of Time', *Angelaki*, 4/2 (1999), pp. 41–52; Allan Stoekl, 'Blanchot, Violence and the Disaster', in Lawrence Kritzman, ed., *Auschwitz and After: Race Culture and 'The Jewish Question' in France* (New York, 1995), pp. 133–48.

69 *Ibid.*, pp. 3, 7, 14, 16, 146.

70 Jorge Semprun, *La Guerre est finie*, trans. Richard Seaver (New York, 1966), pp. 186–7.

71 Antoine de St Exupéry, *Wind, Sand and Stars*, trans. William Rees (Harmondsworth, 1995) p. 15 ['Monsieur de St Exupery, je me vois obligé de demander, pour vous, sanction à Paris, vous avez viré trop près des hangars au départ de Casablanca'].

72 Casablanca's other airport scene, featuring the arrival of Major Strasser, was filmed at Los Angeles Metropolitan Airport in Van Nuys. See Alan Schwartz, *Casablanca: As Time Goes By* (London, 1992), p. 145.

73 *Ibid.*, p. 153.

Photographic Acknowledgements

The author and publishers wish to express their thanks to the following sources of illustrative material and/or permission to reproduce it (excluding sources credited in full in the captions):

AAJHL: p. 47 (top); ADP: pp. 147, 149, 210; AENA: p. 96; Aéroports de Paris: pp. 6, 12, 55, 59; AFP: p. 25; courtesy of Air France: p. 20; AirNikon: p. 233; BAA: pp. 86, 231; courtesy of Barajas Airport, Madrid/P. Lopez: p. 207; Barnaby's: pp. 18, 29, 56, 72, 131, 146; A.W. Besley: p. 18, 56 (bottom); Alexander Brims: p. 72; Kelvin Brodie: p. 249; © Corbis: p. 157; courtesy Dwan Gallery, New York: p. 198; Flughafen Zürich: p. 35; Foster Associates: p. 151; Gianfranco Gorgoni/Colorific: p. 94 (bottom); Hulton Getty: pp. 174, 189, 239, 246; Imperial War Museum, London: p. 90; Jahn Architects/Murphy: p. 227; Jay Gorney Modern Art: p. 205; courtesy of the John Weber Gallery, New York: p. 93; KIA: pp. 110, 111; courtesy KLM Aerocarto Luchtfotografie: p. 75; Udo Kroner: p. 213; Werner Kruger: p. 33; Ludwig Leykauf: p. 139; Lockheed Martin Corporation: p. 137; Werner Loosli: p. 35; Los Angeles Department of Airports: pp. 8, 99, 230; Lufthansa/Lufthansa Bildarchiv: pp. 33, 115, 139, 140, 156, 159 (bottom), 169, 213; Chris Marker: pp. 66, 67, 69; Paul Maurer/Andreu: p. 133; Metropolitan Washington Airports Authority: pp. 234, 235; courtesy of Milan Airport/Fotocielo: p. 10; photo © Ministère de la Culture, France: p. 47 (top); Mitchell Photographic Services: p. 8; J. J. Moreau: pp. 6, 12; Michel Porro: 152; Port Authority, New York: p. 30; Rheinisches Bildarchiv Köln: p. 63; Richard Rogers Partnership: p. 89; Manfed Schulze-Alex: p. 140; Shannon Free Airport Development Company Ltd: p. 220; George Silk/Hellmuth, Obata & Kassabaum : p. 94 (top); Ezra Stoller: pp. 138, 200; Ullstein Bilderdienst, Berlin: pp. 155, 160, 164, 171, 181, 185; UPI/Bettman: p. 61; Ian Walker: p. 29; Photo: J. Wiersema: p. 78; Kazutagi Yagi: p. 13; A. Zeimbekis: p. 56 (top).